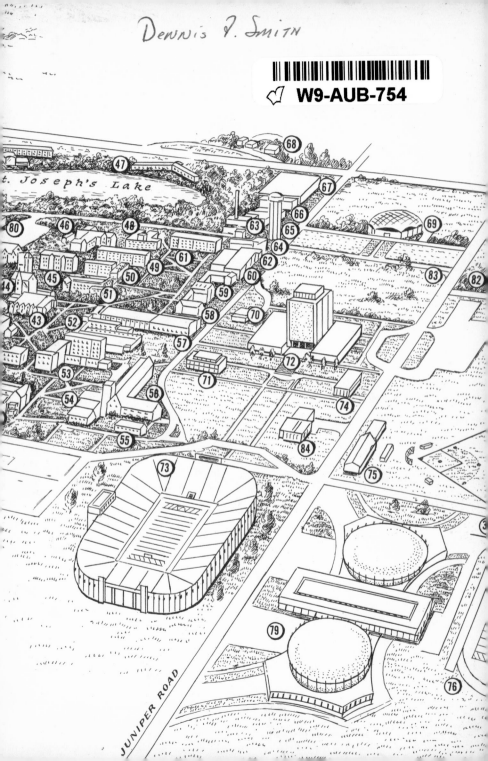

Dennis P. Smith

W9-AUB-754

NOTRE DAME: *Its People and Its Legends*

NOTRE DAME:

Its People and Its Legends

by FRANCIS WALLACE

DAVID McKAY COMPANY, INC.

New York

NOTRE DAME: ITS PEOPLE AND ITS LEGENDS

To

Reverend Theodore Martin Hesburgh, C.S.C.,
Sixteenth President
Who Caught the Pass from Sorin

Library of Congress Catalog Card Number: 78–82506

MANUFACTURED IN THE UNITED STATES OF AMERICA

VAN REES PRESS • NEW YORK

NOTRE DAME CAMPUS

Numerical Listing (for endpaper map)

1 Carroll Hall (1908)
2 Fatima Shrine (1952)
3 Fatima Retreat House (1956)
4 University Village (1962)
5 Military Science Building (1943)
6 Rockne Memorial (1938)
7 Pangborn Hall (1955)
8 Lyons Hall (1925)
9 Fisher Hall (1953)
10 Morrissey Hall (1925)
11 Holy Cross Seminary (1922)
12 Log Chapel (1842)
13 Old College (1843)
14 Architecture (1917)
15 Howard Hall (1924)
16 Cafeteria (South Dining Hall)
17 South Dining Hall (1927)
18 Badin Hall (1897)
19 Hammes Notre Dame
   Bookstore (1955)
20 Dillon Hall (1931)
21 Morris Inn (1952)
22 Main Gate
23 Alumni Hall (1931)
24 Post Office (1967)
25 Walsh Hall (1909)
26 Sorin Hall (1889)
27 Corby Hall (1893)
28 Grotto of Our Lady
   of Lourdes (1896)
29 Sacred Heart Church (1871)
30 Columbia Hall (1895)
31 St. Joseph Hall (1920)
32 Moreau Seminary (1958)
33 Laundry (1934)
34 Bronson Hall (1855)
35 Presbytery (1869)
36 Administration Building (1879)
37 Law School (1930)
38 Lewis Bus Shelter (1953)
39 Tennis Courts
40 Cushing Hall of Engineering (1933)
41 Hurley College of
   Business Administration (1932)
42 Psychology Building (1893)
43 La Fortune Student Center (1953)

44 Washington Hall (1881)
45 St. Edward's Hall (1895)
46 Student Infirmary (1934)
47 Holy Cross House (1961)
48 Stanford Hall (1957)
49 Keenan Hall (1957)
50 Zahm Hall (1937)
51 Cavanaugh Hall (1936)
52 Nieuwland Science Hall (1952)
53 Chemistry Hall (1920)
54 Art Gallery (O'Shaughnessy Hall)
55 Sculpture Studio (1955)
56 O'Shaughnessy Hall
   of Liberal and Fine Arts (1953)
57 Gymnasium and Fieldhouse (1898)
58 Breen-Phillips Hall (1939)
59 Farley Hall (1947)
60 North Dining Hall (1957)
61 Wenninger-Kirsch Biology Hall (1937)
62 Fire Station (1946)
63 Power Plant (1933)
64 Water Tower
65 Ave Maria Press (1940)
66 Mechanical Engineering Lab. (1941)
67 Maintenance Center (1959)
68 Germ Free Laboratory (1951)
69 Stepan Center (1962)
70 WNDU, Radio and Television (1955)
71 Radiation Research Building (1963)
72 Notre Dame Memorial Library (1963)
73 Stadium (1930)
74 Computing Center &
   Mathematics Building (1962)
75 Aeronautical Engineering
   Building (1945)
76 Cartier Field (1962)
77 Geology Building (1855)
78 University Club (1968)
79 Athletic and Convocation
   Center (1968)
80 Lewis Hall (1965)
81 Center for Continuing
   Education (1965)
82 Credit Union
83 East Gate
84 LOBUND Laboratory (1967)

v

NOTRE DAME CAMPUS

Alphabetical Listing (for endpaper map)

FOREWORD AND ACKNOWLEDGMENTS

HOW and why is a book written? It is often hard to sort out the answer from a jumble of notes and events, sometimes unrelated. But in this case the line is clear.

In 1960 Walter Mahony invited me to do an Unforgettable Character article on Knute Rockne for *Reader's Digest*. It served as a base for the Rockne biography I had always intended to write, but otherwise might not have begun. The story of football, *Notre Dame: From Rockne to Parseghian*, then followed logically.

Miss Pat Vanek of the Notre Dame bookstore told me that people were always coming in and asking for a book that would tell the whole story of the people *behind* the football façade and the academic and campus expansion. She suggested that I think about filling that vacuum. While I was thinking, Hugh Downs introduced me on the *Today* show, referred to Notre Dame as The Camelot of Football, and asked *why*. I said Notre Dame people thought of the entire campus as Camelot because it was something, in this age of discord, in which they could still believe, and that millions of "associate alumni" who had never even seen the place seemed to feel the same.

The program of the 1967 Notre Dame–Miami football game led off with an article that never mentioned football. Edwin Pope, sports editor of the *Miami Herald,* had borrowed the first chapter of *From Rockne to Parseghian* which began:

> Notre Dame so dramatizes the American Dream that it might have been invented, as it was, by Edward Frederick Sorin, the young French missionary priest with the physique of a tackle, the zeal of a fanatic, the faith of a child, the practical sense of a business man, the daring of an adventurer.

Editor Charles Heckelmann, a Notre Dame valedictorian in the forties, was helpful in the planning stage. I am indebted to Father Arthur J. Hope for *Notre Dame—One Hundred Years* from which I derived part of the early history and basic characterizations of Sorin, Badin, Corby, and the other pioneers. Their names still live at Notre Dame in buildings, monuments, and warm traditions. And their tombstones are there in the cemetery, where history whispers.

I arrived in 1919 bearing a letter from my parish priest to Father Andrew Morrissey who had been linked with Sorin, and I have known all of the succeeding Presidents, some quite well. As student publicity director, writer, President of the Alumni Association, and (currently) member of the Library Council, I have been on the grounds or thereabouts during the transition from Sorin's woodcut college to Hesburgh's broad intellectual crossroads. By default and by propinquity, I've become a historian of sorts. Like Father Hesburgh, I don't agree "with everything said and done around here" in recent years. As a disciplined reporter, I have tried to give everybody and every group his fair time at bat. I can remember when I was also an angry young man who was kicked out of a class and briefly out of school.

I've drawn upon countless conversations and experiences

with pillars like Dr. George Shuster, Jim Armstrong, Rodge Kiley, Hunk Anderson, Father Cornelius Hagerty, Fathers John and Frank Cavanaugh, Art Haley, Jim Crowley, the Miller brothers, Bill Schmitt, Ed "Moose" Krause, Joe LaFortune. Some of those who have joined the Reunion In The Sky are much represented here—Leo Ward, Dr. Leo O'Donnell, Joe Byrne, Joe Boland, Herb Jones, Arch Ward, Harry Stuhldreher, Rockne, even Gipp. Some are quoted, others are included in groups. Many whom I could not mention may recall conversations before any thought of this book was born.

Most of the Hesburgh material has come from his recorded words, and he made time for me for a wrap-up interview at a very busy time. Father Joyce encouraged me from the beginning. I've had specific help from Father Jerry Wilson, Father Tom McAvoy, the archivist, Father Burtchaell, Jim Murphy, Victor Schaefer, Father McCarragher, and other priests, alumni, faculty, and students, and the many charming girl secretaries of campus officials.

I thought I knew so much about Notre Dame and its people until I sat down to this work. I became fascinated, refreshed, and delighted by discoveries of all I did not know; by insights that come from concentration; by shining little nuggets that turned up in odd places. I am offering it all for those scholars who will later do the in depth books about the miracle we have seen growing for the last fifty years. And if a little of Camelot shines through, that will be all right too.

FRANCIS WALLACE
Bellaire, Ohio
February 21, 1969

CONTENTS

PART I: SORIN

PART II: EMERGENCE

PART III: THE MODERN NOTRE DAME

PART IV: HESBURGH

Illustrations between pages 114 and 115.

PART I

SORIN

1. WHISPERINGS OF HISTORY

A NOTRE DAME student, seeking quiet with his notes before an exam, can find it just minutes away: he need only walk by the Grotto, turn left on the road that separates the two lakes, follow a leafy path into the woods, find a big tree, and sit at its base. The only others nearby will be the men who built the place, each quiet now beneath the small wooden cross that marks the resting of illustrious priest or humblest brother. In stillness like this, Indians trod the first paths, fished, or hunted for deer, mink, black bear, or wildcat; they fought and held councils, and sometimes listened to the Black Robes who came warring for souls while the British, French, and Spanish fought for control of the Northwest Territory.

The early days are still shrouded in the mists of Indian tradition and the sketchy records of the missionaries. Father Marquette is generally thought to have been the first white man in the district, about 1675. It is fairly certain that LaSalle and Hennepin came down the St. Joseph River from Lake Michigan in 1672, left it directly across from the present St. Mary's College, and made portage to the headwaters of the Kankakee, to the Illinois, and down the Mississippi. Father

3

Claude Allouez founded the St. Joseph Mission at Niles, Michigan, six miles north of Notre Dame, about 1680.

The St. Joseph comes down from the northeast, makes a sharp bend, and winds northwesterly to Lake Michigan, thirty miles away. The *south bend* of the river was a natural stopping place for Indian travelers, and the Miamis had a village there. In 1681 the peripatetic LaSalle came again to arrange a treaty uniting Miamis, Potawatomies, and Illinois against marauding Iroquois. They met under a tree with an eight-foot base. It is now called Council Oak, is estimated to be about seven hundred years old and, like any other gnarled senior, shows much evidence of having been baled together after numerous operations. (The site is now a cemetery. Knute Rockne is buried there, and Coach Frank Leahy once brought his football squad to Rockne's grave for inspiration before a big game. Some wandered off to another grave, but Leahy called, "Come back, lads. We will visit Coach Keogan during the basketball season.")

Indiana was admitted to the Union in 1816. In 1823 Alexis Coquillard, a young Canadian, established a trading post and called the place South Bend. He sent for his brother, who opened a tavern, presumably to recapture some of the money Alexis paid the Indians for their furs. A series of treaties opened the territory for settlers, and the Indians were being pushed back by other methods not always honorable. The missionaries had been their friends, and Chief Pokagon may have had this in mind when he appealed to Father Gabriel Richard of Detroit to send a priest to his village near South Bend; but he based his plea on spiritual necessity, and dramatized it by reciting in the Potawatamie tongue prayers he said his people had been taught fifty years before by the last priest to come among them.

Chief Pokagon was in luck. So was the future Notre Dame. Stephen Theodore Badin, born in 1768, had lived under

4

the terror of the French Revolution, seen churches burned, convents despoiled, seminaries banned, priests hunted, Catholics robbed and killed. Already in minor orders, he came to America and in 1793 became the first priest to be ordained there. He was a man for his time and for the Territory—outspoken, impatient, mentally and physically tough. During the next twenty-six years he journeyed over one hundred thousand miles on horseback, "cutting a swath for the Lord," imposing severe penance, lecturing housewives on frugality, storming into barn dances and converting them into prayer meetings. His coming was always regarded as a mixed blessing, and there may well have been a deep sigh over his vast parish when he went back to France. But he returned after ten years and was at Detroit when Pokagon made his plea. At age sixty he mounted his horse, rode to Pokagon's village, and resumed his indomitable flagellations of the settlers.

He decided to start an orphan asylum for the innocents scattered over his domain from Fort Wayne to Chicago. In 1831 he bought 524 acres at St. Marie-des-Lacs, site of the present Notre Dame. But the winds of the cantankerous old hurricane were slowing down. He did build an all-purpose chapel on the shore of one of the lakes before turning the title over to the Bishop of Vincennes and going to Cincinnati to rest for awhile.

Badin's successor, Father Louis Deseille, in contrast to his tempestuous predecessor, was the mildest of men. He had assisted Badin for three years, but no priest ever came to assist *him*. In two years, at age thirty-seven, he was dead. His Indians stood guard over his body, waiting for a priest to come and bury him; but none came, and at the insistence of the authorities in South Bend, he was buried beneath the log chapel.

No priest had come because there was no priest. There was only a seminarian, Benjamin-Marie Petit, a native of Brittany who had begun the study of law when Simon Bruté, Bishop of Vincennes, arrived in France pleading for young men to help him spread the gospel to the whites and Indians of the Northwest Territory. Petit had listened, had traveled to Vincennes, and was hurriedly ordained. At age twenty-six he was frail of body, innocent of nature; but the holy fire within was expressed in a letter to his mother:

> I am a priest. And the hand which now writes you these lines has this very day held Jesus Christ Himself. How can I express all that I want to say and how can I speak things no human tongue is able to tell. . . . In two days I will depart, all alone, and will travel three hundred miles to labor among strangers. God will bear me. I am going in the company of God.

The boy priest became Apostle to the Indians, supporting their cause in one of the moments Americans prefer to forget. The Indians had generally sided with the British in 1812. Now the wave of history broke over them. They were victimized by speculators who got them drunk and used the threat of military strength to move them back from land supposedly protected by treaty. Chief Menominee, supported by the traders and Father Petit, tried to make a stand at Twin Lakes in 1838. He was forcibly moved out, and with eight hundred followers began a two-month journey to the Indian Territory. At the request of the Army, and after receiving the delayed consent of his Bishop, Father Petit caught up with the march at Danville, Illinois, and lent his calming influence to the unhappy journey.

> I saw my poor Indians shuffling in line, surrounded by soldiers who goaded them on under a burning sun amid clouds of dust. Behind them came the wagons, crowded with the sick and with women and children too weak to walk.

6

A Jesuit waited at the Osage River, end of the journey. Father Petit was ill and exhausted. It was six weeks before he attempted the return, with an Indian companion in an open wagon, in rains that demolished roads. On February 11 the Superior of the Jesuits at St. Louis wrote to Bruté:

Father Petit arrived here on the 15th of January reduced to a most pitiable estate by the fever. There were eleven running sores on different parts of his body, his person all jaundiced and in the last stages of debility. God had certainly given him strength to reach St. Louis, for there was none in his body. . . . What patience, resignation and lively gratitude toward all who waited on him! But above all, what tender devotion to the Mother of God who had protected him from his tenderest years!

On the night of the 10th (of February) they came to tell me he was near his end. I asked him if he suffered much. He answered by casting an expressive glance at the crucifix. "You wish to say," I asked, "that He suffered more for you?" He answered: "Oh yes." I placed the crucifix on his lips and he kissed it twice with great tenderness. During his agony we recited the prayers for the dying which he followed, his eyes constantly upon us. He sweetly expired about midnight.

Historically, Deseille and Petit held the spiritual fort Badin had built by the lake. Their bones are under the floor of the crypt, the basement chapel beneath Sacred Heart Church. Through the years, thousands of young men, en route to the altar rail, have walked over them, mostly unaware.

2. THE ROAD TO HEAVEN

REVOLUTIONS spawn unexpected developments, and none less likely than the French Revolution influencing the founding of a Catholic university in the backwoods of America. The reading is legible enough. Badin had fled The Terror and prepared the way for Edward Frederick Sorin, who would also be conditioned by the Revolution for the job ahead.

The Sorin family was one of three in the village of La Roche, half a mile from the commune of Ahuille and its eighteen hundred inhabitants. Their home on a nine-acre farm was a station on the priest underground during the French Revolution. They escaped penalties dealt to other Catholics because of their location, and the warning service of other villagers. Edward, seventh of a family of nine, though born (in 1814) after the events, would have heard the tales and idealized the fugitive priests. At age twelve he was already studying Latin and "saying Mass," using the family bureau as an altar and wearing "vestments" of his own contriving. His devout parents were delighted when he entered the Little Seminary at Precigne and progressed to the Major Seminary in Le Mans.

Sorin has been variously described by schoolmates as

bright, intelligent, gay, frank, polite, dignified, spunky, stubborn, headstrong. He was bigger than his contemporaries, mentally and physically strong, emotionally zealous. "And he knew how to use his strength to boss the rest of us," one wrote. "Edward Sorin was always first. He was born for that."

Ordained in 1838 at the age of twenty-four, he spent the next fifteen months as curate in a small town. His talents demanded much more than that; and again the Revolution touched his life and influenced his future; and that of Notre Dame and all who have been part of it. Rev. Arthur Hope described it this way in *Notre Dame: One Hundred Years:*

> In 1790 the attack centered on the clergy. The spirit of religion was torn from the hearts of the people, and children no longer heard the word of God nor received the sacraments. For over a decade the spirit of godlessness masqueraded under the names of liberty, equality, and fraternity. Even with the coming of Bonaparte the church did not regain her former liberties. Napoleon made a great pretense of restoring the Church to a place of dignity, but in reality he strove by every device to keep the Church subject to himself. As a consequence there arose in France a large number of religious orders, men and women, all of them aflame with enthusiasm for the rebuilding of sanctity and learning.

One of these groups was a mission band organized by the Abbé Moreau to serve neglected parishes. He sought brilliant men of tact and courage, because the opposition was still formidable. He later assumed control of The Brothers of St. Joseph, a teaching, working group originally organized by Father Jacques Dujarié, who had been forced by illness to give up the work. Edward Sorin had met Moreau when the latter was a professor at Le Mans. He joined the new Congregation of the Holy Cross, took the vows of poverty, chastity, and obedience, promised to live in obedience to

9

Father Moreau. At age twenty-six he became a novice, learned the rules of the new community, taught Latin and Greek, preached in surrounding towns, performed menial tasks like sweeping and dusting.

While still in the seminary at Le Mans in 1836, young Sorin had also listened to Simon Bruté, Bishop of Vincennes, plead for vocations to his diocese. The seed had fallen on good ground. In 1839 Bruté appealed to Moreau for a group of teaching brothers and a priest to direct them. Bruté died and the solicitation was continued by his successor, Celestine de la Hailandiere. Negotiations continued for two years with the major stumbling block that familiar five-letter word m-o-n-e-y. The final hurdle, passage money to the New World, was vaulted when "a pious woman of Le Mans suggested a lottery on a gold chain." (Bingo!)

Sorin was chosen to direct the journey of the six Brothers, which was no small sacrifice on the part of Moreau, who had need for the young priest's talents, energies, and capacity to attract souls. "It seems to me that of all the members of our family of Holy Cross, you are the one for whom I have most esteem, to whom I have given the utmost confidence. I will suffer until my death by this separation." It was a prophecy which would unhappily be fulfilled. Both men would suffer, and their mutual bonds be strained by contrasts between the old world and the new world into which Sorin was moving with such impetuous joy, as expressed in his letter to Bishop de la Hailandiere.

Your Lordship:

Never has Divine Providence seemed sweeter, more merciful, more kind. . . . I only wish, Monseigneur, that I had been able to inform you sooner of my great joy and to spare you the painful uncertainty of the past year concerning our coming. But I had to wait until heaven had manifested it's will.

... I will say nothing concerning the Brothers chosen for you. Our dear and worthy superior has chosen them in such a way as to make your heart glad after long waiting. I only hope that you will be equally satisfied with the poor priest who is to accompany them. He is deprived of all personal merits and as you may perhaps expect, without talent or solid virtues; in a word, without any recommendation except his good will. ... I do not pity myself for being so poor. It is rather another reason for abandoning myself entirely to God. ... The road to America seems clearly to me the road to heaven. ... I expect all kinds of suffering, and providing the Good Master continues to protect me, it is all I wish for I have need of suffering. ... How long these six months will be! My body will be in France, but my heart and mind will be with you, Monseigneur! I can only live for my dear American brethren. There is my country, the center of all my affections, the object of all my pious thoughts.

Sorin

Many Brothers had volunteered. Moreau had selected three for teaching: Vincent, Anselm, and Gatian; and three for the manual work: Joachim, a tailor, Francis Xavier, a carpenter, Lawrence, a farmer. Vincent was also a weaver. Anselm was fifteen, Gatian, fourteen years of age. (The Bishop had asked for young teachers, because they would learn the new language more rapidly.) Vincent, at age forty-four, was the oldest of the group. His experience would temper Sorin's enthusiasm.

Boxes and bags were packed with linen, vestments, religious articles, everything they thought might be useful in Indiana. On August 5, 1841, the entire religious community gathered for prayers and encouraging words. The Superior gave the missionaries a final blessing, and they ceremoniously kissed his feet. A layman, M. Léon Dupont, known as the Holy Man of Tours, traveled with them to Le Havre. The

11

passports were not in order, and they were ordered back to Le Mans; but the Holy Man's mundane influence performed a minor miracle. They boarded *The Iowa,* an American ship, only to encounter more difficulties. Sorin was asked to pay three thousand francs for the passage to New York, but he had only three thousand francs to get to Indiana, so their bags were transferred from first class to steerage. Sorin described the place in his first report to Moreau:

> Imagine a large hall below deck sixty feet long by thirty feet wide, lighted at one end by a trap door five feet square. In this space there were over fifty persons, all varieties, scattered pell-mell, without any distinction, sometimes quarreling, sometimes exuberantly merry. . . . With the help of some planks we made a separate compartment and are able to keep it locked. Now all we have to do is put up with the continual tumult of this strange assemblage.

Captain Pell, after a few days, offered an empty cabin in which Sorin said Mass during the crossing. The missionaries began their mission among the ship's company, which included "a number of German Protestants and a company of French comedians." Sorin held informal discussions on matters of faith. He baptized a dying Protestant child and officiated at the funeral.

The passage required thirty-nine days but the arrival at New York was fortuitous. In joyous thanksgiving, Sorin knelt and kissed the soil. He was met by Samuel Byerly, a friend of Bishop de la Hailandiere. His first Mass in America was celebrated on the feast of the Exaltation of the Holy Cross. Mr. Byerly was a man of means who had recently become a Catholic, and welcomed the opportunity to show his respect for the clergy. He also spoke French. He took the voyagers into his home for three days, introduced them to the Bishop of New York. Sorin was overwhelmed:

As he is overburdened with the work of his own business, he got up at three o'clock in the morning to take care of his own correspondence and thus be able to devote the day to us. He completed our provisions and bought us a little bell, a small clock, and several other necessary things. He came himself to pay our fares on the steamboat, to take care of our baggage which he had covered with heavy wrapping paper at his own expense, refusing everything except a remembrance before God.

They were seeing America. Up the Hudson by steamboat, thence to Buffalo, but this was no shuffle off; that phase, by horse-drawn barges on the Erie Canal, took seven and one-half days; so slow that the eager Sorin and staid Brother Vincent could take time out to view Niagara Falls. Father Pax, pastor of a German parish, met them at Buffalo and put them on another steamboat to Toledo. The Lake Erie passage, rougher than anything they had experienced on the Atlantic, seemed to have been booked by the Devil, who also had other hazards in store.

They had expected to go from Toledo to Vincennes by another canal. Sorin made inquiries in his few English words. It finally got through to him: There was no canal.

So how, then, to get to Vincennes? Well, a boat would take them to Napoleon. Ah, Napoleon! Surely there French would be spoken. There would be friends.

French was not spoken in Napoleon. Nor were there friends. One man did offer to take them part way in canoes for ten dollars. Ten dollars! Robbery! Sorin would have none of that. It was a wise decision. He learned that, a short distance beyond Napoleon, the river beds were dry!

Overland was the only way left. For thirty dollars they could buy two carts, each drawn by a pair of horses; and the owner of the carts would send his two sons along as guides. Three "other Americans" joined the cavalcade. After two miles, the road was a joke. It was gutted with mud holes. Trees were down across their path. It was necessary to ford many streams. The horses jolted and tossed the carts. Baggage and travelers were soaked. There was many an anxious moment and much praying. The missionaries could not swim!

But they could fight if they had to; and they had to. First, the two drivers tried to rob them; and when these were repulsed, the three "other Americans" brandished revolvers, "revealing their true intentions." But these were also overcome by the soldiers of the Lord, without violence or loss to anybody. Sorin simply dared the Americans to try to take their possessions. The last stage of the journey was an armed truce. They reached Defiance (always to be a good Notre Dame town), said a hearty goodbye to their fellow travelers, sang "all the hymns to the Blessed Virgin we knew," ate some dry bread and tumbled into their blankets to sleep.

By water to Fort Wayne. By land to Logansport where they were met by the Vicar General, who took them as far as Lafayette (which would definitely not be a good Notre Dame town on certain future fall Saturday afternoons when Purdue would be met). By easy stages—Vincennes! The journey from New York had taken twenty-four days. From Le Havre, nine weeks.

3. PATTERNS ON A DETOUR

THE first land the Bishop de la Hailandiere offered was at St. Francisville, ten miles from Vincennes, across the Wabash River in the State of Illinois. It was a delightful tract of one hundred acres, but Sorin declined, perhaps on the theory that one should never take the first offer. The next parcel was one hundred sixty acres between Washington and Mt. Pleasant in Daviess County, Indiana. It was a pleasant spot, a high plateau, far from the road, in the middle of a forest; but it was healthful, one of the oldest missions of the diocese, and the center of several Catholic settlements. There was a chapel with a sacristy and room for a priest. And two log cabins, one used as a kitchen and the other as a school. The land could be cultivated in due time. Before the altar Sorin and the six Brothers sang the *Te Deum* and a hymn to the Queen of Apostles. And went to work.

The parish of St. Peter's included everything within a radius of five miles; about fifty Catholic families, of German, French, and Irish background. The Bishop had established Sorin's tasks: to care for the families of the parish; to build a school and teach the pupils; to build a novitiate and attract recruits for the priests and Brothers. Father Julian Delaune,

15

who had previously served the parish, helped to surmount the first hurdles, chief of which was the language barrier.

The novitiate came first and was a surprisingly quick success. Brother Vincent was the first Master. In a year's time there were twelve recruits: three Germans, one English, eight Irish. It was a make-do operation with postulants, novices, and members sharing the same crowded quarters, sometimes the same clothes.

One month after Sorin and his band had arrived there appeared in the newspaper of Washington, Indiana, a notice that the Brothers of St. Joseph were conducting a school at St. Peter's and were ready to receive students. Young men of any religious profession would be received. The course of instruction would comprise "all branches of a sound, English practical education: Orthography, Reading, Writing, Arithmetic, Grammar, Algebra, Mathematics, Geography, History (both ancient and modern), Bookkeeping, etc." Tuition and board, including washing and mending, payable in advance, would be $18 per quarter. French or German language, two dollars extra; or both for $3. No extra charge for the services of "an eminent physician."

"We are not mentioning the fact," Sorin wrote to Moreau, "that we shall have to use the attic for a dormitory; we don't speak of the refectory; nothing has been said of the fact that the teachers will probably not understand their new pupils. Tell me, are we not men of faith?" In this case faith would seem to have covered some misrepresentation; nevertheless, it was rewarded. The young Brothers learned the language from their pupils. The school drew thirty girls and boys from the neighborhood and was such a success that Brother Gatian was sent to open another school four miles away. The school buildings "consisted of pieces of wood piled one on top of the other, with open spaces that let in the wind and the light; pleasant in summer, but very cold in winter." But the sons of pioneers were hungry for knowledge and accustomed to rigors.

Sundays the farmers came to St. Peter's for Mass. After a few weeks Sorin began preaching and hearing confessions in English. Some of the parishioners told him they did not understand much of what he was saying, but they continued to come. Protestants also came and were even more confused; and, somewhat amused. Sorin laughed at his own mistakes. They were impressed by the performance, the consuming zeal of a man who had come such a distance to tell them things so few could understand, but which he obviously thought so important. And Sorin learned from them, was impressed by them.

> The Protestants come to our services and conduct them-selves well [he wrote to Le Mans]. Last Sunday we had a Taking of the Habit and most of the people present were Protestants. If we need anything at all they are no less kind than the Catholics. When I see our Protestant friends travel twelve miles to bring us planks, and that for nothing, I can only admire the designs of God and try to respond.... We have the Lord with us. Only tonight we hung up our lovely sanctuary lamp where none had hung before. They tell us we won't be able to afford to keep it burning. But we have a little olive oil and will burn it while it lasts. We can see it as we come through the woods, and it lights the humble home where Our Master dwells. We tell each other that we are not alone, that Jesus Christ lives among us. It gives us courage.

Patterns were being established. Sorin and his helpers would always live by simple faith. Ecumenism would always be with them and the beloved Protestants would always be helpful. Sorin would be surrounded by more and more Irish, be supported by them; but he would never fully approve of them, because "the Irish are not inclined to obedience," which no Irishman would bother to deny. Always there would be poverty and the necessity of pursuing that elusive dollar, without which even men of faith could not produce great results. Almost immediately there had surfaced a dilemma: allegiance to the Bishop of Vincennes or to the Abbé Moreau? It was inevitable that it should come; and it was compounded by the fact that it took three months to exchange letters with the Mother House. The Bishop of Vincennes spelled it out to Sorin:

> Here now I have a letter from your Father Superior. He encloses a contract I should sign that binds me to pay all the expenses of your foundation and leaves me nothing to say about its direction. It is absurd. If I pay the expenses, the members work for me and under me. If Father Moreau wishes still to direct the Brothers, then should he not defray the cost? I have given you land and homes. I have nothing else to give. I am now building twelve churches. I must feed my priests. They get nothing from their parishes.

Sorin could see the logic. He also knew that during the long preliminary negotiations Moreau had understood that the Bishop would support the colony in exchange for their services. This, in fact, the Bishop finally acknowledged, saying that he had had the money at one time, but it had gone to other crying necessities during the long delay. Sorin went to Father Delaune for advice and heard: "It looks as if we will have to put on our begging shoes. I will volunteer if the Bishop will permit."

The Bishop would permit, on the understanding that, since Father Delaune would be acting as a priest of the diocese, the money would come to the diocese, that only part of it would go to the Brothers; and that, on the further understanding that they were Brothers *of* the diocese. Sorin didn't like the new terms but made the best of the situation, and was surprised and gratified to receive fifteen thousand francs from the funds Father Delaune had secured in the East and in Canada. With the new affluence Sorin began to erect a *brick* building to replace the log school; as it progressed his vision widened. Why not a *college?* He enlarged his hopes and designs. Thirty men were busy putting the new building into shape.

The Bishop sent for him. There would be no college. The diocese already had a college. Sorin should not have gone ahead without consent. The matter of control would have to be defined. But there was an alternative.

"I have nothing against your idea of a college," de la Hailandiere said, "but not here. In the northern part of the state there is a piece of land I could let you have. You could try a college there, but I caution you, you will have a more difficult time than here. There would be two conditions. You must establish a school and a novitiate within two years."

Sorin discussed the situation with his people. "If we leave here, we leave the good will of the people among whom we have worked for a year. We leave this land and these buildings upon which we have expended so much money and labor. On the other hand, this land can never belong to us; it is deeded in perpetuity to whomever is the parish priest at St. Peter's. What we want is some property that will be our very own. Here we are too close to the Bishop, and have not gotten along so well as he and we would like. The north is wilder and more sparsely settled. But there we would more likely to be our own masters. There would be less chance of the Mother House in France losing control of the fruits of our labors. Think it over. Pray for the light that we may do God's will."

They decided to go north. The Bishop insisted that the novitiate must remain, for the time being at least, at St. Peter's. He offered his prayers and best wishes. And "three hundred and ten dollars you asked of me, and a letter of credit on Mr. Coquillard for two hundred thirty-one dollars and twelve and one-half cents. My hopes are enormous, as are my desires."

The suggestion of a college in the north part of the diocese had not been a chance thought. Badin's five hundred twenty-four acres had been left in trust to the Bishop, to be given to anyone who would start a school. The deed had been transferred to the Fathers of Mercy, who had made such an attempt in 1840; but after surveying the project, the effort was abandoned and the deed returned, along with one for an additional three hundred seventy-five acres. This is why, and some consider it providential, the modern Notre Dame has had seemingly inexhaustible acreage upon which to build and build.

Only men of faith would have begun such an effort on a bleak, snowy November 16, 1842. They were Sorin and seven Brothers, only two of whom, Gatian and Marie (originally Francis Xavier) were of the colony from France. Four of the five who had been trained at St. Peter's were from Ireland. All were young and robust, as they needed to be. They took turns at riding and walking, and all joined in getting the single wagon out of the ruts of what passed for a road. There is some confusion about the time of arrival, but tradition has settled on November 26th as the date when the two hundred fifty miles to South Bend were completed.

First they had stopped at the cabin of Alexis Coquillard. Now they were being guided by his nephew, seventeen-year-old Alexis. They had crossed the frozen St. Joseph River and put their shoulders to the wagon to help the horses up the steep, slippery road. They had traveled for two miles through dense forest. With a suddenness there had come a clearing, a small, frozen lake whose shores were circled by deep green fir trees capped with snow.

"Is this it?" Sorin asked.

It was. The younger Brothers hastened away, exploring, gesticulating with delight. Sorin was led by Alexis to the little cabin where M. Charron and his wife lived. Both were half-breeds, and M. Charron had long served the missionaries as interpreter.

Sorin paused before the chapel, and its stark history. Inside it was bleak and cold. A tiny strip of worn brown carpet covered a space before the altar. The half-breed pointed: "Priest die here. Priest buried." He pointed to the loft: "Sleep up there."

Kneeling at the grave of Father Deseille, with heads close together and hands joined, they prayed.

A priest had come.

The priest arose to what young Alexis thought was a fearful black height. His black eyes fastened on young Alexis. His hearty voice cried: "You will be our first student!" Which was exactly what young Alexis had feared.

4. BRIGADOON

FIRST there must be a chapel. The one built by Badin was too small and in disrepair. Following the pattern established at St. Peter's, Sorin appealed to the Catholics of the district for help. He urged them on. They worked with enthusiasm, cutting logs, clearing the ground, hauling the timber to the new site a little higher up on the bank of St. Mary's lake. On a given day there was to be a magnificent effort to raise the walls and lay the roof. But alas. The day was bitter cold. The walls went up, but everybody went home and left the roof. Nor did they return. The spirit was willing, but the flesh was weak.

When he left St. Peter's Sorin had been forced to split his community into two parts. Upon the insistence of the Bishop, nine novices had remained under the tutelage of Brother Vincent. When they were later left without a priest, Sorin ordered them to South Bend, and the Bishop did not object. Early in February they loaded a large wagon with beds, pots, pans, religious articles, and enough food to last for the journey. The wagon was drawn by four horses. Eight head of cattle completed the cavalcade. Disaster threatened at the very start. As they climbed the first hill the poorly shod horses found footing difficult on a film of ice. The cattle had more difficulty. Near the top, those in front began to slip backwards. They went down like dominoes, and men, horses, wagon, and cattle were back at the bottom again. It took all the watching neighbors to get them over that hill.

Confronted by a river, they loaded everything on a great flatboat and started across. The cattle grew restive; first one, then all, went overboard and swam—to the wrong shore. There is no record of what the Brothers said while rounding them up. On land, finally, a wagon wheel gave way. They bought a large sled and transferred the load and the damaged wagon. One of the Brothers froze his toes. Two others had frozen faces. When they wished to eat a piece of bread it had to be cut with an axe. They reached Notre Dame on February 27th. Sorin fed them warm soup—and pointed to the unfinished roof. By March 19th, the feast of St. Joseph, Sorin celebrated the first Mass in the new, roofed, chapel. (Faith *and* good works has ever been the Notre Dame formula. In

the Army game of 1928, after Captain Fred Miller had led
the team in a Hail Mary during a time-out, center Tim
Moynihan said: "Let's play a little football, too!")

Clement Ruckers disputed the claim of Alexis Coquillard
to being the first student. Both were there in the winter of
'42. Other students came. Their fathers paid in goods instead
of cash. In his book Father Hope imagined a barter between
Sorin and a parent.

"I got a boy, a right smart lad. I thought we might make
some kind of a dicker for his schoolin'."

"How old is he?"

"Nigh on to fourteen. His maw's dead and I'm thinkin' on
ketchin' me another woman. His maw was a bright woman.
She spelled him and learned him to read and write. What do
it cost?"

"Well, for one hundred dollars we will feed him, mend his
clothes, give him medical attention and the complete English
course—spelling, reading, grammar, bookkeeping, surveying,
astronomy."

"I aint got a hundred dollars."

"How much have you got?"

"Twenty-five or thirty."

"What do you do for a living?"

"Farm. And I got a grist mill. Could you use some corn
meal?"

"Yes."

"A couple of hogs?"

"Fine."

"His maw had a lot of clothes."

"No."

"How about some furniture?"

"Good. Could you pay the thirty dollars cash when he
comes?"

"All right. Do he get Latin, too?"

"That will cost another hog."

"Do he learn to play the piano-forte?"

"That will cost much more. Two big hogs. He will have to bring his bedding, knife and fork, six shirts, six pairs of stockings, handkerchiefs, towels, and so on."

A second colony arrived from France in July, 1843, via New York and Detroit, another hazardous journey, but with more organization and preparation than that of the pathfinders. It included two priests, one seminarian, one Brother, and four Sisters. The first Sunday after their arrival the chapel was packed. The frontiersmen had seen black robes aplenty, but these women in their somber dresses, with flaring French hats, were a great novelty. Sorin explained that the devotion of the Sisters would add greatly to the development of the school. They would tend to the cooking, washing, mending, nursing, milking the cows, and other such duties, making it possible for the men to concentrate on other projects, such as the new novitiate and the new college building already being planned.

The Sisters lived in a loft over the chapel. There was only one window, their fluted caps scraped the roof, the place was dark and stuffy, the bugs came through the chinks in summer, and the cold air came through in winter. For the first few nights they were visited by rats, fleas, and such. Apart from all this, the Sisters were quite comfortable (Sorin wrote in his chronicles) and adjusting to the great adventure in the new land. They were most happy to be serving Mary, Queen of Heaven. Their names were Mary of the Sacred Heart, Mary of Bethlehem, Mary of Calvary, and Mary of Nazareth.

Before leaving Vincennes, Sorin had consulted an architect identified only as "Mr. Marsile," and they had drawn up plans for the college building to be erected at Notre Dame. Mr. Marsile was to arrive in the spring of '43. Meanwhile Sorin was to prepare as much lumber and brick as possible. The lumber was available, and the bricks were made from marl beds on the property. By spring, sixty thousand feet of lumber, two hundred fifty thousand bricks, and the necessary lime were ready. Mr. Marsile was not. Sorin went ahead with a much smaller building he and his people could safely erect. It is what is now called Old College, or The Mission House, located at the right of the old library and (with some patching here and there) is the only original landmark on the campus. Today's visitors will marvel at what Sorin crowded into the small building: a dormitory for the expected students, dining room, bakery, classroom, and clothes room.

When it was finished the architect belatedly arrived, with two workmen. Lumber was available. Bricks were ready. Ah! But the money? Sorin scraped about. The Society for the Propagation of the Faith sent money from France, as it would do in other emergencies. Mr. Byerly, who had welcomed Sorin to America, now had a store in South Bend. He loaned five hundred dollars cash and extended two thousand dollars credit. Father Marivault, of the second colony, turned over an inheritance of twelve hundred dollars. Sorin decided to go ahead with the main part of the "huge" college building and leave the two wings for later. The work began August 24, 1843. After four days the cornerstone was laid. A fire, and winter weather, slowed the pace of building, but all was ready for the twenty-five students who came in the fall of 1844.

As early as December 2nd Sorin had inserted his first ad for students in the *South Bend Free Press*. The building (quoting the architect) would be equal to anything in the United States. Physicians and Sisters would guard the health of students. Discipline would be paternal, but firm. Morals and deportment would be carefully guarded, and reading matter assiduously watched. There would be no whipping. There would be no interference on the part of the faculty with the tenets of any non-Catholic student.

In November, 1843, Sorin drew apart from the Community to make his annual retreat in silence and seclusion. The spot he chose was an eminence between the two lakes and was calld The Island, because it was surrounded by marshland. Sorin experienced such peace that in the midst of his retreat he began to chop down trees and clear the ground. This was where novices would lay the foundation for the spiritual life and receive the godly strength they would need if Notre Dame were to succeed. By December, 1844, two buildings had gone up, the novitiate and the chapel, and the second of the two prime conditions laid down by the Bishop of Vincennes had been fulfilled. The site, now occupied by the Community House, would continue as a spiritual center through the years. Roads soon traversed the marshland.

One year after Sorin's arrival and before the new college building had been finished, John B. DeFrees, a resident of South Bend, had come to Father Sorin and offered to procure from the state senate, of which he was a member, a charter for the college. On January 15, 1844, Mr. DeFrees, a Methodist, expressed his faith in the zeal of his Catholic neighbors:

> Be it enacted by the General Assembly of the State of Indiana, that Edward Frederick Sorin, Francis Louis Cointet, Theophilus Jerome Marivault, Francis Gouesse and their associates and successors in office be, and are hereby constituted and declared to be, a body corporate and politic, by the name and style of the "University of Notre Dame du Lac" and by that name shall have perpetual succession with full power and authority to confer and grant, or cause to be

26

conferred and granted, such degrees and diplomas in the liberal arts and sciences, and in law and medicine, as are usually conferred and granted in other universities of the United States, provided, however, that no degrees shall be conferred and diplomas granted except to students who have acquired the same proficiency in the liberal arts and sciences, and in law and medicine as is customary in other universities in the United States.

Sorin called all his professors together. If they were to be worthy of the Senator's faith, they must organize their studies in such a way as to justify the charter. This was the first faculty meeting.

A traveler coming suddenly upon this secluded place of prayers and meditations, frantic building, and songs to the Queen of Heaven, while kneeling in moon-bright snow, might have thought it a sort of Brigadoon.

5. NOTRE DAME ANOMALOUS

EARLY educators had to be hardy men to establish colleges amid pioneer poverty and indifference. Notre Dame was almost an anomaly. Sorin had been summoned by a French Bishop to what he assumed was still a French Northwest Territory. He had been shocked to find that the French language was not spoken even in the village of Napoleon; to discover that his first task as a teacher would be to learn, and be laughed at as he learned, the language of the new people who had come from New England, Maryland, Virginia, Kentucky, and Ohio. He applied the French educational system (which keeps a pupil so busy that he has neither the time nor the energy to get into trouble) on the sons of pioneers, mostly pugnacious Irish.

The college course, comprising six years, included rudimentary high-school work, plus Latin, Greek, mathematics, and all the religious studies and exercises that could be crowded into a daily schedule that lasted from five-thirty in the morning until nine at night. The boy was supposed to find time for his own fun, which he usually did, and not always on his own time. The teachers, having been boys, knew their tricks, winked at some, were sometimes amused, often outraged, in the eternal battle between authority and youthful vitality.

Sorin made the rules, left their enforcement to others, gave his time and talent to his own problems which were varied and considerable. As the religious Superior, he supervised his priests, Brothers, and nuns. He recruited and trained novices. He was parish priest for the surrounding territory; and when not in his office or at some building project, he could be in the saddle, heading toward administration of the last rites, hearing confessions at a village which had not seen a priest for two months, saying Mass for Indians. The hours on horseback were useful to think about major problems, including those which had to be solved quickly. In his delayed contact with the Mother House he took full advantage of what was known as Presumption of Permission and hoped the Abbé Moreau would not decide he had presumed too much, as sometimes happens in enterprises where the Home Office is far removed from changing conditions on the front line.

He had no illusions about the status of his school despite its charter. He saw his obligation as providing moral training and a workable education to pupils who, in most cases, lacked the background to absorb much beyond that. His teachers were not equipped to give advanced education, but he did what he could with what he had and overlooked no opportunity to improve. He wrote to the Jesuits who had been through these school problems before him, and patterned his academic program after that used at St. Louis University. The first real scholar on the faculty was Father St. Michael Shawe, a secular priest from Vincennes who came in 1845 and remained for four years as teacher and preacher, until requested by the Bishop of Detroit to become pastor of the Cathedral and editor of the *Catholic Vindicator*, the newspaper of the diocese.

Sorin's chief assistants were Brother Vincent and Father Francis Cointet, who had been a classmate at Le Mans, and who arranged his teaching schedule so that he could spend days at a time in the surrounding mission field. "It was to the sons of the forest," a biographer wrote of Cointet, "the remnant of the red race, the poor Irish laborers on the railroad, that he delighted to break the bread of life. Now riding at nightfall to reach some Indian wigwam, or seated in a shanty by the railroad hearing confessions of poor Irish women, or explaining catechism to little children or teaching men their duties as citizens and Christians."

After the diocese of Fort Wayne was created (1858), the Notre Dame priests were relieved of the added duties as missionaries. The average income from the missions of each such priest for the eight years Sorin kept records, was $143.37.

Father Badin returned in 1845 from a long absence in the mission field to see the fulfillment of his dream. He remained the stark individualist. At Mass he would take the missal from the altar, place it on the head of the nearest small altar

29

boy, gesticulate through the sermon, though his right arm was partially paralyzed, as his human bookstand might be before the homily was over. He was loud and long, and the weather made no difference, nor did the comfort of his auditors. One hot Sunday they rose en masse and stood outside listening. Badin ordered the doors closed upon them and resumed his sermon. He would say his office (the daily religious reading required of a priest) in the saddle, and it was said that the faithful horse had been trained to pause momentarily at certain reverent passages.

Badin saw the orphans' home he had visioned appear at Notre Dame in the form of a Manual Labor School, which would become the first Catholic trade school in the country. The orphans were trained in various crafts by the Brothers and given education according to their abilities, which were considerable in the case of James Burns who would become President of the University. Badin proposed a deal with Sorin which may have been the first lifetime annuity contract; he exchanged a piece of property in Louisville for bed and board at Notre Dame as long as he lived. He lived to age eighty-five and Sorin was chided for having been outsmarted by the old man. Sorin said that was one debt Notre Dame could never pay in full, nor could the Catholic religion, which owed much of its vitality in the Northwest Territory to the zeal of Badin. His bones rest under the replica of his original log chapel, exactly under the path his weary feet had trod so often from the epistle side of the altar to the gospel side and back again. Badin Hall, named for him, was long the residence of freshmen who never knew how lucky they were not to have had him for a supervising prefect.

Sorin continued to build, to adapt, as necessity and opportunity arose. There were times when he seemed daring or impractical, but his judgments were sound and so were his intuitions about people. He built shops, an infirmary (hospital), a new church, had himself named the first college postmaster by the good offices of Henry Clay, and used the salary for the good of the Community. In 1852 he added the two wings to the Main Building. The Brothers had become so proficient in the manufacture of bricks from the sticky yellow marl found around the lakes that Sorin went into the brick manufacturing business. Later he sold the concession to an outside company. For years this income was useful, sometimes preventing bankruptcy, and, on occasion, providing luxuries like a new bell for the church or chimes "nothing so fine this side of the Alleghenies." (The affluence of Notre Dame could almost be gauged from the weight of succeeding bells, which signaled formal ceremonies.)

Sorin knew the value of public relations. In 1845 he invited personages from towns in Indiana and Michigan to attend the closing of the school year on July 4th. The ceremonies began with a reading of the Declaration of Independence. There was an address by Father Sorin and a play called *Procida*. Everybody "talked so much about that great night at the college" that a Mr. Keegan, correspondent for "some Eastern newspapers," covered the next July 4th ceremony (1846) and may have been the first outside reporter ever to visit the campus. He wrote in detail about the "upwards of seven hundred persons who arrived in about eighty carriages and four stages. The porticos, dormitories and avenues overflowed with the crowds. There were gymnastics to impress parents that the physical health of their offspring was not being neglected. The band, lately organized, discoursed excellent music." There was great interest in the new museum —a collection of beasts, birds, fishes, reptiles, and antiquities that Father Sorin had recently acquired in trade for two lots in Detroit.

The populace began to rely on the college for the annual Fourth of July entertainment, and the students and faculty responded with such innovations as "Shakespearean plays with painted scenery." There was great disappointment in 1848 when Mr. Nightingale, the pageant director and an obviously sensitive artist, rode into the sunset on the eve of the event and never returned. "The whole thing was botched," Brother Gatian wrote of Mr. Nightingale, "by a choleric individual inclined to overvalue his own capacities and unable to get along with backwoods boys." Everything was bigger and better in 1849 when the first commencement was held with Neal Gillespie and Richard Shortis as the only graduates. Both would become priests and officers of the University.

A new church was consecrated that same year and Sorin always embellished such great events with grace and style. He was in the too familiar situation of being without funds when an insurance man suggested it was time to take out protection, and was told to come back in a few weeks. Before he did, the Sister Sacristan was awakened at midnight by a fire which destroyed the apprentice dormitories, bakery, shops, stables, and altar linens. The loss was three thousand dollars. Sorin wrote disconsolately to Moreau: "All the bread and flour has been burned. I don't know how I am going to serve breakfast for one hundred fifty persons." Help came from the townspeople. Four days later Sorin began to rebuild. Bigger and better buildings arose. Priest "beggars" again went out to get the money.

Sorin had said in a sermon: *If all men fail me, there is one treasury that is always full, that of our Most Holy Lady. When this school shall grow a bit more, I shall raise her aloft so that, without asking, all men shall know why we have succeeded here. To that Lovely Lady, raised high on a dome, a golden dome, men may look and find the answer.*

6. FIGHT TO LIVE!

CHOLERA was an ever lurking danger. In 1854, an epidemic of wide dimensions, which hit the South and New Orleans especially hard, touched down suddenly as a tornado. Three students went home in coffins. Five Brothers, three postulants, and five Sisters died so quickly that, to avoid panic, the bodies were buried at night without religious solemnity. Father John Curley, just over from Ireland and ordained but a year, had been most zealous in caring for the sick. He was taken. Father Cointet lasted but five days. "When I saw he was going to die," Sorin wrote, "I almost lost my mind." Cointet, his oldest friend and closest advisor, was buried with Deseille and Petit whom Sorin considered saints.

A general exodus of students was feared, and Sorin had considered closing the school, but the disease finally abated. Notre Dame had become a leper and was thought to be threatening the countryside. The superstitious said a curse was upon the school. The Know-Nothings proclaimed the cholera had something to do with the Catholic religon brought in by foreigners. Medical opinion centered on the two lakes, the drinking water, or a certain type of fish the Indians had always considered poisonous. Sorin thought the

33

breeding ground was in the marshland surrounding the lakes. He had attempted to lower the water level and drain the marshes through a narrow stream that emptied into the river. But the stream passed through adjacent property owned by a Mr. Rush, who stopped the flow by building a dam. Sorin sought to buy the Rush property, but the owner demanded what Sorin considered an exorbitant price.

The cholera returned and after two more deaths Sorin said: "There are times when a vigorous stand upsets the enemy."

He summoned six of his men, told them to get axes and demolish the dam on Holy Thursday. Then he went to the altar and said his Mass. The dam was demolished. Public opinion supported Sorin. Mr. Rush gave up the land for eight thousand dollars, the marsh dried up, there was no more cholera.

Difficulties arise when the interests of religious communities clash. It was because of the dispute between the Bishop of Vincennes and Father Moreau that Sorin had moved from St. Peter's and founded Notre Dame. He had been so certain that the Bishop would be pleased to have the nuns from France in 1845 that he had not asked permission; so that the first word the Bishop of Vincennes had about their presence in his diocese was from other sources. He wrote Sorin that he already had, at Terre Haute, one community of religious women, and one was enough. The little town of Bertram, Michigan, was just four miles from Notre Dame; after securing permission, Sorin moved the nuns there, and they trudged back and forth each day. After awhile, for reasons not recorded, the Bishop of Detroit rescinded his welcome. Fortunately Vincennes had acquired a new bishop who made no objections, and the nuns were shuttled back to Mishawaka, nearer Notre Dame and in Indiana, but still too far away from the campus.

It was problems like these that Sorin juggled during his lonely jogs on horseback; and for this one his patroness, The Most Holy Lady, had a totally unexpected solution for a pioneer priest to whom m-o-n-e-y had always been something to be begged or borrowed. Small financial showers, the beginnings of *endowment*, had begun to fall in the Fifties.

Reverend Philip Foley, pastor of St. Thomas parish, Toledo, Ohio, gave the University four thousand dollars with the understanding that it would maintain two students each year for a period of twenty years.

William Corby, whose name would rank high in Notre Dame annals, arrived as a seminarian in 1855, with an outright gift of land in Detroit that Sorin later sold for six thousand dollars.

King Louis Philippe of France sent seven hundred dollars to be used by "the tall and grave missionary who had founded a university where the French language and the French culture would always be held in honor." There had been help now and then from The Association for the Propagation of the Faith in France.

Neal Gillespie, of Lancaster, Ohio, one of the two members of the first graduating class, had become a priest. His sister Eliza had become a Holy Cross nun and took the name of Mary Angela. Their father had died some years previously and their mother had married William T. Phelan. She was delighted to have her children in the religious life, but saddened that they had to live in poverty, wear patched clothing, and exist on a skimpy diet. She interceded with her husband. Just before the commencement exercises in 1855 Sorin had received a startling letter from Mr. Phelan:

> My property has a value of $89,650. It is encumbered by mortgages to the extent of $22,500. I give it all to you providing you will assume the obligation of paying off the

mortgages and guarantee me an annuity of $3,000. As security for this annuity, I will expect you to give me a mortgage on the Notre Dame property of $50,000.

Sorin had long had a dream of founding a companion college for women. He wanted to bring the Holy Cross nuns back to Notre Dame. The money from Mr. Phelan had been providential. And that is how St. Mary's, sometimes known to Notre Dame men as "that matrimonial farm across the Dixie Highway," came into being.

Six of the nuns were appointed as a council. Under oath they declared their intention of forming a corporation for the erection of St. Mary's Academy. Sorin gave them fifty of the one hundred eighty-five acres he had bought from Mr. Rush, and five thousand dollars of the money he had received from Mr. Phelan. Sister Angela later became a President of St. Mary's and a biographer of Father Cointet.

There was another problem which could not be solved by money nor, seemingly, by prayer.

A religious community cannot survive without discipline. The subject must bow in mind and heart to the dictates of his Superior; but the Superior has the duty to make his commands reasonable. The Abbé Moreau was essentially a man of action through prayer; Sorin a man of prayer through action. There was the three-month gap in communication. The chronicles also reveal a man between Sorin and the dear friend to whom he had sworn obedience. Back at the Mother House in France, Rev. Charles Moreau, a nephew of the Superior, seemed to look upon most of Sorin's presumptions of permission as unwarranted ambition and arrogant independence.

Sorin's action in immediately rebuilding after the fire of 1849 had brought a rebuke. Another came when he sent a small group to California during the Gold Rush. Success would have relieved the poverty that plagued Notre Dame and the Mother House; but they found no gold, and one of the Brothers died on the trip.

Sorin's yearly accounts were questioned, despite the fact that much of his business was by barter. The switch from French educational methods to those of the Jesuits of St. Louis University had been considered heretical. The very qualities for which Sorin was being widely praised in his new country—his spirit, administrative daring, and accurate adjustments to American methods, were black marks in France. The struggle came to a climax in 1852 and Charles Moreau seemed to have triumphed. Sorin was to be relieved of his post and assigned to India, where the Congregation "needed its best man" to head a mission to Bengal and eventually become Bishop of Dacca.

Sorin was crushed. Letters, some from bishops, went to Moreau, pleading that Sorin *was* Notre Dame, that it must fail without him. When this plea was ignored, Sorin appealed to the American Bishops for advice. They finally reached agreement: The Bishop of Vincennes could, within the rules, release Sorin and all members of the Notre Dame Community from their vows to the Abbé Moreau and the Mother House in France. In agonizing steps for all concerned, the drama was played in these acts:

1. Sorin informed Moreau that henceforth his obedience would be to the Bishop of Vincennes.

2. Moreau, appalled, threatened to take the case to Rome. Meanwhile he was sending a General Visitor to conduct an investigation.

3. The visitor was Father Chappe who had made his vows with Sorin. He was treated courteously, but Sorin held to his position.

4. Without warning, Sorin capitulated.

5. Sorin said a dramatic farewell to his people, and left for France. No one expected they would ever see him again. And what would happen to Notre Dame when a new man came from France?

6. The man who came from France was Sorin. In face-to-face conversations he had convinced Moreau that the man in the field must have a certain freedom of action.

7. Sorin had long maintained that misunderstandings would be few if Moreau would come to Notre Dame and see for himself. In 1857 that happened. Sorin had arranged a welcome: priests, Brothers, and students were lined up. The bells boomed. Moreau described it:

> They run towards me; they almost crush me; for quite awhile I am unable to do aught but bless them and embrace them. Finally we make our way to the church where I intone the *Te Deum* and celebrate a Mass of Thanksgiving.

The next day, in the French manner, they got down to business, discussed presumptions of permission, and the fifteen thousand-franc debt which the Mother House had borrowed from Notre Dame. Sorin resolved this by applying his own patrimony, recently received, to the debt. The financial report revealed that University assets were valued at a net of $159,047.15. The Abbé was well pleased and departed with the customary ceremony.

All that settled, Sorin turned with much less success to a problem which baffles any man: the women of his family disagreed. The Notre Dame nuns, mostly engaged in physical work and living on campus, were fiercely loyal to Sorin. The St. Mary's nuns, mostly teachers housed at the college, were beginning to quarrel with Sorin's educational methods and to demand that they be allowed to progress on their own. This was the first faculty trouble.

Meanwhile there were, and had always been, the students.

7. WILLIE ORD AND FRIENDS

ONE subject on which Sorin and Moreau never lost unity of thought was discipline. No one at Notre Dame had any real freedom of action. Even the few lay professors were bound by rules that governed all their movements. They had to live on the college grounds, conform to all the religious exercises, not go into town without permission, put out the candle by nine o'clock, and under no consideration *imbibe*. Violation of that last stricture could mean the forfeiture of a certain portion of the professor's salary.

Prefects (mostly Brothers) saw to it that students got up on time and dressed quietly; and did not make too much of a clatter on the stairs leading to the chapel in their wooden shoes. (Leather was still a luxury.) If Johnny cut up during chapel, he would get no breakfast. The prefect was charged with seeing that the boys walked, not ran, to the privy. Chewing tobacco was not forbidden, merely discouraged; those who insisted on chewing were compelled to pay the servants who had to clean up after them in study halls and classrooms. The playground in front of the college was divided into two sections, one for the college men and the other for the prep- and grade-school students. Order was preserved. Nobody was allowed to run into the building for a drink of water; he was to ask the Brother in charge, who would bring a pitcher. Theoretically, at least. Boys were not to slouch around in careless postures or unbecoming attire. It was strictly forbidden to blow the nose with the hand. In the refectory, they stood until Father Sorin entered. There was always soup; and the cook was under strict orders to keep it thick and not water it down.

Everything was done to keep the young men away from South Bend. When it was necessary for a student to make a purchase, he had to be accompanied by a prefect. Students had not taken the vow of poverty; it was usually built-in. Patches were always "in." The "good suit" was kept in the clothes room; when a parent was known to be coming the young man was always carefully dressed and shined. Baths were permitted twice a week. The small boys had to see the Sisters to have their feet washed and hair combed. Those with a shaving problem could use their razors twice each week, but only after dinner. Physical punishment was forbidden. (The wrong person might be belted.)

One student, Willie Ord, was a big, strong lad who had not been brought up to knuckle down. After he had attempted, on four separate occasions, to strike his preceptor, the council decided to "give him his trunk," the expression used for an expulsion. Father Sorin overruled the decision. The fact that Willie's bills were not paid could have been a factor. A few weeks later, when the occasion permitted, Willie led a few other lads on a "skive" to town. All they had was a few beers, and all they felt was happy. All Willie really did was start prancing around, yelling at the top of his hearty voice. At the river he decided to swim, and did a striptease. This time Father Sorin almost yielded to the council; but Willie was still in debt.

In a few days Willie was at it again. He slugged Mr. St. Mar, who said that unless something was done about Willie

Ord, the University could find itself another drawing teacher. His services were more necessary than Willie's presence, and in the meanwhile Willie's father had made the mistake of paying his bill. So ended the Notre Dame saga of Willie Ord.

Another student, Tom Bracken, had resisted reform, and the council had decided on dismissal. This time there was no exception by the Rev. Superior. A letter was written to Bracken, Sr., to come and get his lad. He came. He heartily agreed that his son was a rapscallion who deserved everything the school people had given him or might want to give him. Wouldn't they keep Tom and whack him good every time he got out of line? Presumably, Tom, Jr., saw that the odds were against him. He stayed. Nothing more was written about him in the chronicles.

Now and then, on holidays, the boys were taken on long hikes, the idea being to walk all the devilment out of them. These trips were contests between the prefects and those students who wanted to smoke, to steal away and get a few beers or some cider. Sometimes farm girls would be watching, and the boys would yell and be yelled at by the farmers' daughters. If there were pumpkins in the fields there could be pumpkin fights; and ears of corn made good weapons. The boys did return tired, also the prefects.

The records of the Prefect of Discipline indicate that imbibing was considered a mortal sin. "G.D. deserves to have his name recommended for his successful efforts to observe no rule of the institution and not get expelled. . . . Mr. G., a frequent patron of the infirmary, finally got so much spiritus frumenti that he could not carry it or himself. He was permitted to go home permanently, as soon as he was able to make his way to the cars. . . . H.J. returned from South Bend so beastly drunk that he wished alternately to fight and embrace the Prefect of Discipline. He was given his trunk." The "Dirty Nineteen," a roistering group, decided there would

41

be safety in numbers, that the University, always hard up, would not dare a multiple expulsion. They returned from a wild trip to town, ready to settle for a few harsh words, supper, and bed. Their trunks were waiting.

The discipliners were sometimes embarrassed when the most intransigent rebel would return in mature years to receive an honorary degree, or to behave with strict rectitude. Often these successful prodigals eased the situation by crediting the discipline with being the exact medicine they had needed. The sons of pioneers had not been born with silver spoons, nor reared with silken rods.

8. THE CIVIL WAR

A LETTER from Sorin awaited Moreau when he returned to France from Notre Dame:

> During the past week the financial situation has become perilous in the extreme. All our best banks, even those in New York, are suspending payment. We ourselves have been taken for five thousand francs in New York. I hardly know how to face the storm. One might say that we have suspended payments ourselves, for every day we have to refuse to pay our bills, seeing that our treasury is empty. The panic is general.

Moreau was indignant, not so much with Sorin, as with the financial managers of the United States. Among the things Moreau did not understand, but with which Sorin had to cope, were the facts that the market had always been a fortuneteller, and the market of 1857 was registering nervousness over the unrest that was to culminate in civil war four years later. At that time such a financial retreat was called a panic. Now it is a recession or depression.

Students are sensitive to emotional and intellectual change. The University sided with the North and so did the majority of the students; but Notre Dame's students had always been drawn from all parts of the country; there were many Southerners and sympathizers. There were clashes, and when these began to interfere with scholastic decorum Father Sorin issued a firm edict: "Let those who wish take up arms; let those who remain remember this is a school where students may hold as they wish." The first campus military unit, called the Continental Cadets, paraded in South Bend in 1858.

Like most people in the North, Sorin thought the war would not last long. His sentiments were expressed in a letter about a year after the shooting began: "If we are correctly informed the war is to be closed at Corinth for the west and at Yorktown in Virginia. May God give our arms two such victories, as to crush at once this wicked rebellion." When the fall term of 1862 began, the wife of General William T. Sherman brought her young son Willy to Notre Dame and her daughter Minnie to St. Mary's. She wrote her husband that Willy had "more playmates than he could have at home in Ohio, and is very happy." Willy was popular with his minim (grade-school) mates, and when his mother visited him the people of South Bend made her welcome. During the '63 vacation she took her entire family to Vicksburg, where her husband was engaged. Willy became a great favorite with the 13th Regiment, as he rode with his father. They made him an honorary sergeant and gave him a uniform. Willy contracted "camp fever" and died at the Gayso Hotel in Memphis on October 3, 1863. A Notre Dame chaplain, Father

Joseph Carrier, was with him. In the fall of '64 Mrs. Sherman brought her family to South Bend, occupied the home of Schuyler Colfax, and entered her son Tommy in the minims. He was eight, as Willy had been when he entered. Atlanta had just been captured, his father was a hero, and Tommy took some teasing. Indignantly he wrote to his father: "You can count on ONE Notre Dame boy who believes you will have Christmas dinner on the sea-coast."

Shortly after St. Edward's Day in 1863, John B. Walker expressed his loathing for all Southerners so aggressively that Billy Welsh felled him with a brick. The authorities decided that Billy must leave. A goodly section of the student body, though emphatically Northern in sympathy, protested and asked Father Patrick Dillon, who was acting President during a Sorin absence, to reconsider. Fearful of making a mistake, Dillon took days to make up his mind. The students erupted and refused to attend classes. Gradually the ring-leaders were weeded out, "given their trunks," and peace returned to the campus. There was a later affray between "Donovan from Vicksburg" and "Barker from Lafayette, Indiana." Sorin, back on the job, settled this one hurriedly, reminded the newspapers that the dispute between the two boys was not political, that the students were never allowed to discuss politics, that literary pursuits alone occupied their interest. Anyhow, the boy with the fractured skull was doing nicely!

More than thirty years after the Civil War, Sorin was celebrating his fiftieth year in the priesthood. Archbishop John Ireland, in a lengthy discourse covering Sorin's career, said:

"It is a lamentable fact that few priests were sent to the front to minister to the soldiers. Father Sorin's community was weak in numbers, but he sent forward seven to serve as chaplains. He appealed to the Sisters of Holy Cross, and they rushed southward from Notre Dame and St. Mary's to care for the wounded and soothe the pillow of the dying. Few things in the past half-century were done more effectually to break down anti-Catholic prejudice than the sending of our Sisters to the battlefield and military hospitals. There were other priests and other Sisters in the war, but those of Holy Cross made up the greater part of the roster. . . . Father Sorin, you saved the honor of the Church."

Paul Gillen was a native of Ireland who for twenty years had traveled the country as a business agent for the *Boston Pilot*. Shortly before the war, he became a priest and joined the community at Notre Dame. He was in New York in 1861, representing the community in a business matter, when he learned there was a need of priests to accompany Catholic soldiers into battle. Though he was in his fifties, he received Sorin's permission and caught up with the 22nd Regiment of New York Volunteers on the eve of the Battle of Bull Run. He heard confessions until late at night and in the morning gave general absolution. Hundreds of his Catholic boys died on that field, and Father Gillen's horse was "in a fine lather" when he got back to the Capitol after "that ignominious retreat." He contrived a buggy which could be converted, as need arose, into a sleeping compartment, an ambulance, or a chapel. He drove this contraption from one regiment to another, from battle to battle, administering the sacraments and giving comfort to the wounded. Tall and spare, with that wiry robustness that seemed to defy sickness, he served through the entire war, returned to Notre Dame, and lived until October 20, 1882.

Father James Dillon, under Sorin's orders, joined Corcoran's Irish Legion of General Thomas Francis Meagher's famous Irish Brigade in the summer of '61. He was young, enthusiastic, a ready talker. In one battle, when the officers were cut down, he found himself leading and rallying the soldiers; and not until he was relieved by a "more fitting

45

officer," did he think of the incongruity of a priest pushing soldiers into battle. (At the beginning of the war the chaplains were not commissioned officers. In August, 1861, they were commissioned and put on salary.) Dillon's constitution, unlike that of the rugged Father Gillen, was delicate. The rigors of camp life brought on a recurrence of lung trouble temporarily arrested before the war. He persisted until August, 1864, before resigning. He died in 1868.

9. FAIR CATCH CORBY

SHORTLY after joining the Irish Brigade, Father James Dillon had written to Sorin that the work was too much for one man. He suggested that Father William Corby be assigned. It was done; and one of Notre Dame's most colorful and enduring legends was in process.

William Corby, born October 2, 1833, was the son of a Detroit physician. In 1853 he and three younger brothers entered Notre Dame. The next year his father asked about the cost of educating William for the priesthood. Sorin answered: "About one hundred seventy dollars per year. If you would prefer, the entire education can be guaranteed for one thousand dollars." (In advance, probably. Sorin never overlooked an opportunity to pick up cash. There may have been a flour bill to meet.) Corby entered the novitiate in 1854 at age twenty-one, became Prefect of Discipline in 1859, was ordained in 1860, and in 1861 became Director of the

Manual Labor School and pastor of St. Patrick's parish in South Bend. There may well have been some collusion with his friend Father Dillon in the latter's request that Corby come to assist him, inasmuch as Corby was quoted that now there would be "no old women to bother him and no pew rent to collect."

His first engagement was the bloody and indecisive Battle of Fair Oaks, where over twelve thousand were lost on both sides. He was felled by malaria, returned to the field in time for Antietam, Fredericksburg, Chancellorsville, and Gettysburg.

The morning of July 2, 1863, found the Irish Brigade posted on Cemetery Ridge. Across the valley where the town rested, one mile away, the enemy could clearly be seen on Seminary Ridge. At four in the afternoon the Confederates attacked and drove back the Union Third Corps. In a few moments the Irish Brigade would go to their assistance. Father Corby appealed to Colonel Patrick Kelly: "We've been marching constantly for weeks. My men have not had a chance to go to confession. Let me stand on that rock where they can see me." He stood on that rock, told them to make a fervent act of contrition, and they would be restored to grace by the general act of contrition he was about to impart. As he placed the purple stole over his shoulder and raised his right hand, every man, Catholic or not, fell to his knees. The order came: "Order arms!" The troops rushed down to the valley where they would repel the Confederates. For a minute Corby stood motionless on the rock, gazing on the back of many a soldier running to battle "in his grave-clothes."

General absolution was not unusual. The dramatic circumstances of this crucial battle made this incident remembered. Notre Dame officially celebrated it on the battlefield at the Gettysburg centennial. It is recorded in the campus art gallery by Paul Wood's colorful panorama of the scene at Gettysburg. And by a bronze statue on the small campus before Corby Hall where impious students sometimes look at the upraised hand and call out: "Fair catch Corby."

Peter Paul Cooney, a native of County Roscommon, Ireland, came to Michigan at the age of five, but did not arrive at Notre Dame until he was thirty. He taught for awhile, became a priest at thirty-seven, and was a chaplain at thirty-nine. He was a throwback to Badin, "peppery, cantankerously insistent on order and discipline, with an inclination to lecture everyone; but such traits were very forgivable in the light of the truly magnanimous spirit he manifested as a chaplain." He served with the Indiana Volunteers in a smaller theater of the war, but did himself proud in what action he saw. "To Father Cooney, our chaplain," Colonel Mullen wrote after the battle of Stone River, Tennessee, "too much praise cannot be given. He was deeply solicitous, cool and indifferent to danger, and in the name of the regiment I thank him."

Two other priests, Rev. Julian Bourget, from the Mother House in France, and Father Zephirin Leveque, a Canadian, were neither so rugged nor so lucky. Each died in 1862, from illness and exhaustion.

The draft had brought Sorin a serious problem. His Brothers, young and healthy, were subject to the regular draft, and a loss in numbers would bring definite disruption to the daily life of the school. In 1863, when a letter from Mrs. Sherman requested a chaplain for the unit in which her two brothers were serving, Sorin may have decided that what was good for Mrs. Sherman and her two brothers might also be good for Notre Dame and its Brothers. He sent one of his best priests, Father Joseph Celestine Carrier, a native of France who had been marked for a career in science. A man of energy and distinction, Carrier impressed both Grant and Sherman. Upon instructions from Sorin, he prepared a petition which stressed Notre Dame's need for its Brothers, and the contribution it had already made in chaplains and nurses. After Sherman and Grant signed the petition, he had interviews in Washington with Secretary of War Stanton, and with Lincoln himself. The request for exemption was granted, after which the Brothers themselves upset this carefully built diplomatic cart.

Sorin, a superb politician, avoided identification with either political party and maintained pleasant relationships with the people currently in power. Schuyler Colfax, a South Bend native who had been the Republican congressman since 1858, became Speaker of the House in 1863 and had lent his weight to the successful effort to have the Brothers exempted. During the elections of 1864, he suggested that now might be a good time for all Notre Dame voters to come to the aid of the party that had befriended them. Sorin, as lightly as possible, knowing he was treading on thin ice, suggested that for the good of the Order and of the University, it might be well for the Brothers to go along. But the Brothers were mostly Irish, and the Irish were mostly Democrats and not inclined to obedience. So they ignored Sorin trying to tell Irishmen how to vote, especially for a black Republican!

When the voting returns from Notre Dame came in, Colfax was furious. The exemption of the Brothers was canceled. Father Carrier returned to Washington on his most difficult diplomatic mission. Mrs. Sherman wrote again to both Lincoln and Stanton. Her letters (luck of the Irish)! arrived on the very morning her husband had telegraphed the President that Savannah had fallen and the March through Georgia had been concluded. Any friends of General Sherman. And so the Brothers were again exempted. Anyhow, Colfax had been re-elected. (In 1868, on the fifth ballot, he was nominated for Vice-President and ran on the ticket with U. S.

Grant. The Grant-Colfax ticket won. The popular vote was 3,013,313 to 2,703,933. Colfax carried his home state by 10,572 votes, 176,552 to 166,980. History does not record the returns from the Notre Dame precinct.)

More than eighty sisters of the Holy Cross Community at Notre Dame served the wounded and the victims of smallpox, typhoid, malaria, and yellow fever at three hospitals in Memphis, and single hospitals in Cairo, Mound City, Paducah, Louisville, Franklin, Missouri, and near Washington, D.C. They made no distinction between the wearers of the Blue or the Gray. Many soldiers looked for the first time on women in religious garb.

A young soldier was apparently in the last stages of malaria. The doctors wanted to send him home to die, so his bed could be used by somebody else. Sister M. de Sales thought he had a chance. She was sure that the journey would kill him. She persuaded the doctors to give him a few more days. The boy got well. Twenty-six years later the Holy Cross Sisters were opening a hospital in Columbus, Ohio. The Bishop and Governor were on hand for the laying of the cornerstone. Governor Campbell delivered an address and then went to shake hands with the Superior, Sister M. de Sales, who had saved his life. It was the first time they had met since the war.

PART II
EMERGENCE

10. WALK INTO THE FUTURE

THE French Revolution had helped Notre Dame to be born. The Civil War put it firmly on its feet for the walk into the future.

In 1863 a banquet, plus fireworks, celebrated the presence of 236 students. In 1864 there were 400. In 1865 there were 512. From 1859 to 1865 the number of teachers had doubled, from 17 to 34. In 1858 the basic charge was $270.00. In 1864 it had jumped to $320 paper money or $160 gold. It dropped to $230 and climbed back to $245. These changes reflected the currency fluctuations during the Civil War. Afterward, the figure for all basic expenses was stabilized at $300 for several generations. The surprisingly sharp increase in enrollment, contrary to earlier fears, was due to the fact that the majority of Notre Dame students were in the prep-school and minim departments. In upset times, Notre Dame was a safe place for children, as in the case of the family of General Sherman.

Sorin had been the man for his period, the brilliant ad-libber, the doctor with the pulmotor or the soothing syrup, the taskmaster, the one-man band, the publicist, and, when he thought necessary, the con man. He was still all of these, and his talents would now be of even greater value on a higher level. In the chain of command in the Congregation of the Holy Cross, he had been Provincial of Indiana and President of Notre Dame. In the new order he would remain as Provincial and supervise the work in Indiana, mainly Notre Dame. The choice of his successor was almost automatic. Father Patrick Dillon, a handsome black Irishman of strong personality, was the man to erect the planned new college building, because he had already established himself by supervising the building of St. Mary's College.

The Mother House had approved plans, drawn by Mr. Thomas, a Chicago architect, which would utilize a major part of the old Main Building. The Brothers had been gathering sand, lumber, bricks, and stone. They were poised and ready when school ended in June. The building was ready in September, a six-story, box-like structure that packed in classrooms, dormitories, refectory, study halls, and offices—and all for thirty-five thousand dollars! The *white* dome was erected the next year.

Academically, Father Dillon organized a commercial course of two years to supplement the six-year program in arts and letters. The first year included arithmetic, English, bookkeeping, German, geography, history, and writing; the second year, algebra, English, bookkeeping, German, geography, commercial law, and elocution. It is easy to understand the popularity of such a course, and how, backed by the intense hours of study, it produced graduates who could hold jobs and make money. (As time went on, it was purged of some of its high-school aspects. With the founding of the school of Commerce it would be dropped.) Lucius G. Tong, head of the department, noted for his thoroughness, became one of the first faculty "characters."

Father Dillon laid the foundations for the development of the sciences, utilizing the major talents of Father Carrier, head of the "Diplomatic Corps" during the Civil War. The scientific course also took six years of study, the first two of which were really high-school work. An American boy himself who had gone through Notre Dame as a student, the second President of the school realized that the severe French discipline could be applied only to the very youthful scholar. Sorin thought that Dillon's moves to ease restrictions constituted "laxity." Even though he had become too swiftly Americanized in his methods for the people at the Mother House, Sorin never changed substantially on the question of discipline, nor on his concept of the "tight little boarding school." He would grudgingly give ground, and gradually be outmaneuvered by the Presidents who followed him.

Dillon's tenure ended after two years. There had been no time limit set for his term, nor is there any record of personality clashes with Sorin. But Dillon was a strong-willed Irishman, definitely not the type to be dominated, even by Sorin, who, as he would later demonstrate, was definitely the type who might do just that. And Sorin did have a "thing" about the Irish. It reached a point in the late sixties when he forbade the observance of St. Patrick's Day on the predominantly Irish campus, on the ground that it wasted time and was not patriotic. But a lad named Tim O'Sullivan got a key to the balcony at the base of the dome atop the Main Building. At daybreak he serenaded with a cornet solo— *St. Patrick's Day in the Morning*. And the apparently comatose campus erupted with what may have been the first organized cheer from the student body. Timmy O'Sullivan became a priest, and was pointed out in later years as the Irishman who had put the Frenchman down.

Sorin had indeed been chagrined. On the next St. Paddy's Day he forbade even the wearing of the green. Two novices, Dave O'Leary and John Quinn, took a green ribbon from the Mass missal, split it, pinned the parts to their surplices, and marched into the sanctuary. They were given their trunks.

As they were leaving the campus, word came that Sorin had relented, and they could return. O'Leary did return, but Quinn did not come back until many years later when, as Monsignor Quinn, he was invited to preach the baccalaureate sermon, which he accepted as a vindication of the Irish Rebellion in the Sanctuary.

June 7, 1865, was a great day for the Irish and for Father Dillon in one of his last official appearances. The war was over, and the great General Sherman had come for the commencement exercises and to visit his family. At the reception Timothy Howard spoke for the faculty and Tommy Corcoran for the Senior department. Tom Ewing, representing the Junior department, said:

> You have come here, we know, to visit the halls where Willy studied, the groves where he played and the boys who were his friends, a title we are proud to claim. Since Notre Dame is within the limits of your command, it may often be necessary for you to repeat your visit. Should any insurrection among the neighboring tribes of Hoosiers turn your attention that way, you may count on the cooperation of the Notre Dame juniors.

The General replied that he would rather go into battle than try to say the things he felt; he assured them that the boys at Notre Dame would always be dear to him as companions to his sons.

11. THE MARCH IS ON

"The march is on
No brain or brawn
Can stop the charge of fighting men ..."
(from the Notre Dame Hike Song)

WILLIAM CORBY, the third President, had been chaplain of the Fighting Irish, but he was also a calm, urbane person who, having seen so many men running in their graveclothes, seemed incapable of becoming too disturbed by the little skirmishes of peaceful wars. He had long been a favorite of Sorin's, and no hint of discord was ever reported between them. He may have been the precursor of the modern personality college president. He presided between 1866 and 1872 when the walk into the future accelerated into a steady, drumbeat march.

There had been several attempts to launch student journals. *The Notre Dame Literary Gazette* had a brief existence. *The Progress,* a paper of thirty to forty pages "on various entertaining subjects," was begun in 1860 and continued until 1863 when Father Neal Gillespie, its guiding spirit, went to France to study. *The Olympic Gazette* and *The Weekly Bee* made fitful appearances. After Gillespie's return in 1867, *The Scholastic Year* began and has continued through the years, with inevitable changes in form, as *The Scholastic,* a weekly news magazine. It has always been a valuable source for anyone interested in the chronicle of events at Notre Dame. Sorin was delighted with its essays and anecdotes. In each issue he had printed the names of the new students and the exact dates of their arrival so that parents might "ascertain whether their sons had been loitering on their way to school."

From its pages we learn such things as Sorin himself carting a tremendous basket of peaches into the study hall of his "Little Princes," as he called the minims, of Master Page from Milwaukee bringing back a live eagle for which the students built a large cage ten-feet high, but without a roof, which resulted in a forlorn looking eagle when the rains came, and of the arrival of the fourteen thousand-pound bell which was hung in such fashion that two students on each side used their feet to pump it into action. There was great rivalry as to which group could produce the best tone. The bell still hangs in the church tower.

In 1868 Father Auguste Lemonnier, Corby's Vice-President who also happened to be Sorin's nephew, suggested the organization of an alumni association. Father Neal Gillespie became the first President. The first project was the production of a book memorializing the silver jubilee of the school in 1869. The work was largely that of Professor Joseph Lyons of the class of '62. Among other information it noted that the Civil War growth in enrollment was holding; there were almost five hundred students. Illinois led with 118, Indiana had 98; almost every state was represented. A later report (1872) listed 440 students, all except 12 were American-born, and their extractions were listed this way: 183 Irish, 155 American, 75 German, 21 French, 3 Spanish, 2 Scotch, one English, one Italian.

At the general chapter of the Congregation of the Holy Cross in 1868, Father Sorin was elected Superior-General. The power and authority were transferred from the Mother House in Le Mans to Notre Dame. Father Alexis Granger, long the faithful companion and advisor of Sorin, became Provincial. Sorin would continue to keep an eye on what happened at the University, but the gaze would not be so fixed. There would be frequent trips to various parts of the world. (He would make fifty ocean voyages between 1841 and the time of his death in 1893.)

As Superior-General he was regarded with awe on the campus by everybody but his Little Princes. A contemporary wrote: "His sense of dignity was almost majestic. He seldom laughed although he would smile kindly in conversation. Perpetually serious, he bore his great responsibilities with an air of grave confidence, his mighty frame moving with measured stride, his gigantic head and flashing black eyes on the alert for any irregularity. To the students his word of correction was suave but firm. To the faculty his word was not so suave. Even though he was no longer President, nor even Provincial, everyone at Notre Dame knew who was master. None but the minims ever approached him with anything like exuberance. Toward them he was surprisingly tender."

When, in October, 1868, Sorin was leaving for France, the students took the occasion to "manifest their good will and respect in the form of a public ovation." Such attentiveness was not forgotten. From France came an odd-shaped contrivance and a note: "I send you a new invention, the latest thing from Paris, a beautiful velocipede. That it will be a source of new and great enjoyments I have no doubt. After you have tamed it, you will please give a ride upon it to Eddie, Willie, Charlie, and Georgie of the minims."

It was a courtly campus. The European custom of extending New Year's greetings to superiors and officials was strictly adhered to, with speeches, of course, and the customary banquet at which "the choicest luxuries of the season were plentifully displayed." Father Carrier continued to excel in diplomatic missions. He came back from France with a fine telescope, a gift from Napoleon III to "Notre Dame, an outpost of French culture and power."

One spring morning Father Corby responded to a knock, received three students. They were blushing and embarrassed. "What can I do for you gentlemen?" the President asked. Would he step outside, please? There the entire student body awaited. It was April 1st, and he suspected some little trick. The crowd opened and revealed a magnificent black charger decked out in ribbons and a saddle. There was a presentation speech by Bill Walker of Marysville, California. The President responded, the students cheered, the band played a martial air, and the horse, or so it was said, danced to the music. Recreation for the rest of the day, naturally.

The law school was opened in 1869. It was a two-year course, with the prerequisite that entrants were obliged to have completed some work in the liberal arts. Notre Dame was emphasizing that hitherto the legal profession had had more than its share of "shysters and pettifoggers"; it was assailing the practice of "making a lawyer out of anyone who could buy a few law books and study in a lawyer's office while running errands for his would-be mentor." To raise the standards of law, Notre Dame sought to impress her students with the intimate relation between law and religion. *The University Chronicle,* student paper at the University of Michigan, was "agreeably surprised that Notre Dame demands of its law students some previous education," and bemoaned that, at its own institution, "law students have only to prove that they are eighteen years old and present a certificate of good moral character." (Issue of January 16, 1869.) The first law graduate came in 1871. In the first eight years there would be only twenty-one.

No one, in those days, was thought to really have had much schooling unless he could sing a few tunes and play an instrument. Sorin always gave great attention to this most graceful of the arts. Maximilian Girac first came to Notre Dame from France in 1848, having fled the Revolution. His execrable English and his tantrums only added to the reputation of this artist. Already established bands, orchestras, and choirs took on new life under his direction. He wrote Masses and other sacred music. Unexpected musical talent was sometimes revealed by the modest Brothers, notably Leopold and Basil.

The cornerstone of the present Sacred Heart Church on the campus was laid May 31, 1871. It would be ten years abuilding.

In 1871 the students put on a benefit for the victims of the Great Chicago Fire, which was a personal thing to Notre Dame because so many of its people came from that distressed city. The first special train originating from Notre Dame carried students home to Chicago for the Christmas holidays that same year. And Salmon P. Chase, Chief Justice of the Supreme Court of the United States, was a distinguished campus visitor.

On June 7, 1872, shortly before he was to retire from the Presidency, the students had another gift for Corby. This time they "manifested their affection" by giving him "a splendid four-seated carriage worth four hundred fifty dollars manufactured in South Bend by Studebaker." There were the usual addresses by representatives of the seniors, juniors, and minims; and Corby's usual witty and urbane response. After which the band struck up a tune so lively and the students shouted so vociferously, that the team of fine horses that came with the carriage, became excited and plunged away, across flower beds and other vegetation carefully tended by Brother Landscape. (The Brothers were more known to students by their occupations than by their names: Brother Candy Store, Brother Book Store, and so on.)

12. THE IRISH LOSE ONE

AUGUSTE LEMONNIER had begun the study of law in France before the urge came in 1861 to become a missionary and follow Sorin, his uncle, to America. He was a gentle youth who adapted to the language and customs as quickly as he advanced through the posts of Prefect of Discipline, Prefect of Religion, Director of Studies, Vice-President, and at thirty-two, President. Sorin later wrote: "I never left him a chance to benefit by our relationship." Lemonnier, sensitive to nepotism, worked incessantly to make it on his own. (Sorin had sent another nephew back home, saying, "If you insist on remaining French it would be better if you returned to France.")

As President, Lemonnier steered a charter change through the state legislature which beat back attempts by St. Joseph County to tax the Manual Labor School. He also made an important change in the format of the Labor School by giving the orphans a chance to become something more than craftsmen if their capabilities warranted. He saw the obligation to cultivate artistic and intellectual talents, regardless of the economic state into which a gifted student had been born. This would be difficult, at Notre Dame, to which poverty clung as a fungus.

Because of the lack of money, superior lay teachers were almost shut out. There were, as yet, few outstanding Catholic scholars in the country, and the six hundred dollars salary Notre Dame offered was hardly an inducement. Orestes A. Brownson had applied and had been "appalled" to learn that his services would be required daily from six in the morning until ten at night. It would be generations before non-Catholic teachers would be hired. (One of these, noting his contract made no mention of his faith, was told: "Professor, you take care of the physics. We'll take care of the religion.")

Lemonnier tightened up the requirements for graduation and scrutinized the day-by-day performance of teachers as well as students, so that there would be no cheapness about the degree. He made the first move toward filling the glaring need of a library, commissioning Professor Jimmy Edwards to begin collecting books. The first year's catch (1874), with meager funds, was twelve hundred volumes. For almost forty years Edwards would devote himself to this work (among many other duties and interests); and he is largely responsible for the rich archives of American Catholic history shelved at Notre Dame.

Lemonnier was generations ahead of his time in the work associated with the office of Prefect of Discipline. He substituted compassion for harshness, understanding for severity. Students saw him as he was, decent, sincere, and spiritually stalwart. When Maurice Williams, a former student, was dying of tuberculosis, he returned to the scene of his childhood piety, to prepare for eternity. He was visited every day by Lemonnier. When the end came the young President was sad, but also happy, because he had seen the proof that Notre Dame not only taught a boy how to live, but how to die.

In 1874, when they learned that their President was breaking down from overwork, the students sought to cheer him up by organizing an entertainment to end all entertainments, at a school noted for its entertainments. It included music

63

by the band, a selection by the orchestra, six separate theatrical performances, interspersed by readings in Spanish by a student from Montevideo, and climaxed by an address by the minims department that took three of the tykes to complete. It was hardly what the doctor would have ordered for a weakened body, but it was balm to a gentle soul.

Lemonnier sat through his last Commencement, but was not strong enough to make his customary speech. Told by the doctors that there was no hope, he said: "I came into the world with nothing. I take nothing with me. I desire nothing but the grace of God." He suffered through many crises before dying on the evening of October 29th at the age of thirty-five. Above all, he had been what every good priest desires to be above all—a good priest.

The obvious choice to succeed Lemonnier was Vice-President Patrick J. Colovin, who had taken over the duties during Lemonnier's illness. He was a man of many and definite talents—orator, theologian, disciplinarian, and an outstanding teacher whose lectures were clear and analytical. Sorin had appointed him Vice-President at his nephew's insistence, but he had never really liked the man, thought him lacking in respect for authority and with a spirit so contentious as to be almost a personal affront to the Founder. He was, though born in Canada, another aggressive Irishman; and when an Irishman opposed Sorin, he automatically blamed his national origin. (In one of his letters at a much later date, he noted that a Bishop was being harassed by some of the priests in his diocese. "And all of them are Irish.")

Sorin delayed the appointment for two months. At the faculty banquet on New Year's Day a lay speaker, probably a politician and undoubtedly an Irishman, dwelt pointedly on the virtues of the Irish and climaxed his speech by turning to the Founder: "And now, does the most Reverend

Superior-General have an announcement that might give this banquet historical importance?"

So neatly trapped, the Superior-General made the announcement, and it would have historical importance, not of the type anybody would have preferred, but predictable. Externally the principals behaved with the charity expected of priests, who happened to honorably disagree on some basic, but negotiable subjects. In 1875 Sorin was thought lost at sea for two weeks, and Colovin led the daily prayers with such sincerity that it was thought the threatened tragedy might have effected a private reconciliation.

Colovin ran a tight Administration. The students were handled justly but firmly. The first moves were made in relations with Latin America that would become historic. Free rein was given to Father John A. Zahm, a young priest who would (as will be seen), loom large as scholar, scientist, author, educator, and administrator. He is still considered by some to have been the most brilliant mind Notre Dame ever had the opportunity to nurture.

In October, 1876, the first mention of football appeared in the annals—but only because the weather was "too inclement" for the more popular sport of baseball. Football was a form of soccer, played with forty-two men on a side, with the prize a barrel of apples. There were no national reverberations when the contest ended in a *tie*. There were few spectators. Everybody got good and tired, ate apples, and went to the dormitories peaceful and happy. If Sorin knew of it he would have approved; for in his scheme, games, like long walks, were designed to use up that extra animal energy which otherwise might explode dangerously.

March 17, 1877, had a double significance. In addition to being St. Patrick's Day, the national day of the majority of faculty and students, it was the anniversary of President Colovin's ordination. It was celebrated with éclat, regardless of previous controversy and the well-known thoughts of the Founder about the Irish.

In August Notre Dame had a new President.

The change was accomplished with the usual amenities. Colovin would exchange jobs with Corby, become President of Sacred Heart College, a Holy Cross operation in Watertown, Wisconsin, while Corby would return as Notre Dame's sixth president, and the only man who would ever hold that office twice. It was understood on campus that Colovin was a martyr to the Irish cause. There was resentment, but no rebellion. Corby, also Irish, was a military man accustomed to the chain of command. The bland peace and orderly forward march of his previous tenancy was resumed.

A spelling bee was held, emphasizing that fundamental in which even college students were (and are) so often deficient. The first female invasion occurred when two dozen young ladies arrived from South Bend in a four-horse carryall, using the cover of a Literary Club and accompanied by "much swishing of skirts and soprano cacophony." The announced purpose was to gaze through a new telescope sent over by Napoleon III. The heavens were so heavenly that the ladies were "loath to leave," while they themselves were being observed by certain mustachioed students of the law school, who carried canes in order to appear mature.

The art of fencing flourished because of the growing number of dramatic productions employing that form of athletics. A fencing class was disturbed when a stranger asked to take a hand and proceeded to defeat not only the pupils, but the instructor, who was probably much better at parsing. The stranger, oddly attired, had dropped off at the kitchens to accept food always available for such as he. Sometimes these Knights of the Road tarried for awhile in shacks built against the back of the fence circling the baseball field, an area known to students as Rockefeller Hall. They were known in those early days as hoboes or bums. The one who demeaned the fencers, obviously a gentleman of manners, may have been the first hippie ever to make the Notre Dame scene.

Father Zahm's experiments had reached the fascinating subject of sound. When he produced a machine which he said would record and repeat whatever was said, a cynic asked: "How are you, Mr. Wise Guy? When are you going to take a bath?" The machine repeated the question and thereafter no wise guy students messed around with Father Zahm.

George Sampson, a third-year student from New Jersey, went hunting in October to try out his "magnificent new fowling-piece." A priest walking along the banks of the St. Joseph River, saw him stumble and fall, heard the shot. He swam the cold stream and was there in time to hear the boy's last confession. The priest was the same Tim O'Sullivan who had played the cornet solo from the roof on a well-remembered St. Patrick's Day. Occasionally students died tragically; when it happened, the campus was also killed. Death was not on the curriculum.

13. "IF ALL WERE LOST..."

APRIL 23, 1879, came on a Wednesday, which was a free day. It was pleasantly warm, with a breeze, and the minims frolicked. Workmen finished a job on the roof and came down. At eleven o'clock sharp, young eyes saw flames close to the railing that ran around the dome. Shrill voices gave the alarm. People came from everywhere. The college building was on fire.

If water could have been brought to the roof at once the blaze could easily have been extinguished. Buckets had been placed at strategic spots for just such an emergency, but there was no water in the buckets. When the first buckets finally reached the roof the carriers could not get to the flames because the door to the dome railing had been locked by the workmen; they had followed orders; the lock was a safety measure to keep students like Timmy O'Sullivan from venturing there.

Before the door could be opened the pitch roof was on fire. The bucket brigade was now working, but the water was no match for the hungry flames. Water was finally forced by steam pressure to the tanks on the roof; the bucket carriers worked from there, but were soon driven back. The supports of the dome burned and the statue of The Virgin crashed to the ground six stories below.

South Bend had a fire engine of sorts, but the engine needed repairs before it would move. By the time it huffed and puffed to the campus the building was doomed. Everybody was trying to save what could be carried out or thrown out the windows, but now there was danger of being caught inside, of being cast down among the burning timbers as the upper floors began to give way. Those on the outside whose job it was to carry the stuff to safety, were endangered by desks, chairs, beds, and other furniture that came hurtling down among the smoke. There was no order or plan. In the panic things were lost that could have been saved, and these included historical documents, letters, records, and manuscripts. The library was a total loss. Within three hours the college building, Infirmary, and St. Francis's Home were in complete ruin.

68

Sorin was in Montreal, preparing to embark on one of his European trips. The students were told to go home, that a new building would be ready in the fall. Those who could not leave were to do as best they could in Music Hall, the only building of substance, apart from the church, which had been spared. This they did, with whatever bedding had not been burned. Some sang: "The old gray home she ain't what she used to be." South Bend people brought food and clothing.

Sorin was now sixty-five years of age and there was concern over what effect the destruction might have on him, so that the news was deliberately withheld from him until Professor Jimmy Edwards could get to Montreal *by train* to break it gently. Sorin's return was described by Professor Timothy Howard in a letter to Father Hudson of *The Ave Maria:*

He walked around the ruins and those who followed were confounded by his attitude. Instead of bending, he stiffened. He signalled all of them to go into the church with him. I was then present when Father Sorin, after looking over the destruction of his life work, stood at the altar steps and spoke to the community what I have always felt to be the most sublime words I have ever listened to. There was absolute faith, confidence, resolution in his very look and pose. "If it were ALL gone, I should not give up," were his words in closing. The effect was electric. It was the crowning moment of his life. A sad company had gone into the church that day. They were all simple Christian heroes as they came out. There was never more a shadow of a doubt as to the future of Notre Dame.

There was no further indulgence in useless regrets or unmanly sorrow. Every cart, wheelbarrow, and wagon was put into service. Again Sorin was the leader, as he filled the first barrow and wheeled it away. Every member of the community felt it his duty to show how he also could labor, even some of the students. An impious *Scholastic* editor reported:

> Everyone agrees that Very Rev. Father General can wheel off a load of bricks with grace and dignity. We do not wish to discourage the efforts of a conscientious worker, but still, regard for historical accuracy compels us to state that Father Granger would scarcely command a large salary among the horny-handed sons of toil. It may be the want of skill of the loader that makes the cart almost immediately capsize, but we don't by any means say that this is the unquestionable fact.

It was decided to give degrees to the seniors whose work indicated they would have graduated in June.

The loss was estimated at two hundred thousand dollars. Only forty-five thousand dollars was forthcoming from insurance.

W.J. Edbrooke, a Chicago architect, submitted plans for the new building. Every precaution was to be taken against future fires. The city of South Bend would extend its water mains to the campus. Ground was broken May 17th. By June 21st the stone foundation was imbedded. The record reads like an architectural marathon. Three hundred workmen were employed. There was no eight-hour day or forty-hour week, no stoppage by dispute. A constant stream of stone and steel came by rail, an unbroken train of wagons brought brick from the kilns of South Bend and Bertram. Some bricks had been saved from the fire. The rubble was used as a base for the road that went by the community house, to the cemetery and toward St. Mary's.

Once again it was build now—pay later. With the work in progress Sorin began the familiar search for money. Alexis Coquillard, one of the first two students, donated five hundred dollars and impressed upon other South Bend businessmen the value of Notre Dame to the city and district. The

St. Mary's girls contributed their pocket money and put on a gala concert. Chicago, which remembered how Notre Dame had responded to its fire, was generous with money and with credit. A critic wrote to *The Chicago Tribune* protesting aid to a school which had "no other purpose than making converts among its Protestant students." Judge T. G. Turner responded vigorously, concluding: "Aid is being asked only of persons whose generosity is not blinded by bigotry, however religiously disposed. I am not, sir, nor have I ever been, nor do I expect to be a Catholic, but I am a friend of honesty and truth." Notre Dame came to national attention for the first time because of the fire. There was widespread respect for its fighting spirit as expressed by the patriarchal founder; but when he tried to collect seventy-five thousand dollars in unpaid student bills he said: "Shall I say how much I received? Why not? It may be profitable for all of us to know the answer. I received twenty-two dollars."

As always in the Sorin pattern, a bigger, better building arose from ruins. Except for the two wings and the dome, to be added later, it is the main building that still stands, with the church and Washington Hall, as an enclave of a "prim French seminary." The architect called it Modern Gothic, but modern architects are puzzled by its countless angles and corners, jutting points of masonry, numerous gables and turrets, the classic pillars that support the dome and statue; and the rotunda, festooned by frescoes, extending from the second floor to the dome. The enrollment did not improve, but those who came in the fall were delighted with such innovations as gas illumination, steam heat, hot and cold running water.

The Great Fire, instead of undermining Sorin's health, seemed to invigorate him. When he sang Mass his deep voice seemed richer and stronger. A long beard had given him a majesty that inspired awe. He became a social lion to the

71

more prominent people of South Bend, who brought their visitors to observe his "old world courtesy." His mood expanded under these attentions. When the Studebakers, the Stanfields, the Hubbards, the Millers, or other prominent South Bend people came, they "would assemble about five in the evening in the parlor, with introductions and pleasant exchanges, and a bit of an appetizer, perhaps. At six they were ushered into the Senior Refectory where three or four tables were fairly groaning under their wealth of viands. After dinner the guests repaired to the parlors, where wines were served, or to the porch where the gentlemen were regaled with the choicest cigars. When all had rested perhaps Mrs. Stanfield or Mrs. ex-Mayor Miller would perform on the piano. As they drove off in their carriages the chimes would sound in the church tower."

As a first-class public relations man, Sorin gave such potential benefactors what they wanted; and it was the same with the press. On New Year's Day, 1881 the two South Bend papers received identical gifts: "a huge pyramidal cake, flanked by bottles of Bordeaux of the vintage of '75 and California wines of 1878 and a good flagon of Chartreuse." With each present went these admonitions:

The following Parisian etiquette must be strictly observed in disposing of the accompanying articles, otherwise no one can say what might happen:

1. They form neither a meal nor a lunch; for in either the people eat and drink, and the disposition of the above is neither the one nor the other; it is a Parisian dessert.

2. This dessert is intended for twelve joyous guests; for whom the cake is divided into two parts, perfectly equal; one facing east for Bordeaux, the other straight west, towards San Francisco. The company are thereby divided into two respectable bodies.

3. The eastern show first in most elegant style, how to

finish both cake and wine without eating and drinking, viz: by carefully and cautiously, and politely, dipping the one into the other.

4. Ten minutes after the disappearance of both, the Chartreuse is poured into 12 liquor glasses and leisurely degusted to the last drop, each one looking at someone else inquiringly, trying to ascertain how he or she or they like it.

5. If the little Parisian dessert has given satisfaction, the party will show their appreciation in one same way, viz: by returning basket and bottles to Notre Dame for another supply twelve months hence; otherwise, the giver could not persuade himself that he had succeeded in pleasing his best friends.

It is not surprising to learn that Notre Dame always had a good press. It is hardly likely that the ink-stained wretches of the press wasted time following instructions, especially that part intended to ascertain if they liked the gift. It can be assumed that the injunction about returning the basket and bottles was faithfully followed. Historically, it is of interest to know that the journalistic custom of "free-loading" is embedded (and embottled) in the past.

Sorin returned from his fortieth ocean crossing in 1882, got off the train at two in the morning. For the first time no one was there to meet him. So he walked the three miles to the college. And the walk may not have seemed long because he had another problem. He had been spending more and more time with his Little Princes, had promised them a "great Parisian dinner" when their number reached fifty. It had stopped at forty-eight, and the little ones were getting very impatient. Ah! Invite Bishop Dwenger of Fort Wayne, make him an honorary minim, and because of his exalted station, let him count for two minims. And so it was done. Except that the Bishop smoked. And a minim told him he was not a good minim, because minims didn't smoke.

14. "#1"

FOOTBALL was no longer a substitute for baseball on an inclement day. It was still a form of soccer, played by as many as sixty on a side, but the players now were "resplendent in their gay colors," and the game was watched by students, workmen, and faculty. In 1881 the Reds won over the Blues after a hard struggle. The prize was a barrel of cider, presumably not pillow-soft because the Reds were "slightly unmanageable" that night and required firm words by Father Corby to quell them.

As the school emerged from its pioneer days it had, about 1880, taken the first poll of alumni graduated from the classical and scientific courses. The results: 18 percent priests, 27 percent lawyers, 10 percent businessmen, 8 percent educators, 4 percent farmers, 3 percent editors, and two "doing nothings." Eighty percent were Catholics, three were "Israelites," and the remainder Protestants. These figures also seemed to fit the Sorin concept of the "tidy little boarding school," content to prepare its graduates to make a good living, with no effort to proselyte those of other faiths.

Other figures were not so pleasing. The enrollment had dropped steadily from 512 during the Civil War to 324, including seniors, preps, and minims, who returned after the fire, even though the tuition had been lowered to $125 a semester. "We should remind our friends," a *Scholastic* editorial said, "that this sum is at about the rate of but six dollars a week—scarcely more than the price for board and room at a good boarding house. The tuition is a gift."

Why? That was Sorin's major problem. It could no longer be blamed on Colovin's lack of congeniality, or the postwar depression. Father Corby was a popular priest, a good administrator, a loyal man who followed policy. But perhaps too much of all these? Was it time for a change? For someone who would *initiate*, rather than *preside?* Regretful of course; and how could it be done nicely?

Early in February, 1882, Father Corby was thinking it was time to add the first of the two wings to the college building. There had been an increase of twenty-five students over the previous year. The Continental Cadets, a military group and a source of recreational and physical culture, not forgetting the disciplinary angle, had been well received. He was particularly proud of new Music Hall (the present Washington Hall), and its ventilating system which eliminated the foul air that caused those fatal diseases of the lungs and throat so common in the country; many young priests of Notre Dame died, most recently Father Edward Lilly, the school's musical pride. (The band, en route to the cemetery, had played one of Lilly's own compositions, a death march he had composed a year previously for the funeral of George Sampson, the student who had accidentally shot himself.)

Father Corby was unprepared for the letter from Sorin. It said that Rome had heard with some astonishment that Father Corby was both Provincial and President of the University. Ecclesiastical authorities thought that was much too much responsibility for one man. Accordingly, it had become Sorin's duty to relieve Corby of one of the offices. Corby replied that he would be glad to yield the Provincialship.

Sorin thought it better that Corby should do as he, Sorin, had done in a similar situation—remain Provincial and give the Presidency to a younger man. "It is time we should look to young Father Walsh and try him in the office of President."

Father Walsh was a Sorin protégé, but he was young, and he was thinking in terms of scholarship. If Sorin wanted to cling to *his* idea of a "tight little boarding school," shouldn't he have sensed the thinking of young Tom Walsh before appointing him? Perhaps he had. Sorin was imperious, but not reactionary. Perhaps he realized that Timothy Howard had been right, that after the recovery from the Great Fire, the future of Notre Dame was no longer in doubt; that it could no longer be controlled by one man, or impeded by clashing ideas of any number of men; that it was ready to begin a life of its own through its own young men. Perhaps that was why, as grandfathers gradually do, Sorin had been spending more and more time with his Little Princes.

Thomas E. Walsh was a Canadian, son of Thomas Walsh and Winifred McDermott, fourth of nine, born May 15, 1853, in the village of Lacolle, near Montreal. At age fifteen he enrolled at nearby *Collège de St. Laurent,* a Holy Cross institution often visited by the Superior-General, who decided that this young man, who had already decided to become a priest, was a student of great promise and deserved the best possible training. It is possible that Walsh may have been the first Notre Dame student ever recruited as a future President. In 1873 Sorin sent him to the *Collège de Ste. Croix,* near Paris, and personally followed his progress while visiting France. By 1876 the need at Notre Dame was so pressing that he brought the promising young man back and immediately thrust him into the high echelon. Tom Walsh taught Latin and Greek, continued his own studies necessary for ordination, became a friend and admirer of Colovin, and steered

76

safely through the diplomatic shoals of the latter's situation with Sorin.

Altogether he was so universally regarded, that when Corby succeeded Colovin he petitioned that Thomas Walsh, though *not yet ordained,* become his Vice-President and Director of Studies. He was ordained in 1879 the year of The Great Fire, and played a fruitful role in the restoration of order and reorganization of classes after the loss of the records. During the next two years he so thoroughly demonstrated his ability to get things done with smooth efficiency, that Sorin felt he could safely appoint him President. And young Walsh proceeded as if he had written the book. He was described by contemporaries in superlatives; name it and he had it: intellect, charm, poise, "the innocence of a child and the wisdom of a man." His one weakness, a tendency to obesity, was excused by his biographer: "When he had moments of leisure he preferred to stretch out on the grass under some leafy tree and find relaxation in the *Pensées* of Pascal, or Bossuet's *Histoire des Variations.*"

Father Walsh was a builder of men, of academic departments, and of physical facilities. During the twelve years of his presidency, Notre Dame emerged into a new era with many of its modern foundations firmly set, or planned.

Academically Walsh worked through the method of giving a man responsibility, and turning his creative energies loose. He began with the Law School, which had declined after a prosperous start. His man there was William "Colonel" Hoynes, who may well have been known personally by more Notre Dame students over a longer span of years than any other individual. "Colonel" was an affectionate title. Born in Ireland, brought to this country at age seven, Hoynes at fifteen (after swearing he was seventeen) was wounded at the Battle of Prairie Grove, Arkansas, and discharged. He reenlisted, was wounded again but remained in service until honorably discharged at the age of eighteen, on November 15, 1865. He graduated from Notre Dame in 1872, became a newspaperman, got his law degree from the University of Michigan in 1877, was admitted to the Illinois bar, practiced before the Supreme Court of the United States.

Father Walsh took him from a Chicago law practice in January, 1883. For fifty years it was according to Hoynes, not only in the law school, but on the entire campus. His appearance, his actions, and his speech, like his title, were all parts of a benevolent exaggeration. He loved the boys and it showed through his pomposities. Whenever he came into Washington Hall he would be applauded. He would smile, bow to right and left, and raise his wide-brimmed military hat. His every appearance was a tidbit, relished most by himself. And he developed the first Catholic law school in the country, attracting and holding students.

Father Joseph Carrier, between tours as war chaplain and roving ambassador, was the first man of science at Notre Dame. He was greatly interested in botany and biology, and passed the baton on to his pupil, John A. Zahm, before becoming curator of the Notre Dame museum of natural sciences and (1874) President of St. Mary's College in Galveston, Texas. Father Walsh, impressed by John Zahm, decided to build what became known as Science Hall. The cornerstone was the gift of John B. Cassidy, the first student to receive the degree of bachelor of science at Notre Dame. The building itself, designed by John Zahm, provided for things scientific on a grand scale for those days. It became the locale of later important work by Father Alexander Kirsch, who had studied biology under Abbé Carnoy at Louvain, and for Albert F. Zahm.

(Rev. Louis J. Neyron, a secular priest, had taught "the science of anatomy" in the early years. It is to be hoped that his dialogue in this field was more precise than the tales he

78

told of his experiences as a surgeon in the army of Napoleon and of his capture at Waterloo. It is hardly likely that even Napoleon could make do with a surgeon of only twelve years of age. Father Neyron was advanced in years when he arrived at Notre Dame, and his memory may have been victimized by his imagination. Nevertheless, he became the campus authority on the Napoleonic Wars and was frequently interviewed by the local and Chicago newspapers.)

In 1879 Albert F. Zahm, younger brother of Father John, came to Notre Dame and was enrolled in the classical course, a flagrant case of miscasting, remedied when he switched to science. Fellow students thought him peculiar when he would stop and ask: "Don't you hear them? Airships carrying passengers from Chicago to New York without stopping?" He had ideas about the rocket propulsion of boats. He invented a gun that would shoot around a corner. In his senior year he designed a rotor plane to be driven by a heat engine. He moved from the helicopter idea to that of the airplane. In 1882 he built the first wind tunnel (the forerunner of the world's first large wind tube which he built in 1901 at Catholic U.).

In 1883, after graduation, Father Walsh persuaded Albert Zahm to remain at Notre Dame as a professor of mathematics. Aeronautical research became his passion. To further it he studied French, German, Italian, and Spanish, took practical courses in the engineering shops, joined the American Society of Mechanical Engineers, studied bird flight, bird anatomy, and animal mechanism. He developed gliders capable of steady flight, used the ceiling of the roof of the museum in Science Hall to suspend a flying machine operated by foot power. He would use his foot to keep from bumping the wall. Brother Benedict, curator of the museum, saw the marks, figured that only the devil could walk up the side of a wall, blessed himself, and sprinkled the place with holy water.

In the late eighties, Dr. Albert Zahm launched gliders from the roof of Science Hall. In 1893, his last year at Notre Dame, he helped organize America's first International Aeronautic Congress, and at the engineering congress at the Chicago World' Fair, he gave a paper which was the first to disclose the modern method of launching an airplane and controlling it in flight. He had degrees from Cornell and Johns Hopkins, was Chief Research Engineer of the Curtiss Aeroplane Company (1914–1917), for thirteen years (1916–1930) was in charge of the U.S. Navy Aerodynamic Laboratory; in 1929 he became Chief, Division of Aeronautics (Guggenheim Chair) Library of Congress.

15. "BELLES LETTRES"

FATHER WALSH, disappointed by the number of dropouts from the basic classical course, placed the blame on compulsory Latin and Greek. He permitted electives for these dusty subjects and offered a new course which emphasized English and American authors, studies in rhetoric, style, essays, poetry, and drama. In all this he was guided by a shadowy, almost ethereal figure who never taught at Notre Dame, but had a subtle influence on its teaching.

Daniel Eldred Hudson was born at Nahant, near Boston, December 18, 1849. After his primary education he worked for awhile in a bookstore publishing house where he came in contact with Hawthorne, Lowell, Holmes, Whittier, Emerson, and other great New England writers. Longfellow took more than a casual interest in the bookishly inclined youth. "Young man," he asked, "are you going to be a writer when you grow up?" The reply came quickly: "No sir. I'm going to be a Catholic priest and missionary to the Indians." After studying briefly with the Jesuits at Holy Cross College in Worcester, Massachusetts, Hudson decided to become a Trappist, and in 1870 was headed for an Iowa monastery. On the train he met Father Paul Gillen, the former Civil War chaplain, who preached Notre Dame so glowingly that Hudson stopped off for a visit which lasted sixty years.

He entered the Novitiate March 7, 1871, was ordained (with John A. Zahm) on June 4, 1875, and almost immediately was put in charge of the now-venerable *The Ave Maria,* which had been founded in 1865 by Sorin as a weekly periodical, whose principal object was to increase devotion to the Blessed Virgin. For fifty-five years he remained as editor. His taste and discrimination attracted the best Catholic authors. He seldom left the campus, but bishops, priests, and laymen made pilgrimages to his rooms on the second floor of the presbytery. He was a wisp of a man, an almost disembodied spirit. His annual closing sermon for the month of May was described by Brother Florian: "He won't be long. He'll talk to you for five minutes, and then he'll turn to the Blessed Virgin and talk to her for five minutes, and I swear to Heaven, the tears'll run down your cheeks." This will not seem an unusual statement to those who remember Brother Flo.

In the pages of *The Ave Maria* there had been occasional articles by Charles Warren Stoddard, author of *Idylls of the South Seas.* But he had indicated in letters to Father Hudson that he was getting tired of being a "literary tramp," and longed to settle down in some peaceful monastery. Perhaps, Hudson suggested to President Walsh, here was the man to head the new course in "Belles Lettres." Stoddard said he would be delighted; after which came some second thoughts to Father Hudson. What would be the duties? How many classes? How old the students? How much time to himself?

> Could I write freely to my friends and receive letters which would not necessarily be open to inspection of the Rev. President or the Rev. General or anyone but myself?
>
> I have been for some years what is known as a *free liver*. I have taken wines and liquors with my friends whenever I felt like it and have sometimes taken more than what was good for me.
>
> I am a smoker—but have never in my life *chowed*. I have been through the pipe and cigar stages and now smoke only *s*igarettes.
>
> I like regular hours, method, a quiet life. I think I could prep*air* myself for the Chair of English but could not attempt anything outside of it at your University.
>
> One thing—I am a confirmed misspeller. It is an open secret and it is a constitutional weakness which is beyond all human aid.

Stoddard arrived for the spring term in 1885, gave up his post in 1887. His forebodings had been prophetic. The idea of being warned by Father Regan, the Prefect of Discipline, not to give *s*igarettes to the boys! And that Indiana climate!

His successor, Maurice Francis Egan, was the other side of the literary, social, and pedagogical coin. He was a poet, had done some fine novels. After the Great Fire in 1879 he had written a book of verse especially for the benefit of the University. In 1889 he was editor of the New York *Freeman's Journal,* and his friends gasped at his intention to assume the "Chair of Literature" in a place called Indiana about which most of them still had strange ideas. Father Walsh built a two-story home on the edge of the campus for Egan, his wife and three children. Egan christened it "The Lilacs" and (though by Notre Dame standards it was considered rather elegant), called it a cottage and asked his friends to send lilac plants for planting. He settled down for a comfortable stay, became, along with the two Zahms, part of the prestige front Father Walsh was building for that school out in Indiana. Egan became a social lion, enjoyed finding himself the criterion by which the native Hoosier judged social practice and conduct. His opera hat, the only one in the area, was frequently borrowed for amateur theatricals, and finally became a prop for the University theater. By that time Sam Adler, the local clothing merchant, was selling toppers aplenty. What Mr. Egan did, society did. He wrote charmingly of this period in his *Recollections of a Happy Life*.

The Walsh building program reflected the steady growth during his term. The minims were given their own building in 1882; and the next year the arrival of the hundredth minim was celebrated with another Royal Parisian Banquet and a play, performed by the lads, written by the Superior General. By 1887 there were two hundred minims, and the building had a new wing. (Eventually it would become St. Edward's Hall.) The two wings were added to Brownson and Carroll Hall in the Main Building.

In 1882 the dome was completed—first the brick foundation, then the iron framework, the supporting columns, and the dome itself. The statue, a gift of the girls from St. Mary's, had been waiting for three years. It is 19 feet high, made of cast iron, weighs 4,400 pounds. The perilous job of erection, with the equipment then available, took a day and a half to complete. Finally it was done, and a great cheer welcomed Our Lady's return to reign over the campus, 125 feet above the roof and 206 feet above the ground. This time, "a golden statue on a golden dome, so that all men might know why

83

we have succeeded here." The statue, executed by Giovanni Meli, is a replica of that erected by Pope Pius IX in the Piazza di Spagna in Rome, to commemorate the promulgation of the dogma of the Immaculate Conception.

In 1886, after the completion of Science Hall, Walsh turned to the completion of the Sacred Heart Church, which had been in limited use for almost ten years. The temporary back wall was knocked down and The Lady Chapel added, with its altar imported from Rome, a product of one of Bernini's pupils. The bronze main altar, from the shops of Froc-Robert in Paris, had originally been displayed at the Centennial Exhibition in Philadelphia. The design is Gothic, but there is no clear record of the architect of the church. Original plans by Patrick C. Keely had been discarded as much too expensive. Another set had been submitted by J. Brady of St. Louis. The church as it stands today has been credited to Brother Charles. Overall supervision of details through the years had been entrusted by Sorin to his faithful "Tonto," Father Granger.

16. LIFE WITH FATHER WALSH
(1881–1893)

IN the evenings the priests and lay faculty would have a leisure period on the porch of the college building. Conversation would turn to the events of the day, but more especially to the society they were helping to build. Father Walsh was always alert for the new thing; and people like Zahm, Egan, Carrier, and Jimmy Edwards were idea factories. Religion and education were much discussed. Someone mentioned that the members of the American hierarchy did not encourage or direct the work of the laity. Others immediately pointed to the lack of educated Catholic laity (which it was Notre Dame's basic function to improve). Jimmy Edwards thought the University might do something specific in this field by giving a medal annually to a Catholic layman who excelled in "faith, morals, education, and good citizenship." And so was born the Laetare Medal.

For centuries it had been the custom of the Holy See to award on Laetare Sunday, to some outstanding royal personality, the Golden Rose. Father Walsh decided that Notre Dame should give a medal. Had he been alive, the first recipient would undoubtedly have been Orestes A. Brownson, the American philosopher and educator who had become a convert, and had long been a friend of Sorin and of Notre Dame. (He had no official connection, but he is buried in the crypt, and Brownson Hall was named for him.) Instead, the initial award was given to Patrick Keely, the architect "who more than any other changed the style of ecclesiastical structures and modified architectural taste in this country." Through the years the Laetare Medal has acquired distinction by its awards to people like President John F. Kennedy, Chief Justice of the Supreme Court Edward Douglas White, Alfred E. Smith, generals, educators, artists, writers, scholars, and businessmen. (A complete list will be found elsewhere.)

The Laetare Medal was another hash mark on the sleeve of Jimmy Edwards, one of the unsung heroes of the swaddling days, who was almost entirely responsible for the creation of the library, and of the Bishop's Memorial Hall. He taught some classes, mostly history, was involved in the Museum of Natural Sciences, and other projects. When not otherwise occupied, he might accompany Hal Jewett, the first great Notre Dame track star, to important meets. For fifty years Professor Edwards worked feverishly for Notre Dame, wherever he happened to be. Many times during that period he resigned, but nobody ever paid much attention to his flurries of temperament. Once when he seemed to mean it, Father Walsh told him to take a year traveling in Europe. Edwards came back with many articles to add to the various collections in which he was engaged. He died in 1911.

A few private rooms had been made available in the new college building for students of superior talent and conduct. Inevitably the idea came, this one from Father Zahm: Why not a separate residence hall for such students? It was a revolutionary thought and quickly opposed, because the open dormitory and open study hall had been traditional in Catholic schools. That, Zahm argued, had been because most Catholic schools were primarily prep rather than college. Walsh authorized the building of what was to become Sorin Hall, opened for occupancy on New Year's Day, 1889. It was later enlarged, but originally there were fifty single rooms "large enough to encourage study and small enough to discourage visiting." (The latter was never achieved.) After two years Maurice Francis Egan, in an article in *The Catholic World,* hailed it as a successful new departure. It was also a departure from Sorin's French concept, but he made no objection, nor to Walsh's other innovations. Ironically, Sorin Hall is about the only large-scale reminder to the casual modern visitor that a man called Sorin ever had anything to do with the place. It was first of the residence halls which have substituted nicely for the fraternities and clubs at other schools. Out of them naturally evolved the system of Interhall athletics which would later be adopted by Ivy League colleges (Intramural), as one of the antidotes to commercialized athletics.

In today's world of scientific miracles the unusual has come to be expected, but in the latter part of the previous century each innovation was hailed. A telegraphic office was installed at Notre Dame in 1873 with appropriate ceremony. In 1878 the first telephone service between Notre Dame and South Bend developed into quite a social affair as "music sung at either place was heard at the other. Several songs were sung by the ladies from the St. Mary's Academy and listened to by the audience in South Bend. The senior orchestra gave several selections, with violin, cornet, flute, and guitar solos. The instruments worked admirably and the music was listened to by a large audience, chiefly ladies." The students, of course, "amused themselves similarly."

Gasoline lamps had been the only source of artificial light. When coal-gas lights came in, the University planned its own gas works, but the project fell through when Zahm's experiments produced arc lights in 1881. Notre Dame claims (supported by the *Electrical Review*) to have been the first college in America to be lighted by electricity. Installation of "the incandescent electric light just developed by Edison" was a major event in September, 1885. When the crown on the statue of Our Lady and the crescent at her feet were illuminated for the first time, some startled natives thought they were looking at "a new comet that had suddenly appeared above Notre Dame."

In the midst of all this American change, the French discipline remained. Smoking had become a privilege of seniors, with consent of their parents; but no student was yet allowed to go to town without permission or a chaperon. Standing ads were run in the papers threatening prosecution of any who sold or gave liquor to students. Another printed warning was given to young ladies "to cease prowling about the University grounds, especially Sunday afternoon and evening. Their names are known and will be published." Father Walsh, elastic on most subjects, was a total abstainer who also preached what he practiced. "I was rather amused," Egan wrote, "when Dr. Walsh said that if whiskey could be publically condemned by the authorities of the Catholic Church, the progress of the Church could be endless in the world. Having a great sense of humor, he had a great tolerance, but he always declared that if the Jews had drunk whiskey, Our Lord would never have performed the miracle at Cana."

In October, 1890, Walsh's determination was tested by a group of thirty-two, mostly from the Preparatory Department, who went to town without permission, toured the taverns and returned safely—except for two who "had a real problem trying to find the campus, due to the varied routes suggested by the spirits they had so joyously consumed in town." At a special meeting the faculty decided to suspend the two who had given the greatest scandal, but inflict milder punishment on the thirty. As on an earlier day, the group thought there would be safety in numbers, and demanded that the same punishment be given to all. It was done. Their trunks were packed, and carriages took them to South Bend.

The incident received wide publicity, despite a University policy (still in operation) to avoid embarrassment to students who were being disciplined. Father Walsh explained: "It is better to have a small attendance at the University with good discipline than a large attendance without it. The rules will be preserved at any cost." He received messages from educators throughout the country. The President of Northwestern wired: "You are the first college President to take so bold a stand for law and order."

Politeness was stressed, and in the French tradition, the social arts. "There is something rude and uncouth about the term 'Stag,' " the *South Bend Register* said. "It recalls beer, brawls, and bloody reminiscences of mining camps and cowboy society. But at Notre Dame one sees how, at an all-male school, gentlemen dance with gentlemen without shocking the proprieties, or violating the rules of decorum. It is at once a diversion and an exercise in spiritual grace." But a more masculine diversion and exercise in physical grace was much more appealing and enduring.

George W. DeHaven and W. Harless, who had played the soccer-type football at Notre Dame, shifted to the University of Michigan. They wrote to Brother Paul, in charge of athletics, that the Michigan team was now playing according to the rules of rugby football and would be leaving Ann Arbor the latter part of November, to play a series of games with the teams of leading cities and colleges of the Northwest. It was proposed that they stop at Notre Dame and play a game with a picked team of the senior department. Rugby, which featured running with the ball rather than merely kicking it, was a new thing begun in the East. Notre Dame would gladly play if Michigan would first explain the rules.

On Wednesday, November 23, 1888, the first Notre Dame varsity football team lined up: fullback, H. Jewett; halfbacks, J. Cusack and H. Lunn; quarterback, G. Cartier; center, Rush, G.A. Houck; rush line, F. Fehr, Pete Nelson, B. Sawkins, W. Springer, T. O'Regan, P.P. Maloney. Notre Dame lost to Michigan in a game that lasted only "one inning." There was a noon dinner. Father Walsh invited the visitors to return, everything was just peachy. Notre Dame organized a Rugby football association, and new uniforms were provided for the two campus teams: "The jacket and trousers are of canvas, the stockings are the best quality of wool and the caps are jersey. The trimmings are brown and black by which colors the teams will be distinguished."

The next season Michigan came to give the Irish neighbors

89

another lesson. On Friday, April 27, 1888, before four hundred spectators at Green Stocking Ball Park in South Bend, Notre Dame was defeated 26 to 6. The next day they were at it again, but the Irish were getting the hang of it. The first "rhubarb" developed when Notre Dame "alleged" an unfair ruling by the Michigan man who was refereeing. It went into the records as a 10-4 Michigan victory, but there were no more games between these natural geographical rivals for a decade; and future relations would be intermittent and stormy.

The first "away" game was played in 1889 at Northwestern. Brother Hugh, before he would fall asleep at the dinner table at football banquets, would tell this tale, which, like his belly, would expand with the years. The players, according to his version, were still arriving in ambulances throughout the next week, and the impression he gave was that any man able to make it on his own power had not done his full duty to his alma mater. Notre Dame won, of course, 9–0. It was the only game in that first "undefeated" season. No games were played in 1890–1891. In 1892 the long string of winning years began, and football had become a definite part of this masculine scene. The opponents were anybody available, including the Illinois Cycling Club, Indianapolis Artillery, and Chicago University. Changes were being made, the suits were padded; but the game would not begin to assume modern outlines until 1894 when the first "coacher" was named. H. Jewett who was fullback on the first football team and in 1891 also became a national sprint champion with marks of 9:8 in the 100-yard dash and 21.6 in the 220. As an engineer he pioneered in the automobile business, became chairman of the board of the Paige-Detroit Company. Quarterback G. Cartier was of the family for whom Cartier Field was named.

The first Notre Dame baseball team was organized in 1865

by Matthew Campion, who became a priest and pastor of St. Mary's Church in that Purdue town of Lafayette, Indiana. Adrian "Cap" Anson, who would go on to the big leagues and become a diamond immortal, played with the Juanitas, one of the dozen campus teams. Outside games were the exception until the nineties. The first colleges played were Chicago and Michigan. Notre Dame upset the previously undefeated Michiganders in 1892, but the sports editor of the *Scholastic* admitted: "The local team, being weak in the points, secured the services of Willie McGill, who used to be a student at the University several years ago. Willie allowed only three hits. Without him Notre Dame would surely have lost the game." Because it sent a steady stream, including men of the stature of Roger Bresnahan, Ed Reulbach, and Cy Williams, to the big leagues, Notre Dame was known nationally as a baseball school—until Rockne.

Boating, both rowing and sailing, was popular. Intramural races were always held on St. Joseph Lake, as part of the entertainment for St. Edward's Day and Commencement.

17. HIGH NOON

SORIN had become a world figure. In addition to Notre Dame he guided the destinies of the Congregation of the Holy Cross, with its houses, schools, and colleges, in America, Canada, and France; and its missions in Guadeloupe and

India. He had many visits with Pius IX and Leo XIII, who valued his knowledge of ecclesiastical affairs. The patriarchal figure with the stern visage, the white hair, the long white beard, became familiar at such places as the Provincial Council in Cincinnati and the Plenary Council in Baltimore. His wisdom, experience, and prestige had won wide respect and lifelong friends among the hierarchy and laity. His towering position was fully recognized in 1888, on the occasion of his golden jubilee as a priest. Two celebrations were held, one for the student body on May 27th, and the other for the public on August 15th.

The student celebration, marking the 50th anniversary of Sorin's first Mass, began Saturday afternoon with a reception in Washington Hall that included the usual musical entertainment and congratulatory speeches by representatives of the student departments. After supper a band concert, punctuated by artillery salutes, was held before the Main Building, while Sorin and faculty observed from the porch. A handsome open barouche, drawn by two coal-black steeds, came up the shady path. Professor John Ewing made the presentation speech for the students, alumni, and faculty who had contributed. "After several trials had been made and it was proved to the satisfaction of all that docility as well as fleetness was a quality of the horses," Sorin, Zahm, Corby, and Professor Jimmy Edwards climbed into the carriage and drove off, amidst cheers.

Dusk gave way to darkness, and the campus was illuminated with Chinese lanterns hanging in the trees and around the fountain, while the façade of the Main Building was draped with flags and banners. "And out of every window—spacious study halls, lecture, class, and private rooms, from roomy libraries in the halls—there beamed the noonday brilliance of the Edison light." All this became background for "a magnificent display of fireworks." The next day, Trinity

Sunday, a solemn high Mass was sung by Sorin, whose deep and vigorous voice seemed to deny that he was seventy-five years of age. The sermon, on the life and works of Sorin, was preached by the Provincial, Father Corby. After Mass Sorin blessed the cornerstone of the new hall that was to bear his name.

At noon a French dinner was followed by a series of toasts —to the Pope, to Sorin, to America, and to Alma Mater—by senior James Burns, who had come up from the Manual Labor School and might therefore have been thought to also speak for Father Badin, who had bought this place as a hospice for orphans.

The student celebration ended on Monday, with a boat race on St. Joseph's Lake in the morning between the crews of the Evangeline and the Minnehaha, followed in the afternoon by a competitive drill between companies A and B— military units known as Hoyne's Light Guards.

The principal jubilee celebration was held in August. Once again the grounds were colorfully decorated. Arches were erected at different points on the campus, adorned with American, Papal, and Notre Dame colors. At the main gate which was then just in front of the present statue of Father Sorin, a log cabin was built—a reminder of all that was visible at Notre Dame forty-six years before, when Father Sorin first came to it. Before the church a canopied double arch was built, decorated with the papal colors and golden roses. In front of the steps of the Main Building there was an evergreen arch surmounted by a Cross and Mitre with the motto: "Welcome—1838–1888." The façade of the Main Building was draped with bunting, while hundreds of American flags fluttered from its windows and those of other buildings. Notre Dame Avenue, leading to the University, was decorated with arches flying the Papal and American colors.

The most distinguished guest, Cardinal Gibbons, was delayed several hours because he had had to attend the funeral of General Philip Sheridan. A large escort, attended by the band, finally came up the avenue, followed by the Ancient Order of Hibernians, the local Polish Lancers, and Father Sorin's jubilee carriage with Cardinal Gibbons and Father Corby. The campus, at dusk, with its gay colors, lanterns, and electric lights, presented a rare and exciting scene. As the carriage and escort approached the Main Building, cheers of applause from the hundreds of people filled the air, while the big bell and the chimes from the church rang out a joyous welcome.

As he alighted at the Main Building, His Eminence found many members of the American hierarchy waiting to greet him: Archbishop Ireland of St. Paul, Archbishop Elder of Cincinnati, Bishops Dwenger of Fort Wayne, Burke of Cheyenne, Spalding of Peoria, Ryan of Alton, Jansen of Belleville, Ryan of Buffalo, Watterson of Columbus, Gilmour of Cleveland, Phelan of Pittsburgh, Richter of Grand Rapids, Keane of Richmond. After an informal exchange of greetings, Father Walsh read to His Eminence a Latin address of welcome from Notre Dame.

The ceremonies of the morning of Wednesday, August 15th, began at six o'clock with the consecration of the new Church of Our Lady of the Sacred Heart by Bishop Dwenger. The ceremony, closed to the public, continued until nine o'clock. Then Bishop Maurice Burke of Cheyenne, who had attended Notre Dame twenty-two years previously, blessed the mammoth seven-ton bell and named it for St. Anthony of Padua.

At nine-thirty the doors of the church were opened to the public. A large procession of uniformed Catholic societies—Ancient Order of Hibernians, Knights of St. Casimir, and St. Hedwig Society—had marched out to the University, accompanied by three bands. These organizations and other

94

people filled the church for the low Mass said by Father Sorin. A procession of acolytes, priests, and prelates escorted Cardinal Gibbons to the church where he celebrated a solemn Mass. The music was Haydn's Third, sung by the choir of the Jesuit Church of Chicago. The sermon (as previously noted), delivered by Archbishop Ireland, traced the growth of the church in America and the part Father Sorin had played in it. At one o'clock a French dinner was served in the two refectories on the ground floor of the Main Building, followed by toasts and tributes to Father Sorin. The toasts were proposed with water; neither wine nor liquor was served at this French banquet.

At four-thirty the several University buildings were blessed by Bishop Watterson and placed under the special protection of Our Lady. Then from the steps of the Main Building, Archbishop Ireland delivered an address on Christian Education. Cardinal Gibbons followed with a short expression of tribute to Father Sorin's work. A Solemn Benediction of the Blessed Sacrament given by Bishop Watterson closed the religious ceremonies. The evening supper was followed by a display of fireworks and a concert. It had been a long, long day, celebrating a long, long life.

Bishop Keane, recently appointed rector of the new Catholic University of America, to be located in Washington, D.C., remained at Notre Dame for a month, combing Sorin's experience, as he composed the statutes for the new institution. The original draft is in the Notre Dame archives.

18. THE YEAR OF GREAT SORROW

DURING the jubilee there must have been the thought that when Sorin could not go on, his successor would be Father Walsh, who at thirty-five had already been President of Notre Dame for seven bounding years.

Five years later, as he dedicated the statue to the Sacred Heart in the middle of the quadrangle, Father Walsh must have had the thought that before long he would be gathered in those outstretched arms of Christ.

He had been in bad health for two years. Travel and medicine had not arrested the decline. It was obvious to the people at the commencement exercises in 1893 that he was not well. He was taken immediately to St. Mary's-by-the-Lake Hospital in Milwaukee. Dissolution began with swelling of the feet. He was anointed and received the Viaticum while still in possession of his faculties. His last words: "I should have liked to labor longer for the University." He was only forty years of age and had been President for twelve years.

Alexis Granger was born at Daon, France, June 19, 1817. He was ordained at Le Mans at age twenty-three. Four years later he joined Sorin at Notre Dame and began the long and devoted walk in the shadow of the Founder. He was not brilliant, just steady, reliable, pious, charitable. As pastor of the church before, during, and after it was built, he saw to the stone and brick, the windows, the frescoing, the chimes, the bronze altar. But above all else, he was the confessor. In the confessional his power came from his self-effacing humility. A letter from an old student expressed the sentiments the boys felt:

In 1891 I went to confession to Father Granger in the chapel of the basement of the church. He gave me as a penance a decade of the rosary. He asked if I had a rosary. I told him I had lost mine in a fire at our home two months before. He reached in his pocket, handed me a rosary around the outside of the confessional. Whether it was his own or not I do not know, but I always obeyed his injunction to keep the rosary with me. I went through the Spanish War in Cuba, and World War I in France, and many other tight situations where an engineer must go. By day that rosary has been in the left front pocket of my trousers and by night in the pocket of my pajamas or under my pillow when I slept in a bed.

Once, in going across the "Shoe Swamp" (Cienga Zapata) I was mired in the mud and so deep, the muzzle of an automatic I carried in a shoulder holster was in the mud. My pockets were all filled with mud. In cleaning them out I took out my rosary and washed it in the water of the swamp. Three colored Cuban boys who were with me were much surprised to see an American take a rosary from his pocket.

The rosary has had only one broken link. The beads have worn down. Half a century is a long time to have one rosary. However, in remembering in my prayers each day those whom "we have loved long since and lost awhile" is included Father Granger.

C. C. Fitzgerald, C.E. '94

It was Father Granger who had cut away the underbrush on the northern edge of St. Mary's Lake for the first Novitiate. He had survived the cholera. He was a member of the University Council which met with Moreau. It was his job to meet visiting parents. When Sorin became Superior-General he had appointed Granger Provincial of Indiana. He had watched nervously as the minims tried out the velocipede Sorin had sent from France, calling: "Watch out. You break zumpsing." He had heard Father Lemonnier's death-bed confession. He had helped wheel the bricks away after The Great Fire. When anyone, high or low, lay dangerously sick, it was Father Granger they asked for. Remembering these, and a thousand other incidents, Father Sorin wept when, on Wednesday, July 26, 1893, he was told that Granger had died. "First, Father Walsh, and now, *mon cher* Alexis! Who next?"

Sorin knew. The previous year, the oaken body had been stricken with a startling sickness, with hemorrhages and a great weakness. A specialist from Chicago diagnosed Bright's Disease. On St. Edward's Day, for the first time in all those years, Sorin was unable to attend the celebration of his Saint's feast. The best he could do was make the porch of the presbytery where he lived. The band was there, and the students. He smiled, waved, and returned, with some assistance, to his death-chamber. Two weeks later he could not get out of bed. His eyes were closed. His lips moved in constant prayer. The minims wanted to see him once more. The Sisters took them to their chapel.

The evening of October 31, 1893, Sorin opened his eyes, gazed at the religious kneeling about him. It was farewell. Had he lived until February he would have been eighty. Typically, he had supervised his funeral in a letter in his own hand:

When I die the Community shall not be disturbed by any extra preparations or invitations to strangers for my obsequies. On the contrary, I wish the Community to remain completely at peace, exclusively occupied with the needs of my poor soul. I want nothing more than is prescribed by the Rule: a simple wooden coffin with simplest purple vestments. No strangers of any sort are to be disturbed by telegraphic announcements, no invitations whatever to attend; none present but my own dear children of the Holy Cross around my bed; no delay to wait for friends at a distance. When laid in state, I want no strangers to look at me and prevent my own dear children from praying undisturbed around my mortal remains. Indeed, I want no visit but from my own (religious) family for which alone I have lived and whose affection I so much prized since my entrance into the Congregation.

The order was ignored. The patriarch was a personage. The strangers came from all parts of the country. In his sermon, Archbishop Elder said: "I do not think it likely that in all of our country or in any country, there is a place where one single man has transformed a savage wilderness into such a city of splendor and culture as this University of Notre Dame." Sorin has his little wooden cross among the whisperings of history, in the community cemetery.

A casual visitor, if he looks real hard, will find a statue of the Founder, camouflaged by progress, where it once stood sentinel at the entrance to the old quadrangle. After World War II a smaller statue disappeared. Postcards came from all parts of the world to Notre Dame: "Having a good time. Wish you were here. Father Sorin." And one day the statue was found in a rowboat bobbing on the lake surface. Sorin would permit a frosty smile; after all, he was a traveling man. He had spent most of his life coping with student wit and energy, had been inclined to be personally soft about his own hard rules. He would understand that, while Notre Dame boys could see the human foibles of priests, and humanly take some advantage of them, they never forgot that a priest paid a very stiff human price to stand somewhere between man and God. Sorin himself had written that only this feeling of respect had prevented campus uprisings when mass student energy threatened to become combustible. That glue still holds.

19. ZAHM VS. MORRISSEY

WHEN a dominant leader passes there is the immediate matter of succession. With Walsh also gone the Congregation of the Holy Cross passed over the aging Corby and returned the seat of power from Notre Dame to the Mother House in Le Mans, with Father Gilbert Francais as Superior-General. One of his problems would be an unavoidable personal contest at Notre Dame between Andrew Morrissey, the President, and John Zahm, the Personality.

The University chronicles are crowded with Zahm's achievements as scholar, builder, lecturer, scientist, writer, traveler. He had extended the bridge with South America, had been given a doctorate by the Vatican, was providing the image of scholarship Notre Dame needed for national recognition. He had been elevated to the Vice-Presidency under Walsh, and in the latter's absence had presided over the Golden Jubilee. Morrissey had come to Notre Dame from

Ireland at age twelve, was ordained at twenty-four, had served as director of studies for seven years. His intellectual formation had been hampered by the necessity to teach, study, and perform a multiplicity of small duties. Physically he was unimpressive, pudgy, with a fat face, and small hands and feet. Their personalities were contrary. Zahm was described as cold, standoffish, intellectually arrogant—Morrissey, as bright, clever, warmhearted, blunt, emotional.

By almost any standard Morrissey was a pigmy in comparison with Zahm. Yet in 1892 Zahm had been replaced by Morrissey as Vice-President; and on his deathbed Walsh had recommended that Morrissey be elevated to the Presidency. The assumption was that Zahm would best serve the University as ambassador, and Morrissey as administrator. Zahm was a buy-now-pay-later man with a cavalier disregard of money. Morrissey, who had twice seen the University on the brink of bankruptcy, worried about meeting the payroll. As priests they were amicable. As opponents Morrissey's political acumen compensated for Zahm's superior mind. His Irish sensitivity was shocked by Zahm's sincere, but indiscreetly expressed opinions that under Morrissey the University could not possibly grow in intellectual stature. They had been set on a collision course by Sorin, who had sponsored both and left them to wrestle with the future.

Morrissey might not have become an intellectual giant even if he had been given the opportunity. He was competent, liberal on most questions, and no enemy of scholarship; but he firmly felt that Notre Dame had made it in its own sphere and should not try to foolishly compete "with all those schools so heavily endowed." Under his leadership, Notre Dame did continue the momentum established by Walsh, and in the path Walsh had set. Things progressed, seeds came to flower, new ideas and experiments within the range of reasonable fiscal common sense, were encouraged. New people were brought in. The enrollment continued to rise; in Morrissey's time it reached seven hundred.

In the fall of 1894 Notre Dame needed a new professor of electrical engineering. Father Morrissey and Father Corby went to Chicago and brought back Jerome J. Green. He was born near Somerset, Ohio, got his primary education at a country school, entered Ohio State, became interested in photography, built his own camera, and made enough money from it to earn a degree in electrical engineering. He was teaching in a Chicago technical school for two dollars and fifty cents a night, and that's where Morrissey, following a tip from the city engineer, found him, six years after gradution. He had been experimenting with wireless on his own. Father Morrissey found enough money to subsidize his work, and in 1889 Jerry Green sent what is generally believed to be the first wireless message in the United States from St. Mary's to Notre Dame, an event witnessed by reporters from Chicago newspapers. He constructed the first x-ray machine in that part of the country, and it was put to use by the doctors of the section. Except for a year's leave at the University of Paris, he remained at Notre Dame until 1914, teaching and experimenting.

Because of The Year of Great Sorrow, the Golden Jubilee was delayed two years, until 1895. To commemorate the event, the Alumni Association commissioned Timothy Howard, a former student and professor, to write the history of the first fifty years. For a full week in mid-June, Notre Dame men came back to relive escapades and pranks, thrills and heartaches, with humor and exaggeration and an occasional flagon of inspiration. The Governor of Indiana appeared with Father Morrissey, as politicians will do whenever voters are assembled. There was the sobering moment when all gathered in the church to pray for those who were celebrating in, it was hoped, the sky. And this became the first Reunion.

A caustic English professor, Dr. Austin O'Malley, took full advantage of academic freedom, saying what he thought and encouraging students to do the same. "You have here," he once said to a class, "such a lovely church. And right next to it that monstrosity, Sorin Hall, which looks like an old-fashioned icebox turned upside down." Not to soothe O'Malley, but to make room for one hundred more students, the practical Morrissey added two wings to Sorin Hall. Next to the church another hall was erected for the use of priests. It was called the "Professed House." But it was also needed for the students, and the name was changed to Corby Hall after the death, in 1897, of the venerable Provincial. (In recent years Corby has again become a residence for priests.)

The Manual Labor School had been withering away under the heat of progress. The old frame building, between the sites of the present Walsh and Badin Halls, had acquired the name of St. Joseph's Hall. It was replaced by a new St. Joseph's Hall which later became the central portion of the present Badin Hall.

The Spanish-American War brought some heat but little fire to the campus. Many students joined up, but few saw action. Yet *Remember the Maine* became remembered through a sequence revolving about a baseball player named John Shillington, who was "given his trunk" for failing to return on time from a game in Chicago, his home town. He joined the Navy, wrote to classmates hoping "old Notre Dame would remember Old Shilly," because remembering Notre Dame still brought a tear to Old Shilly's eye. Shilly was on the *Maine* when it blew up. A granite monument, topped by one of the shells resurrected from the *Maine,* is somewhere among the nooks of the old Brownson campus around the Main Building. So old Notre Dame still remembers Old Shilly.

Father Morrissey, as his appearance indicated, was not a

practitioner of athletics, but believed in a relationship between physical and intellectual culture. In 1898 he built a gymnasium which promptly burned down; all but $20,000 was covered by insurance, and with the speed of a Sorin, he built "one of the largest college gymnasia in the United States," *The Scholastic* proudly reported. It was dedicated March 11, 1899, with a track meet in which the Universities of Chicago, Illinois, and Michigan took part. Notre Dame was proud of the new facility, which seated seven hundred.

The covering story in *The Scholastic* revealed the surprisingly modern attitude toward athletics at that time. No student was allowed to compete unless his general average in class work was 75 "percentum." The faculty advisory board, headed by the President, had jurisdiction in all matters pertaining to finances and the amateur standing of the athletes. A student committeee elected the managers of the different teams and "requires to be informed at its weekly meetings of all negotiations that are undergoing with other institutions." A statement of policy said: "The faculty and students of Notre Dame University are united in the determination to bind the pursuit of knowledge and the practice of athletics together, much as they were in the days when Pindar sang. To be sure, athletics is held to be subordinate to morals and the attainments of the mind."

One could, as they say, "write a book" about that old dirt floor anachronism known as "The Gym," and its basketball, track, and other events through the years. Rockne and Westbrook Pegler shook hands there to end a famous feud—which broke out anew the following day. Max Houser and Frank Doriot had a "preferred room"; Houser would pretend nightmares and chase Doriot around the running track at three in the morning. The occupants of tables in the Carroll Hall refectory would run relay races, with the winners getting all the tarts the next time that luscious dessert was served. In

1930, with snow outside, Rockne used the gym to work his National Champions—at the same time basketball and track teams practiced. The highlights of Notre Dame football history could have been preserved, if tapes or written records had been made of the pep meetings before big games.

20. GROTTO, GREEK, GROWTH

UNDER Morrissey Notre Dame was becoming a cautiously growing town. It had added a central heating plant, a railroad spur, shops, and utilitarian buildings. A new bakery featured the old staple, "The Notre Dame Bun," about which J.P. McEvoy wrote a poem. Dr. John Talbot Smith, a visiting lecturer, always took a sack of buns home. They served many student purposes, including doughballs for throwing in the refectory.

The curriculum was constantly under revision. The school of journalism, which emphasized history, economics, and philosophy, was designed to discipline and stoke the mind of the future writer rather than merely to teach the mechanics. So constantly close to his own grim economic problem, Morrissey was wary of daring economic theory that might lead to experimental legislation. The political philosophy was liberal: Great private interests must be gradually adjusted to public welfare. Morrissey warned: "We must be prepared for a clash."

Thomas Carroll, a student who had become a priest in the diocese of Erie, gave an idea to Corby, and the Provincial grasped it. In the spring of 1896 workmen came to a spot behind the presbytery. There was some digging. A foundation was laid. Big boulders were hauled in, some weighing two tons. A statue of Our Lady was placed in a niche on the right and facing her, on the pavement below, a replica of St. Bernadette. And that's how Notre Dame got its Grotto, a replica of Lourdes, a charming, undemanding spot, dear to old students, who bring their wives for a silent prayer; and young students, who bring their dates after a dance at the student center or, as recently observed, following a John Davidson network television performance on campus. Seldom in the normal waking hours has there been a moment through the years when the Grotto has been unattended. Visitors are deeply impressed. A New York sports writer and war correspondent, known for several reasons as "Broadway Bob" Brumby, called it "that outdoor cathedral."

Latin, Greek, and the classics, deemphasized by Walsh, were again stressed by Morrissey. Father Nicholas Stoffel organized the play *Oedipus Tyrannus* in the original Greek. Each morning he drove up from South Bend, where he was pastor of St. Joseph's Church, "his faithful dog trotting beside the buggy," for the endless rehearsals. It was worthwhile to the director, if not necessarily to the tyrannized performers, when on May 1, 1899, Archbishop (later Cardinal) Martinelli, the Apostolic Delegate, witnessed the play. Father Stoffel edited an *Epitome of the New Testament* in Greek, and set the type himself in *The Ave Maria* shop.

The College of Law was flourishing under "Colonel" Hoynes. Father Morrissey flattered the Colonel's "little vanities," and the students added to his law library (or *The Scholastic* said they did), such volumes as *J. Sullivan on Prize*

Fights, Booze on Spiritous Liquors, and *McNichols on Street Car Fares.*

On the campus everybody knew everybody else, and in case of doubt, said hello. The fun was mostly homemade, much of it in the "rec" rooms of the Halls.

The President was still paterfamilias, his door was always open. In the spring of 1905, John F. Cushing came to say goodbye, because he could not afford to return the following year. Father Morrissey told John he was so well-known as a good boy and a good student, that he should come back next year and get his degree, and not bother his head about finances until he was able to pay. John Cushing really got around to it in 1931. In a letter to President Charles O'Donnell he wrote:

> I find at Notre Dame the conditions that make for the two-fold training of great engineers in all the departments of engineering, a technical training that ranks with the best and a training in character foundation nowhere excelled. Because I feel I owe Notre Dame a debt of gratitude I can never fully discharge, I ask you to accept from me a gift of three hundred thousand dollars towards the erection of a hall of engineering to serve the immediate needs of the College of Engineering and to meet the expectations of older men like me who confidently look to Notre Dame to produce the men that are to carry on.

In case of doubt parents wrote *personally* to the President himself. "Allow George to smoke one cigar twice a week. . . . I sent a box to my brother, and he writes that it did not reach him. Will you kindly visit the Express office in South Bend . . . it was a box of edibles . . . and see if they have the box? . . . Will you please see that Harvey is not required to take a bath in cold water as the attack of congestion he had last spring was due to taking a cold bath. . . . My son has never been a bad boy. His worst failing was he did not want to go to school regular. . . . Johnny wrote home that he had something in his ear. He says he cannot here [sic] well but we thought it was because he wants to come home. Would you see his ear and tell us about it? . . . Why do I have to pay for Edward now? My intention was to pay when he was through. . . . I am sorry to have to tell you something against my dear son Edoard. He has an extraordinary love for reading interesting books, viz: novels, and amongst them the *Voyages of Julius Verne*. You will be able to help him, I'm sure."

All students did not have Edoard's addiction to culture. On many it had to be applied by various methods, including the artistic performances in Washington Hall. An Egyptologist sought to impart some knowledge and enthusiasm for the pyramids; but while the lights were out many a pebble and peanut found its mark. Terror was struck in the hearts of actors who might have made better plumbers, but the prep-school rascals from Carroll Hall might also have hissed a John McCormick or laughed through the death scene by Sarah Bernhardt. To visit St. Mary's it was necessary to have a relative there; so phony cousins were numerous; and any mail in girlish handwriting that had a South Bend postmark was carefully inspected. Social life of the proper type was encouraged. In April, 1905, the first class dance, the Senior Ball, was held in the apparatus room of the gymnasium. "The room had been decorated with bunting and streamers, the orchestra was concealed behind a forest of palms and a punch bowl was ensconced in an artistically decorated booth."

Football began to stabilize in 1896, with the arrival of Frank E. Hering, who had played quarterback for A.A. Stagg at Chicago and coached for a season at Bucknell. At Notre Dame he coached and played football, a common practice then. He also took law and taught English. He became one of Notre Dame's important men, a President of the National

Alumni Association, a lawyer, an orator, a poet, and editor of the magazine of the lodge of Eagles. On February 7, 1904, he addressed a national convention of the Eagles at the English Opera House in Indianapolis. In 1930 the War Mothers, after an investigation, declared that in this speech Frank Hering had been the first to propose an annual day to honor mothers. On May 10, 1931, the Eagles unveiled a tablet on the site of the speech.

The rosters of the football squads during the Morrissey tenure reveal interesting names. Louis "Red" Salmon is still listed among the all-time gridiron immortals as a fullback. John "King" Farley was a great all-round athlete familiar to later generations of students as a hall rector who might very well handle any young buck who got out of line. Even in a wheel chair after the amputation of a leg, The King was a fearsome figure on campus. Angus McDonald would return often as Chairman of the Board of the Southern Pacific Railroad. Frank "Shag" Shaughnessy, later of the top councils of baseball, was captain of the 1904 football squad; and Dom Callicrate, 1907 captain, still tall and straight, returned for his sixtieth reunion with an autographed football of a 17–0 victory over Purdue for the Sports and Games collection. . . .

In 1894, on a European trip, Father Zahm met the Superior-General and presented the case for the establishment of a house of studies close to Catholic University in Washington, designed to advance the higher education of Holy Cross priests who would return to the campus as teachers and administrators. Corby and Morrissey opposed Zahm's action as "going over the head" of the Provincial and President. Father Francais, the Superior-General, ruled for Zahm and put him in charge of the Washington project.

Father Dion, Procurator-General based in Rome, died in February, 1906. One month later Zahm was summoned to Corby's office and handed a letter from the Superior-General, ordering him to Rome to become Procurator-General. If it was "a kick upstairs" engineered by Corby or Morrissey, it backfired. In Europe Zahm would be in frequent contact with Francais.

In 1897 Corby died. Zahm returned to Notre Dame as Provincial. He was now superior to Morrissey. They worked together for seven years without surface discord.

At the meeting of the Indiana Provincial Chapter in 1905 Morrissey, "forced to the conclusion that if he did not retire Father Zahm would ask for his resignation," submitted it. The matter was handled with superficial grace. It was announced that the "great burden of the Presidency" had undermined Father Morrissey's health. A trip to Europe and a year's good rest were recommended.

Father John W. Cavanaugh, a "Zahm man," was installed as President. The Notre Dame arrow, in the persons of more highly educated future leaders, was henceforth aimed away from the Sorin concept of the "tight little prep school" and toward scholarship. Zahm, already an outstanding exponent of *teaching* and *research,* moved into the third University function of *inquiry.* Darwinism was immensely popular in secular colleges, but not accepted by religious fundamentalists. Zahm wrote a book designed to show that whatever was of proved scientific value in the theory of evolution was perfectly reconcilable with Catholic doctrine. His statements about the origin of man's body ran afoul of the Congregation of the Index. The doctrine he defended was never condemned as heretical, but the Holy See made it clear that it did not approve of the sentiments of the professor of science at Notre Dame. He was ordered by Rome to withdraw his book from circulation. And for the Province of Indiana, on August 20, 1906, there would be a new Provincial—Andrew Morrissey.

Zahm, according to an ancient priest who still lives at

Notre Dame, "took it very hard." But he remained the good priest, the good sportsman. The glue held. He continued to bring prestige to the University. His last gift to Notre Dame was his Dante collection, one of the best in existence.

Morrissey, Provincial for many years, was elevated to Co-adjutor Superior-General. He died May 27, 1920, in Paris, one day after having been received in audience by the Pope.

Eighteen months later, November 11, 1921, Zahm contracted a cold and died in Munich. He had been en route to Baghdad to verify certain details before giving his manuscript, *Berlin to Baghdad,* to the publisher.

Each has his little cross in the cemetery.

21. THE PUBLICIST

JOHN WILLIAM CAVANAUGH, the ninth President, was born at Leetonia, Ohio, May 21, 1870, the son of Patrick Cavanaugh and Elizabeth O'Connor. He arrived at Notre Dame at sixteen, was ordained at twenty-three. His formal education was limited to a bachelor's degree, probably because the University had urgent need of his talents. He had a facile style in speaking and writing, the air of a great man, and could "walk with kings nor lose the common touch." He was striking in appearance, had courage and charm, was altogether a personality whom political kingmakers would have loved. He was also custom-made to lift Notre Dame from the rustic image and give it an impressive national appearance. As a high-powered public relations man, the forerunner of the modern college president, he presented Notre Dame as a national asset, asked not for charity, but an investment in the public interest. The money did not come in his time, but he cut through the wilderness and paved the first road. He was also, and never ceased to be, a priest who would select and train young priests for scholarship and leadership.

His gifts were so preeminently literary that even before his ordination he had been assigned to work under Father Hudson at *The Ave Maria,* where he remained for eight years; during this period he also taught English and registered as a preacher. ("Smell the flowers," the blunt Morrissey would say.) He was Superior of Holy Cross Seminary at Notre Dame from 1898 until 1905 when he was made President. He was inclined to be dictatorial, something of a one-man band, but he got things done.

In his first sermon to the students as President he spelled out the traditional policy: Notre Dame must manage somehow to educate Catholic young men superbly, even though it lacked the wealth and endowment of most other schools. It could do this because of the personal sacrifice of its dedicated religious. The moral life would be fostered by instruction that would augment faith. Disciplinary regulations were for the student welfare and should not be considered as punishment. Discontent and disobedience from "the sporty element" would not be tolerated.

One of his early activities was to tidy up the historical past. He raised $25,000 for the heroic statue of Sorin which still stands sentinel on the old quadrangle. On that same day, May 3, 1906, he moved the bones of Badin to the replica of the log cabin the pioneer had built. (The rebuilding was done by William Arnett, a former slave, who could still wield a broadaxe.) Present at the interment was Father Louis

L'Etourneau who had served Mass for Badin in the old building.

Academically, the primary job of Cavanaugh, the flowery man, was to cultivate the garden planted by his predecessors, to add to its harmony, beauty, and usefulness. The student body grew toward the one thousand goal. The number of master's degrees increased. The head of the City News Bureau in Chicago wrote: "I think you have the best body of men in the West to work on." The faculty was being enlarged and enriched by the first products of the higher education program initiated by Zahm: Matthew Walsh, Charles O'Donnell, John O'Hara, and, among the Irish, a Belgian, Julius Arthur Nieuwland. He was born February 14, 1878, in Hansbeke, Belgium, son of John Baptiste and Philomena (Van Hoecke) Nieuwland. While still an infant he was brought to South Bend, eventually entered Notre Dame, where he became the ultimate vindication of Zahm's program for higher education. After graduation Nieuwland went to Holy Cross in Washington, earned a doctorate at Catholic U., was ordained in 1893, immediately joined the faculty at Notre Dame as a teacher of chemistry, and in that same year performed the first reaction that would lead to the preparation of "Lewisite," the most deadly gas in World War I. Though his early work was in chemistry, he switched his principal interest to botany, and "derived an almost illegal pleasure from his tramps through the woods and swamps." In 1909 he founded and edited a bi-monthly magazine, still published at Notre Dame, called *The Midland Naturalist,* which dealt largely with plant life in the prairie states.

As a teacher he is said to have been mediocre with mediocre students, but for those with the talent and courage to work he was an inspirer and director. The late Dr. Leo O'Donnell of Pittsburgh, one of his students, confirmed this attitude. "He would talk to Rock as if he were an equal. And

113

Rock would stand there and argue with him." (Rock was Knute Rockne, who might have been another Nieuwland if he hadn't been channeled by events, rather than choice, into other fields.)

Nieuwland had never strayed far from chemistry, and in 1918 returned to it as a major field. Vincent Sweeney, a brother-in-law of O'Donnell, became Nieuwland's secretary and told this story: "We went out in the open campus before old Science Hall. Father Nieuwland had a substance he was going to test. The only trouble, he said, was that he didn't know whether it would burn; but if it did burn the best place to be would be away from there. So he lit it and I established what must have been a new Notre Dame record for the 100-yard dash. Nieuwland was just behind me—the only reason I beat him was because he was wearing a cassock. The substance did not explode. We walked slowly back. Nieuwland inspected it and said: 'Vincent, this is synthetic rubber.'" Specifically, it was the base from which synthetic rubber would come.

The story gives validity to a fear the University had about Nieuwland. It was a common thing for him to stay long stretches in his laboratory. He had a thin leather pallet laid on a long table, and here he would doze while waiting for some chemical reaction. The fear was that while he relaxed, something might go wrong, and he and Chemistry Hall would be blown up! The American Chemical Society publicly lauded him for the work he had done with dangerous chemicals with no thought of material benefit for himself. Notre Dame, with its constant need for money, was not quite that disinterested. It received annual grants from patents on Nieuwland's work until the patents ran out.

Nieuwland was attached to Doctor Edward Lee Greene of the Smithsonian Institution and also to Dr. Greene's "magnificent herbarium." He extracted money from Father Mor-

The campus today. Father Badin's original 524 acres grew to over 1,000, though more land may be needed for the building years to come.

Rev. Edward Frederick Sorin CSC
1842-1865

Rev. Patrick Dillon CSC
1865-1866

Rev. William Corby CSC
1866-1872   1877-1881

Rev. Andrew Morrissey CSC
1893-1905

Rev. John W. Cavanaugh CSC
1905-1919

Rev. James A. Burns CSC
1919-1922

Rev. J. Hugh O'Donnell CSC
1940-1946

Rev. John J. Cavanaugh CSC
1946-1952

Rev. Theodore M. Hesburgh CSC
1952-

Auguste Lemonnier CSC
1872-1874

Rev. Patrick J. Colovin CSC
1874-1877

Rev. Thomas E. Walsh CSC
1881-1893

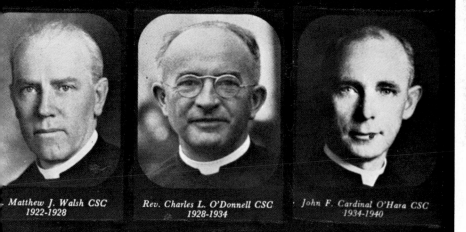

Matthew J. Walsh CSC
1922-1928

Rev. Charles L. O'Donnell CSC
1928-1934

John F. Cardinal O'Hara CSC
1934-1940

Sorin, born in 1814, La Roche, France. Dillon, soldier of the Irish Brigade, born 1832. Corby, born 1833, son of a Detroit physician. Lemonnier, nephew of Sorin, born in France, 1839. Colovin, born in Canada, of Irish parents. Walsh, born 1853, Lacolle, near Montreal. Morrissey, born in Ireland, 1860. Cavanaugh (John W.), born 1870 in Ohio. Burns, born in 1867, in Michigan City, Indiana. Walsh (Mathew J.), born 1882 in Chicago. O'Donnelly (Charles L.), born 1884, in Greenfield, Indiana. O'Hara, born Ann Arbor, Michigan, 1888. O'Donnell (J. Hugh), born 1885, Grand Rapids, Michigan. Cavanaugh (John J.), born 1899 in Michigan. Hesburgh, born 1917 in Syracuse, New York.

MINIMS OF 1880.

Sorin's beloved "Little Princes" had their own building by 1882 and some went on to become Notre Dame scholars. Sorin gave them "royal Parisian" dinners.

1863. Top: Rev. Patrick Dillon, Dr. K. O'Hanlon. Lower: J. J. McCormick, Rev. J. Dillon, V. Rev. Wm. Corby.

3rother Basil's band. He taught music for 50 years—front row, leaning
»n his horn. Criticized for long hair, he replied, "It takes all kinds."

Old College or Mission House, built 1843, with bricks made from loc[a]
marl.

The Log Chapel, built in 1831 by Father Badin, first priest ordained i[n]
America, in 1793. This replica, rebuilt in 1906, contains his morta[l]
remains.

Physics class circa 1910. In 1889 Professor Jerome Green sent first wireless message in U.S. from St. Mary's to Notre Dame. Invented an x-ray machine.

Father Julius Nieuwland, in his famous chemistry lab after World War I.

Photo of 1865. The Sacred Heart Church and the Main Building, with a white dome, completed in 1862. The latter burned down in the Great Fire of 1879.

The Grotto or The Retreat, a replica of Lourdes built in 1896. In th
niche are statues of Our Lady and St. Bernadette. Photo of 1958, durin
a TV performance.

Student political meeting. Standing is Richard Rossi, Student Body President, '68, an advocate of Student Power. Controversy dominated the year 1968.

Rev. Bernard Longe, still going strong. His hobby is photographing athletes in action. He was awarded the title of "biggest chest in the world."

Knute Rockne. His "magic sword" won half a million dollars a year. He lived to see the stadium built.

The Four Horsemen of Notre Dame football, so named by Grantland Rice in 1924. Harry Stuhldreher, Don Miller, Jimmy Crowley, and Elmer Leyden.

Notre Dame stadium opened informally October 4, 1930, capacity 59,000. During the '20s the old bleachers held only 22,000.

Pope Paul (then Cardinal Montini) with Father Hesburgh at commencement 1960.

Dr. George N. Schuster with Cardinal Montini. At right, seated, is Dr. Tom Dooley.

Father Sorin, founder of Notre Dame, 1857.

Father John A. Zahm, scholar, builder, scientist, writer, guiding genius of the University at the turn of the century.

Rev. Cornelius J. Hagerty, "the spirit of Notre Dame," now retired. He taught philosophy to generations.

Two quiet lakes, St. Mary's and St. Joseph's, border the campus.

rissey, never an easy task, to have Greene come to the campus, asserting: "He seems glad to get away on a little trip from Washington, and this would be a good occasion to settle the terms by which he would leave his specimens with us and thereby make Notre Dame a mecca for scientists who must consult his library and herbarium." The library did come, but Nieuwland himself would become the mecca; though he probably never gave a thought to that.

He was a "character" only in the sense that he wore a smelly raincoat he had cooked up in his laboratory. He avoided all pretense, had none of the mannerisms of the self-conscious great, persisted in giving the impression that he was just another man on campus, doing his job, enjoying it hugely. A sportswriter alumnus who had known him returned on an exhibition trip with the New York Yankees, and solely because of that propinquity was assigned a place at the faculty table in the dining hall. When Nieuwland pointedly joined him, he thought it a good opportunity to interview the great man about Rockne's credits as a chemist. Nieuwland did the interviewing. He wanted to hear every small item about his idol—Babe Ruth.

In the later years of his presidential term, Father Cavanaugh would meet a person to whom he wanted to sell Notre Dame as a university of growing academic importance, and therefore worthy of assistance, preferably financial. He would grow irritated when his auditor seemed to be more interested in the growing importance of the Notre Dame football team. His successors, in varying degrees, would have the same trouble; but all learned to live with it, some even happily.

22. LUCK OF THE IRISH

FATHER TOM CRUMLEY was slow-moving, slow-talking, solemn. His philosophy classes would be interpolated with such observations as "a gentleman is a man who could play a trombone but won't." In his poetry class he would dawdle over "summer is acumin' in, murry sing cuckoo," until his students could never be quite sure they weren't being put on. He had a firm jaw and the smouldering eyes of an Airedale. As Vice-President he was automatically chairman of the Athletic Board, and the inheritor of a chronic problem.

In 1896 the Western Conference, known as the Big Ten, had been organized to bring some order into the conduct of the burgeoning sport of college football. It was composed of nine state universities and Northwestern. Notre Dame was shaken off as small fry, which it was in the number of students; but so was Northwestern; and the Irish had held their own with the two or three Big Ten schools they played each year. There were also insinuations that Notre Dame's standards were not up to those of the Conference schools. Under Coach Tom Barry, who had played for Brown University and had taken law at Harvard, the Irish voluntarily conformed to Big Ten requirements, and let it be known it was available. When Michigan, after some disagreement, withdrew from the Conference in 1905, Notre Dame applied; was again rejected; and in the well-known Irish manner, reacted. Father Crumley retired from the fray with the tart observation: "The matter seems to have been settled on theological rather than athletic grounds." A schedule "freeze" went into operation and in 1909, with its best team in history ready to prove Notre Dame could hold its own with the best, there were no Big Ten schools to play against.

But there was Michigan, which had just high-hatted the Conference and which, under their famous coach Fielding "Hurry-Up" Yost, annually pretty much justified the claim of their school song "Champions of the West." The ambitious Irish had ideas about that. In their last three seasons, they had won twenty, lost two, and tied one; they had lost to Michigan the year before by the close score of 12–6. Furthermore, their new coach, Frank "Shorty" Longman, had recently played on one of Yost's famous "point-a-minute" Michigan teams.

The dressing-room speeches on the afternoon of November 6, 1909, had they been taped, would be jewels in the new International Sports & Games Collection at Notre Dame. Both teams were undefeated. Yost, a vigorous orator, no doubt called upon his champions to put the upstart Irish in their place—*again*. Longman, a thespian thunderer, was undoubtedly inspired by the relentless urge of a pupil to upend a famous master. His theme was psychologically and emotionally sound: Beat Michigan for the first time; avenge the Conference snub of Notre Dame by defeating the school which had snubbed the Conference.

It came to pass. Touchdowns then counted five points. Notre Dame scored twice and added both extra points. Michigan was held to a field goal, and the final score, 12–3, reverberated through the Midwest. Thereafter, in his annual indoctrination of freshmen, Father Matt Walsh, in a soft voice and with a straight face, would tell how Pete Vaughan, the Irish fullback, had hit the Michigan line so hard and so bent over that the mark of the goal post (then on the goal line) he had knocked down (along with numerous Wolverine defenders) plainly showed *on his back*.

The scheduled return match between the Irish and the Wolverines was eagerly awaited. There had been recriminations and ultimatums, but Notre Dame was en route to Ann Arbor when Michigan canceled. The dispute was over player eligibility, a lively subject at that time, with each "alleging" about the other, and each could have honestly thought itself right, because the definitions and practices were not yet clear. In the publicity battle that followed, Notre Dame was outweighed and outpointed, but retired with this stinging jab from the student editor of *The Scholastic:* "Michigan backed squarely away."

The event affected college football history. Notre Dame's relations with Michigan were so scarred that these neighbors became, in a quiet way, the Hatfields and McCoys of the Midwest. People still occasionally want to know why Notre Dame doesn't belong to the Big Ten. The answer had a lot to do with the Irish-Wolverine squabble that spilled over into the Big Ten which, without formal action, decided back in 1910 that life would be simpler without the pushy and contentious Irish. President Cavanaugh was entirely amenable to playing the smaller neighborhood colleges and forgetting the big time; but as an entity Notre Dame was a vital youngster, eager to test the growing power it felt in its young body. There was no formal statement, such as Sorin's "If all were gone I would not give up," but in a gridiron way Notre Dame picked up the wheelbarrows and rebuilt in such a bigger, better way as to have important effects on its future as an educational institution and upon the entire collegiate football scene.

Longman was succeeded by Jack Marks, a Dartmouth man and one of the unsung heroes of the Notre Dame football tradition. He gave it the future trademark of speed and cleverness. He experimented with the forward pass, which had been added to the game in 1906. In his two seasons he won thirteen, tied two and lost none. One of the wins and one of the ties were with Pittsburgh; and let the record show that Pitt gave Notre Dame the opportunity to show it could play the best at a time when it desperately needed such a showcase. Let the record also show that the Irish baseball team had given a valuable assist in establishing the pivotal relationship with West Point.

Jesse Harper, another Stagg quarterback at Chicago, had been recommended to Notre Dame by The Old Master when Marks left. (Coaches at that time were usually post grad students who got needed credits and moved on.) Harper took off his coat and stayed awhile. "I needed some games so I sat down and wrote a few letters." One went to West Point, where the Irish baseball team had dropped in that spring. It arrived at a time when the Army had decided to add schools from all parts of the country to its grid schedule. Harper saw an opportunity, and what he did about it would, despite a brief career, place him among the coaching immortals. His squad, tough and seasoned, was led by a quarterback and end who were going to spend the summer working at Cedar Point, a Lake Erie resort. Harper gave them a football and told them what to do. The quarterback was Charles "Gus" Dorais.

The end was Knute Kenneth Rockne. He had never made the football team at Tuley High in Chicago because he was too small. He never got a high school diploma because he was a member of the track squad which put more emphasis on the sport than on academics and was dropped en masse. He worked five years in the Chicago post office, became an amateur track star, saved one thousand dollars from an average annual salary of around nine hundred dollars, decided to go to college, intended to go to Illinois University, but was detoured to Notre Dame by Johnny Plant and Johnny Devine, track athletes who had preceded him there, because it was "a poor boy's school where he would have a better chance of getting by."

In his own words Rockne came as "A lone Norwegian Protestant on the Irish Catholic campus." He was twenty-two years of age, moody, balding. The job they gave him was cleaning up "the slops" in the chemical lab. He wore a sweater; if he wanted to go to town in cold weather he would have to borrow a coat. The football coach, Longman, was not impressed by this little runt. Rockne was so bashful around girls that he would never get a repeat date. "He was older than the rest of us," Dorais remembered, "and seemed to have that many more problems. His thoughts came so fast he was inclined to stutter." The truth was, nobody but a few close friends knew he was on campus, as a freshman, nor cared whether he stayed. Several times he did pack his suitcase, but he was always caught in time by Plant, Devine, or Fred Steers, another track man. (Steers, a Chicago lawyer and member of the Olympic Committee, was not a Catholic, but remained a most enthusiastic supporter of the University until his death in 1968. Devine became the father of Sam Devine, an Ohio Congressman and Notre Dame alumnus.)

Rockne, a model student, engaged in football, track, and theatricals; he played the flute in the orchestra, was one of the editors of the yearbook, frequently played the part of the local "checkers champion" in "goofing" escapades. In the classroom he was deadly serious, graduated from the stiff science course with a general average of 90.52. The 94 in philosophy might have revealed the future psychologist; and anybody who was ever exposed to Genung's Principles of

Rhetoric will appreciate the 93. Kittie Leeper Devine, who had double-dated with him, never could understand how that bashful, blushing, tongue-tied boy could develop into an orator with "the ease and poise of a great personality."

Rockne was never a disciplinary problem, though he might have been if authorities had known he sometimes went out on a Saturday night to pick up five or ten dollars fighting at local clubs under assumed names. Authority for this was his "second," Joe Gargan, a halfback and campus character in his own right who later became, by marriage, brother-in-law to Joe Kennedy and uncle to his famous sons.

If Longman had remained as coach, Rockne might not even have returned for his sophomore season; but Jack Marks knew what to do with smaller men with fast feet, staunch hearts and quick minds. The bashful, balding boy learned other things than how to catch a football on the sands of Cedar Point that summer. A girl named Bonnie Skiles also worked there. She later said: "These two devils said they were going to beat Army with the forward pass." And beat Army they did in one of the all-time stunners. "We hadn't originated anything," Rockne later wrote, "just systematized a weapon that had been lying around. By completing fourteen of seventeen passes for 220 yards we had demonstrated for the first time in a major game that the forward pass could be used as an integral part of offense."

Rockne lost out on two coaching jobs after graduation. Dorais beat him on the toss of a coin for one; and he was balked from studying medicine at St. Louis University when the admissions' officer decided he couldn't do justice to the medical course while coaching a high school. It was only then that he returned to Notre Dame as assistant to Harper in football, head track coach and instructor in chemistry. With his immediate future secured he got married, began to raise a family of three boys and one girl, and to perfect the ideas and artifices that would thrill a nation.

Harper continued to write letters asking for football games. One resulted in the most horrendous disaster since The Great Fire, a 28–0 loss to Yale in 1914. "All of us but Harper," Rockne wrote, "went to New Haven with nothing between our ears but fat." In 1917 Wisconsin broke the solid Big Ten front by returning to the Notre Dame schedule. Purdue and Indiana followed, and Notre Dame was out of the Big Ten penalty box. Harper had uncovered the rich vein of intersectional football which Rockne would mine.

While still an assistant coach, or so the story goes, Rockne discovered an unknown student in street clothes dropkicking in front of a residence hall. A few weeks later the student had put a 62-yard dropkick into the collegiate record book. That is the story, and the kick is a matter of record; but George Gipp was not exactly an unknown. He had come to school on a baseball scholarship on recommendation of "Dolly" Gray, a former Irish player who had made the big leagues. Notre Dame's brightest athletic star was another dividend of the Sorin ecumenical movement, the son of Rev. Matthew Gipp, a Congregationalist minister.

23. WOODCUT COLLEGE

THE catalogue in the Cavanaugh era was illustrated by woodcuts of a rustic scene with an aura of leafy charm. Father Crumley once observed "the entrance has a shoe factory to the right and a pigsty to the left." The "shoe factory" was Chemistry Hall, where Nieuwland brewed his potions. Admittedly it was a box-like structure built for use rather than beauty. The "pigsty" was the boundary of the University farm (now occupied by the posh Morris Inn) where Brother Leo, the farm director, kept his prized porkers. Rome Dugan, a prep-school character, once tried out a new rifle on Brother Leo's prize pigs. It cost him twenty dollars. He presented thirty dollars, said the extra ten was for Brother Leo whom he would shoot the next time. Paul Kennedy, track captain, worked off part of his expenses as Padrone of the Prize Pigs. He said Brother Leo took much better care of his pigs than Rockne did of his prized athletes.

Regardless of opinions to the contrary, athletes are students, and they have more fun. Dan Young, a lineman of the Gipp era, recently laughed over a Nebraska game: "We laid on the sidelines in straw. There were no benches for the visiting team, just taunts from the crowd about Fish Eaters. Rock got us out of the hotel lobby because the gamblers were operating there. He wasn't afraid of our morals, but that we might become overconfident, since they were making us favorites. Gipp told a prefect that, if cleanliness were next to holiness, as the Bible said, he must be the holiest guy on campus because he lived next to the shower room."

(Dan Young is typical of the athlete who doesn't get his name in the record book. In the fifty years since he was a "dumb guard," Dan Young had circled the globe on engineering projects. His stationery reads "Foley Brothers, Thailand." His credits as general manager include the San Gabriel and Shasta dams; a tunnel under the Hudson River; the George Washington Bridge; air bases in the Caribbean and ports on the Persian Gulf during World War II; a railroad through Brazilian jungles; piers in Chile and Peru; a $120 million copper plant in the Andes. After completing the world's largest iron ore benefaction plant in northern Minnesota, Dan offered a Mass of Thanksgiving for three years on the $300 million project without a fatal accident.)

On a pleasant evening President Cavanaugh would stroll the campus, drop in at a hall for a bull session. At Sorin, Father Gene Burke would play the piano and sing his versions of folk songs, which revealed that hall prefects were not as easily fooled as they sometimes seemed to be. Ice cream or hot dogs would materialize. Protocol was out the window. Students could talk as equals. But no cigarettes. (Cavanaugh was as passionately opposed to tobacco as Tom Walsh had been to alcohol.) When he left, it was usually with an idea of what the boys were thinking at that moment.

But not always. On a February evening the President, returning from town, came upon a disturbance near the entrance to Cedar Grove Cemetery which edges the campus. The carriage was stopped by a gang of students. One explained that two students had been beaten up by company thugs on the Hill Street trolley. The reinforcements had come looking for the bruisers. The President sympathized, said he would look into it, ordered the boys back to their halls. They obeyed meekly. At the Main Building, Father Cavanaugh talked it over with his Vice-President, Father Matt Walsh. Everybody who ever visited Notre Dame knew about the trolley and its deficiencies, its erratic schedule and its sometimes irascible motormen. Boys were not always gentlemen, the employees were not always diplomats. But violence was not the answer. In the morning he would . . .

Father Walsh was not listening. There was a glow in the sky. *Fire.* The lurking enemy of Notre Dame! The two priests hurried to the scene, found the trolley burned to the tracks. The ringleaders were punished, but when the company demanded damages, Cavanaugh read them a lecture about equipment, diplomacy, and the introduction of physical force. He was also never again quite so sure of student reaction, or so trusting of a meek demeanor in a mob.

Student government was informal, but effective. For the extreme case there was always the lake, for the naïve there was the psychological hazing known as *goofing*. If anybody were so unwise as to admit he was good at anything, everybody agreed with him. He was lauded, laureled, promoted, fawned upon, led down the garden path through a series of exhibitions of his specialty or contests (which he always won), with the campus "champion." It went on until somebody (seldom the goof) cried "enough." Freshmen learned to be modest; seniors were reminded they had better be. Boys learned to live together in close quarters.

Occasionally, the death of an old-timer recalled the early Notre Dame in which he had had a part. Timothy Howard, for instance, had graduated "way back in '62," joined the Union forces, was wounded at Shiloh that same year, lay close to death for awhile, but returned to Notre Dame to teach the classics, study law, teach law, become a State Senator, and Chief Justice of the Supreme Court of Indiana. He wrote the history of the first fifty years. Notre Dame gave him an honorary doctorate, awarded him one of the early Laetare Medals.

In the midst of all this lived the uncomplicated people who furnished much of the *work* and *pray* in the Notre Dame formula of work-pray-think-laugh-fight. For forty-three years Sister Al (Aloysius) was mother, tyrant, and final board of appeals to Sorin's Little Princes. Brother Paul, the Hermit, was also known as The Hornet. Generations of older students remember Sister Cecilia, empress of the Infirmary, whose first treatment for every disease, from broken leg to sunburn, was a stiff dose of calomel. She entertained few gold-brickers. Brother Bonaventure was a small sprite with a nimble gait. He would approach each new student who looked as if he might be an athlete, get his vital statistics, and then compare these with the great exemplars of the past. He was a walking encyclopedia of weights and records, never missed a contest of any sort in any sport, remembered every detail. He was lowly of heart, sweet of disposition, innocently playful, with a wonder-working smile. If one of his favorites passed, he would nod and say: "His father must have been a daycent man." In March, 1916, the athletes bore the body of Brother "Bonny" to his little cross.

Brother Cajetan, marshal of the minims, carried a sawed-off broom handle which he called his "wand," and when one of his charges got out of line on a walk, he would be reminded by a gentle tap. He was a man of such great prayer that Cavanaugh was surprised to receive a complaint from a parent that the Brother's cursing shocked his little son. The minim confirmed that Brother Cajetan did swear a lot after he went to bed at night. A sentinel was posted, and sure enough, he did hear sighs and groans from Caj's chamber, and loud exclamations: "Lord! God! Lord, God! Be merciful, to me, a sinner. Oh God Almighty! Have pity on me, a sinner." Cavanaugh replied to the parent: "If Brother Cajetan's prayers are not heard in heaven, they certainly have been heard on earth."

In 1852 Brother Basil (John Magus) came from Germany, performed the most menial tasks, until by accident, somebody heard him at the organ "charming forth such exquisite improvisations as the angels may have leaned down from heaven to hear." Also an artist on the piano and violin, he taught music for fifty years, was too humble to be a great teacher, but so talented that he inspired. He would cease to play if people watched. The night before he died, frail, and with long gray hair falling to his shoulders, he was at the console, playing for Benediction. The President once spoke to him about his hair, and grooming. He listened, said, "Father, it takes all kinds." And made no changes. The title for a book of poems by Father Charles O'Donnell, *The Dead Musician,* was taken from the first poem, a tribute to Brother Basil:

> "Widowed of him his organ now is still,
> His music-children fled, their echoing feet yet fill
> The blue, far reaches of the vaulted nave.
> The heart that sired them, pulseless in the grave.
>
> Only the song he made is hushed, his soul
> Responsive to God's touch, in His control
> Elsewhere shall tune the termless ecstasy
>   Of one who all his life kept here
>   An alien ear,
> Homesick for harpings of eternity."

The Brothers were men of faith and good works and humility. Brother Florian was the exception, "a lovable old rascal whose pompous bearing was an imitation of Cavanaugh's gracious gait; and it would come off quite well except when his feet hurt." His job was porter of the Main Building, but he played it as an ambassador. When he conducted tours of the painting collection, his voice boomed with authority; and if he exaggerated the worth it was only because "these people must realize they are seeing something of immense value." He liked to create the impression that he was so overworked he was bereft of appetite and could only nibble at his food; student detectives discovered that he always ate with the workmen ahead of the regular dinnertime. He was a collector of discarded items, which he would dispose of at a profit. He was in a position to do small favors, but let it be known that gratuities were in order. A visitor was so obviously a bishop that "Flo" made an elaborate genuflection, kissed his ring and asked His Excellency to follow him to the Bishop's suite. The Bishop introduced his son, explaining he was an Episcopalian bishop who had merely come to look at the paintings. "Flo" was a natural-born con man and hustler, who had found a happy outlet in an unusual niche.

Brother Alphonse, rector of Brownson, was a grave, imperturbable, impartial dispenser of justice. He gave his verdict; what the superior did thereafter was the superior's problem. His great reward was to have a boy ask for a volume from his private collection of spiritual books. He trudged the fields with his glasses, was so expert a bird-watcher that he contributed regularly to Nieuwland's *Midland Naturalist*. The students dedicated the 1918 *Dome*, the yearbook, to him.

24. "OVER THERE"

NOTRE DAME had been founded in troubled times that led to the war with Mexico. The Civil War marked her twenty-fifth anniversary. The war with Spain came about the time of her fiftieth birthday. The nation was again at war in 1917 when the Diamond Jubilee was observed with ceremonies appropriate to both occasions.

On Friday, June 8th, James Cardinal Gibbons arrived for the first time since Sorin's jubilee. Now he was twenty-nine years older, and he rode in a motor car instead of a carriage in the parade from the railroad station to the campus. That night Father Walter Elliott, C.S.P., the great Paulist preacher who had been a student during the Civil War, told the assembled alumni and guests how things had been in Sorin's time.

Saturday morning there was another parade from the station and through the town. This time the honored guests were the Apostolic Delegate, the Most Reverend John Bonanzo; and Admiral William Shepherd Benson, Chief of Naval Operations, who received the Laetare Medal from Cardinal Gibbons; and there were telegrams of congratulation from President Woodrow Wilson and Secretary of the Navy Josephus Daniels.

Sunday morning the Cardinal pontificated. The procession from the Main Building to the church included the graduating class (many in uniform), the faculty, and the large group of visiting priests and prelates; and finally His Eminence, in brilliant scarlet, under a canopy of gold and white. The Archbishop of Chicago and later cardinal, George Mundelein, read a letter of congratulation and benediction from His Holiness, Pope Benedict XV. Eight seniors, bearing an American flag, entered the sanctuary for the blessing of the flag by the University President. Later the flag was raised; and because of the war, this annual event was given a touch of grandeur.

Eighteen priests had applied to the Provincial to serve as chaplains. The eight chosen were: Father Charles O'Donnell, the poet; Father (later Bishop) George Finnegan of the Mission Band; Father Edward Finnegan, who had been Prefect of Discipline; Father John McGinn, professor of sociology; Father Ernest Davis, a gifted professor of chemistry; and two younger priests, Father James O'Brien and Father Frederick McKeon. Of these, Father Walsh saw the most service, and Father Davis was badly gassed.

The enrollment, which had dropped at the beginning of the war, improved when the government installed, in 1918, the Students Army Training Corps (SATC), an innovation which permitted students to continue studies while being militarily trained. The War Department agreed to pay the tuition, then $120 a year, plus $30 a month for subsistence. As the campus became an armed camp, ordinary college routines were subordinated, and all was not salubrious for the academically oriented, but Father Cavanaugh found a compensating pleasure. He wrote to a former student:

> I have read of the miracles in Lourdes but have seen greater wonders at Notre Dame. Charley McC. hasn't missed

a single morning since the time he reported at 5:31 a.m. instead of 5:30. He was "bawled out" with eloquent fluency and spent the rest of the day washing the toilets of Barracks No. 1, formerly Corby Hall. Charley hasn't missed the 5:30 since. . . . I have a great idea. I should like to organize mental and moral boobs of the past and march them all over the place.

[Later]. . . . We have gone through serious experiences since my last letter to you. The influenza was almost the death of all human joy. We had more than two hundred cases of the disease and there were nine deaths among the students. [The Spanish Influenza ravaged the country in 1918.]

In January, 1919, Father Cavanaugh wrote to John Talbot Smith:

The soldiers are gone, with only slight damage to Brother Philip's campus. Mentally, morally, and socially, the University was never so well-conditioned before. The old spirit has come back with a rush and Notre Dame is perfectly herself again. It is the sweetest miracle of my life.

Over twenty-two hundred Notre Dame men had been in the fighting ranks. Forty-six had died in the line of duty.

In April, 1919, Father Cavanaugh celebrated the twenty-fifth anniversary of his ordination very simply. He thanked the students for not going to the lengths of a great oration he had once heard: "It reminded me of the wisdom and mercy of God, the wisdom which is unfathomable, and the mercy which endureth forever."

After the Provincial Chapter meeting in the summer of 1919 Cavanaugh wrote to a friend:

In accordance with the provisions of the new Canon Law, I have been replaced by Father Burns. He is profoundly skilled in educational problems and school life. I expect to be very happy next year. I am to reside at our house of studies in Washington, not as Superior but as a member of the community. I will be permitted to arrange my own work in my own way. This will give me a chance to do some writing.

After being President for fourteen of the most formative years, John William Cavanaugh was retired at forty-nine, in full vigor. In Washington he briefly resumed his ambassadorial duties, was rated one of the best orators of the capital. He returned to Notre Dame to teach, also intending to do "The Story of the Little Crosses" in the community cemetery. Father Zahm discouraged the idea: "Why don't you do something more serious?" The story remains to be written. His lecture class—*Shakespeare, Dante,* and the *Bible*—was a positive joy; and not just because, since it was held at eight in the morning, he did not call the roll until the end of the hour.

One of his last presidential appointments was not his least important. When Harper decided to give up football and return to his Kansas ranch, Rockne was the logical successor. Cavanaugh thought he was too young; but Harper, Fred Steers, and others persisted.

PART III

THE MODERN
NOTRE DAME

25. APPRENTICE TO PRESIDENT

JAMES ALOYSIUS BURNS was born in Michigan City, Indiana, February 13, 1867. At age fifteen he entered the Manual Labor School at nearby Notre Dame and took advantage of Lemonnier's decision to give the more promising apprentices opportunity to advance. He took full advantage of all college life, including athletics where, typically, he drew the hardest task, that of baseball catcher and had the honorable marks of the receiver to prove it—bunged-up thumbs and disjointed fingers. He graduated at twenty-one, followed the teach some—study some program for future priests, before and after his ordination in 1893. Always he had his eye on the next rung of the ladder. Here are entries in his diary:

> June 30, 1895. . . . I asked Father Morrissey last night about going to the Cornell summer school. He would not grant permission. . . . I asked him bluntly if he did not admit that the more a man knows about the subject, the better he is prepared to teach it, even in its elements. He didn't believe it. . . . How long, O Lord, how long?
>
> July 5, 1895. . . . I got permission, after all, to attend the summer school so here we are, Father Ill and myself, at Cornell.

February 18, 1896. . . . Father Morrissey is sincerely anxious for Notre Dame's advancement but it is his and our misfortune that he is not himself a "University" man. He is broad-minded, liberal, energetic, talented, with winning personal qualities. But he lacks the substance as well as the polish of higher education, and is himself, I think, sensible of his own limitations. He does not seem to believe in higher education-university education for college teachers.

1898. . . . Father Zahm Provincial! I first learned the news on the evening of the 2nd when Father Cavanaugh came over and read me the General's Circular Letter (which he had been commissioned to translate).

In 1900 Father Burns was appointed Superior of Holy Cross College in Washington. He remained for nineteen years, supervising the training of young priests who would become teachers. During this period of anonymity he earned a doctorate at Catholic U., wrote three books on Catholic education, and helped found the Catholic Educational Association. The new Canon Law, which brought to an end the practice of keeping superiors in office for long periods, supplanted him at the same time it ended Cavanaugh's presidency at Notre Dame. Burns hoped to be assigned to the new seminary in the Diocese of Dacca, India. Instead he was elected President of Notre Dame by the Provincial Council in July, 1919. His first goal was to tighten up the internal structure in the various colleges, but his immediate problem became how to handle the college population explosion that followed World War I. In addition to the returning students whose education had been interrupted, and the normal freshmen from high school, there were the unexpected number of veterans who had no urge to go back to the farms and the mills after they had seen Paree.

The academic problem was solved by enlarging classes. Rooms in South Bend homes took care of the overflow, but also created a disciplinary problem; it was obviously impossible to stricture drinking and enforce study hours off-campus, especially among those accustomed to the social freedoms of military service. With every indication that such conditions would exist for future years, it would be necessary to look for more lay teachers, to find the money with which to pay them, and to increase the salaries of lay teachers already at hand, to forestall raids from other colleges with similar problems.

The long-term solution for housing was new residence halls; but Burns, so much like Zahm on education, was, perhaps because of his poor-boy background, more kin to Morrissey on money matters. And there was a more immediate remedy: bring the "Day-Dodgers" back from town, make Notre Dame a university in fact by *getting rid of the prep school and the prep-school image.* The older priests were horrified; even Zahm protested: "throwing away a ready-made prep school is folly." But it was done; after which Burns, capitalizing on his contacts and prestige among educators, gave a new direction to the old custom of begging by going to the financial Foundations with the pitch Cavanaugh had already initiated:

Notre Dame was now a national asset. It had grown because of its Living Endowment, the free services of dedicated religious, translated into financial terms at around $150,000 each year. Its endowment was a mere $100,000, and part of this was restricted to scholarships. It asked for money which would be used for faculty improvement and buildings.

He came back, not with a few thousands, but with this offer: The Rockefeller Foundation would provide $250,000 and the Carnegie Foundation $75,000 *if* the alumni and other friends of the University would prove their faith by raising $750,000. The project was received so enthusiastically that Father Burns decided to raise two million dollars instead of one, with the first million going to faculty improvement and the second to new buildings. The first drive was inaugurated in 1920, at a great meeting in Washington Hall. The spirit, alas, was willing, but the pocketbook proved weak. It was only by strong efforts of the Chicago alumni that the original goal of one million dollars was reached.

Father Burns had spent one summer school at Harvard, and admired the manner in which the University invested its extensive endowment. With his million in sight, he proposed that Notre Dame should have a Board of Lay Trustees which would administer all permanent funds. The first meeting was held in January, 1921, with Hon. William P. Breen of the class of '77 as chairman. In 1922 the presidential term of Father Burns came to an end; by the provisions of the new Canon Law he could have served another three years, but he chose to give all his efforts to the new task of fundraising. In 1926 he became Provincial, and in 1938 was elected First-Assistant-Superior-General. During the next two years he was frequently sick. He died September 9, 1940. Like so many of the Presidents, the last days of this good and faithful man were spent in agony. He was 73.

"In all the history of Notre Dame," Father Hope wrote, "there was hardly a priest who carried himself with comparable dignity, restraint and modesty. He had a heart as warm as Cavanaugh's, but only those in deep trouble ever suspected his profound and sympathetic understanding." In 1920 these qualities influenced a decision which would affect football history and live unseen in an enduring legend of the gridiron that surfaced briefly in, of all places, the American political campaign of 1968.

Rockne's first full squad (following the abbreviated wartime card of 1918) was one of his greatest and included names still familiar: Eddie Anderson and Roger Kiley at ends, Buck Shaw at tackle, Morris "Clipper" Smith and

Heartley "Hunk" Anderson at guards, Slip Madigan, Harry Mehre, and George Trafton at center, Walter Miller and Chet Wynne at fullback, Arthur "Little Dutch" Bergman, Norm Barry and Johnny Mohardt at halfback, "Pete" Bahan and Joe Brandy at quarterback. Gipp had been the outstanding star of that undefeated group in 1919; since most were returning even greater things were expected in 1920—until Gipp was dropped for nonpayment of his scholastic dues. He could have gone to many other schools with no questions asked; but now that he had lost it, he wanted Notre Dame.

So, on a September afternoon in 1920, a grim Rockne and a repentant Gipp came to the President's office on the second floor of the Main Building and were moved in ahead of the sophomore who was next in line. It was all right with the sophomore, who also wanted Gipp back in school, as did everybody, not merely because he was a potential All-American, but because he was a likable, modest guy, his own enemy, but nobody else's. This was the approach Rockne used: George had made the mistake of thinking he could cut classes and get away with it. He now knew better; all he asked was a chance to prove that he could pass his work, right now, *orally,* without any opportunity to cram.

George got his chance, passed the exam, was reinstated as a law student and football player. There was still punishment— he could not be captain. So he accepted that demotion, led his teammates to another undefeated season; became player of the year after a sensational game against Army. He contracted tonsillitis, which developed into pneumonia and a strep throat. Penicillin would have saved him, but there were no miracle drugs. The nation watched the daily bulletins from the bedside of the football player-of-the-year, who had also been signed to a baseball contract by the Chicago White Sox. George became a Catholic the day before he died. He weighed eighty pounds. There was a campus heartbreak as the student body marched in his funeral, the football team in formation with the left-half vacant. The snows of Christmas powdered the grave of Thanksgiving's Hero.

None of this would have happened if Father Burns hadn't made it possible. Was he just another college President bending another ethic to keep a football star eligible? The sophomore who also waited that afternoon was no football star, but another poor boy who wanted to stay in school. Father Burns practically carved out a job, put him into the newspaper business. Three months later his first page-one story would be George Gipp's funeral. Eight years later he would complete the circle of that afternoon by writing the newspaper story that would launch the "Win-for-the-Gipper" legend.

26. THE QUIET MAN

FATHER MATTHEW WALSH was a tall, slender, soft-spoken, soft-appearing academician to whom things that were not supposed to happen often did, like being a war-time chaplain, building buildings, calming a prison riot, disciplining a temperamental artist like Rockne, presiding over an expanding university, supervising an amazing athletic success story. He asked little, made no commotion, was a happy, contented man who could handle just about any situation that came up anywhere, but didn't especially want to.

He was a native of Chicago, of the usual Irish parents, and by propinquity seemed destined to become a great man of Notre Dame. At age eleven, in a Holy Cross Brothers school, he was called out of line to meet Father Thomas Walsh, the seventh President, who was on his way to Wisconsin where he would die within one month. Young Matt went to Notre Dame at age fifteen, was welcomed by President Andrew Morrissey, directed to Provincial William Corby, delivered to future President John Cavanaugh at the seminary. He was one of the first to benefit from the educational program sponsored by Father John Zahm, and in Washington was trained by Father James Burns.

In 1907 he received his doctorate in history at Catholic U., went to summer school at Columbia, enrolled in economics at Johns Hopkins, was ordained at Baltimore, taught history and economics at Notre Dame, became Vice-President at twenty-nine, and at thirty-five was a chaplain.

Walsh got to France in time for the heavy fighting around the Marne. Many intelligence officers had been killed and there was the problem of finding college graduates among the enlisted men for replacements. Walsh recommended a Notre Dame man; and when the latter pointed out that he had enlisted before actually receiving his degree, Walsh said: "As Vice-President of the University of Notre Dame, and in the absence of the President and other members of the faculty, I confer on you the degree of Bachelor of Laws." So Dan McGlynn received a battlefield degree as well as a battlefield commission.

Transferred to Paris to administer to the Americans in hospitals there, Father Walsh became aware that there were fourteen hundred American prisoners in the Bastille, and that no priest had visited them in months. He arrived in the middle of an attempted prison break. The marine officer in charge called to the milling men in the yard: "Here is a

Catholic priest from Notre Dame University. All you fellows who are Catholics, right face." About one-third of the group went to confession with the threat of physical, as well as moral penance, over their heads. The guards, holding guns, took no chances, and the riot subsided.

When he became President in 1922 Walsh moved with battlefield dispatch. On the theory that new dormitories would pay for themselves, he built temporary, barracks-like Freshman and Sophomore Halls; the permanent complex of Howard, Morrissey, and Lyons Halls; and the new dining hall and cafeteria. With the downtown student brigade brought back to the campus compound and the enrollment frozen (so it was thought) at twenty-five hundred, classrooms were added to existing buildings, and all sorts of mechanical problems regarding light, heat, water, and plumbing were met and solved. The faculty was increased to one hundred seventy-five, and for the first time lay teachers outnumbered religious. The academic processes were tightened under the supervision of Father Charles Miltner, Dean of Arts & Letters, and one of the superior men produced by Notre Dame. Other campus figures were emerging.

Father Francis Wenninger, Dean of the College of Science, formed the Notre Dame Academy of Science, an honor society limited to upper-classmen with an average of 85 percent or better. Notre Dame had been the first Catholic college in the country to have a school of engineering, and for more than forty years "Marty" McCue was its first citizen, as student and as a teacher of the old school whose dignity commanded respect. Father John O'Hara would later say of him: "His cultivation of the life of his soul was as intense as his pursuit of mathematics. He loved to serve Mass but sought out a dark corner of the chapel to exercise this act of devotion." Father Alexander Kirsch, a native of Luxembourg, with two years at Louvain, was a scientist of such whimsy and concentration that he would shuffle through the corridors croaking like a frog and imitating the noises of other animals he discussed in anatomy or zoology. He was a big man with a booming voice, and would disconcert strangers in lonely corridors.

Father Timothy Maher came to Notre Dame two years after its founding, and remained until his death in 1925, at the age of ninety-one. He was Secretary of the University under Sorin, later became postmaster, and, by election of his colleagues, "President of the Young Men's Club." Father Daniel Spillard, another "lifer," is generally thought to have held more jobs in more places in the Congregation than any other individual.

Brother Columba, a shoemaker by trade, seems to have been the only man in University history associated with miraculous powers. His intercession was sought, his reputation was widespread, he went where the sick called, and in many instances he "is said to have worked cures." After his death in 1923, pilgrimages were made to his grave, and people took handfuls of the soft loam from his resting place. He was Sorin's nurse in the latter's last illness, but rebuffed eager young religious people who adulated the memory of the Founder. "Pshaw. He was no saint."

In the twenties religious intolerance reached one of its peaks under the robes of the Ku Klux Klan. Al Smith was the major national casualty; and in the Indiana hotbed Notre Dame was a shining target. The South Bend Chamber of Commerce sponsored a meeting, ostensibly to clear the air, which developed into a confrontation between Protestant ministers and Fathers Walsh and Cavanaugh. The meeting was adjourned without a meeting of minds. The Klan proposed to parade in South Bend. Permission was denied, but members advanced upon the town from all directions. There were skirmishes with Notre Dame students, and Father Walsh, the chaplain who had calmed the prison riot, had to mount a cannon before the courthouse and call upon his own students to return to the campus. Again, the glue of respect held.

Eventually the fires burned themselves out, but for quite a few years Sorin's precious ecumenism was strained. There has never been a serious Town-and-Gown dispute, nor even a threat after Knute Rockne came along to bring prestige and considerable economic benefit to the South Bend dateline.

27. A HAND OF POKER

IN Chaplains' School the Major had asked: "You come upon a group of soldiers playing cards, gambling for money. How would you handle the situation?" Father Walsh had answered: "I think I'd take a hand." He probably would have done well. Certainly he did so in a quiet game with a good friend for high stakes.

Knute Kenneth Rockne is a prime example of the legend that Notre Dame always produces its man for the occasion, on or off the field. He arrived as the "tight little boarding school" was ready to flex its muscles and expand. His success was the wedding of his own plethora of talents and the fertility of the campus. He provided the favorable publicity that attracted students and the money to pay for their housing and instruction. Burns, supported by Walsh and Father John McGinn, had struggled to raise $750,000 as the college's share in the first endowment drive. Rockne's football endowment would produce as much as half a million dollars a year, tax free and immediately available for buildings and salaries, because there would be more where that came from—as long as Rockne kept swinging his magic sword. Football profits, still large, are no longer of vital importance; but for many years they were, and Notre Dame has always acknowledged this debt to Rockne and to football.

In 1919 the bleachers at Cartier Field seated 2,500, and the season's attendance (the Army game was still played at West Point) was 56,500. In 1924 the wooden stands had been augmented to 22,000, the season's attendance was 318,000, over 50,000 saw the Army game at the Polo Grounds and the Stanford battle in the Rose Bowl, the only bowl game Notre Dame has ever played. In his first six years Rockne won 55, lost 3 (to Iowa in 1921, and Nebraska in 1922 and 1923) by a total of 18 points, and tied 1 (Army in 1922). A Notre Dame appearance became a style show, with the smooth precision of a well-rehearsed motion picture from which the brutality had been erased. Charlie Caldwell described it: "The 1924 Princeton team was better than average; yet I felt as if we were being toyed with. I had been sold—hook, line, and sinker—on Rockne football. I wanted to learn everything I could about coaching a sport in which there were apparently a hundred and one opportunities to advance new thoughts, to develop partially explored theories and to blend the traditional with the unorthodox."

The Rockne teams usually gave away weight, but never speed, imagination, intelligence, or sophistication. His graduates were in demand, and they spread the Notre Dame gospel in all parts of the country. Some became household names on their own. Frank Thomas at Alabama, Eddie Anderson at Iowa and Holy Cross, Slip Madigan at St. Mary's, Hunk Anderson at Notre Dame and North Carolina State, Buck Shaw at Santa Clara and in the Pros, Noble Kizer at Purdue, Rip Miller at Navy, Rex Enright at South Carolina, Elmer Layden at Notre Dame, Harry Stuhldreher at Wisconsin, Jimmy Crowley at Fordham, Adam Walsh at Bowdoin and in the Pros.

The Rockne men were bright because he would have no other type around him. They used their wits, as well as their brawn and minds, in whatever they did. (When Crowley and Layden were commissioners of the rival National Pro League and All-American Conference, Layden playfully asked if the AAC owned a football. Crowley showed up at their next confrontation with a football under each arm.) Roger Kiley, Norman Barry, and Don Miller became judges; Eddie Anderson, Johnny Mohardt, John Weible, and Harvey Brown, doctors; Joe Brandy and Danny Coughlin, newspaper publishers; Vince Harrington, an Iowa Congressman; Joe Boland was the first of the player-coaches to hit the national network as commentator. Bernie Coughlin became a priest. There were lawyers and businessmen galore.

Gipp lent his name to a legend. Harrington was killed in World War II after he left Congress to become an Air Force major. Max Hauser transferred from Lafayette, was billed "another Gipp," never made it, and became the subject of Rockne's famous gag: "Max, I'm saving you for the Junior Prom," and died an unsung hero trying to save a girl from drowning.

They come back for reunions. They talk of the old days, tell the old tales; and a favorite is the one about Dave Hayes, a second-string end who made up in heart and character what he lacked in weight. After he graduated in 1922 he called on Father Burns, contributed all of his earthly wealth, two hundred fifty dollars, to the endowment drive, said: "I came here on a freight train; that's the way I'll go home." Dave's son also came to Notre Dame, and is a sculptor.

College groups fortunate enough to play two or three years together have an advantage. The 1924 squad was in its third season when Grantland Rice sat down to compose his "lead" after the Army game:

> Outlined against a blue-gray October sky, the Four Horsemen rode again. In dramatic lore they are known as Famine, Pestilence, Destruction, and Death. These are only aliases. Their real names are Stuhldreher, Miller, Crowley, and Layden. They formed the crest of the South Bend cyclone before which another fighting Army football team was swept over the precipice at the Polo Grounds yesterday afternoon as 55,000 spectators peered down on the bewildering panorama spread on the green plain below.

Rice's lead might have been just another bit of pretty prose had not George Strickler, the student publicity director, arranged to have the team met by four livery stable horses when it arrived in South Bend. The Rockne teams of '25, '26, '27 did not have the advantage of either poetry or continuity; the personnel are mostly Forgotten Men, and their records of 7–2–1, 9–1, 7–1–1, were considered "ordinary" for Rockne. Actually, nothing about Rockne nor his squads was, or could ever be, ordinary. Always there was drama, excitement, surprise, sometimes more intriguing off the field than on. The attendance kept going up, and the newspapers gobbled the "copy" that was always coming out of the school with the French name, Irish nickname, and melting-pot personnel.

Even a defeat was news. In 1925, after the Four-Horsemen and Seven-Mule squad had departed en masse, the moment of truth came: Army 27, Notre Dame 0. And the three thousand students arose at five, trudged downtown through heavy snow to welcome the losers. . . . At half-time that year, it was Northwestern 10, Notre Dame 0. Rockne did not appear in the locker room until the signal had come to take the field again. He said: "Fighting Irish! You can tell your grand-children you played on the first Notre Dame team that 'ever quit.' " The final score: Notre Dame 13, Northwestern 10. Rex Enright, who tore up and down the field during the second half, wrote: "You will recall that was the morning Rockne had accepted the Catholic faith and made his first Communion." Rex, who was not a Catholic, had, with the rest of the squad, been too tensely trying to give the coach a commemorative victory. Rockne had loosened them up by shaking them up. (He credited his conversion to the example of his players and to his immediate family; had delayed be-coming a Catholic until after the death of his mother, a devout Lutheran. There had been a generally accepted story that Rockne had been a Mason. A check with the fraternity proved it untrue.)

Rockne, a jumping jack of excitement, broke out crying during a locker-room talk in 1925, was so close to a break-down that Joe Byrne engineered him into a European vaca-tion. He came back so refreshed, that in 1926 another un-defeated and national championship seemed in prospect— until Carnegie Tech pulled one of the stupendous upsets of all time with a 19–0 victory while *Rockne was in Chicago at an Army-Navy game*.

Rivaling his coaching record was his success as Director of Athletics. He had built the gold-bond schedule by box-office attraction, but also because of personal magnetism. He was in Chicago at the Army-Navy game because the Big Ten schedule meetings were being held there over that weekend; and Carnegie seemed no threat. Other schools were continually making him offers. One was Southern California. Rockne recommended his friend, Howard Jones, and then scheduled Southern California as the Pacific Coast opponent. There are scraps of paper in the archives of a dozen universities which purport to be "agreements" signed by Rockne to coach their teams. He was often tempted, but never wholly serious; and he always protected himself with a verbal reservation: "If Notre Dame will amicably agree." It was part of the poker game he was playing with President Walsh.

Rockne wanted a home stadium. So did Notre Dame; but first things first; it would build the stadium after the academic problems of faculty and building had been met. And *if* Rockne were still around to fill it, instead of at one of those other schools with whom he constantly flirted. The situation climaxed after the 1927 season when Columbia University announced that Rockne had signed to coach football and teach chemistry for a then-stupendous salary of $25,000. Rockne fell back on his verbal agreement, and Columbia withdrew; after which Father Walsh dropped his bomb: "If Mr. Rockne wishes to better himself, Notre Dame will not stand in his way."

Rockne threw in the winning hand, issued a statement that in effect told people looking for coaches to look elsewhere. With that settled, the first moves were made toward erecting the stadium. Nobody knew that Rockne had only three years to live.

But what years.

In accord with Canon Law, Father Matt Walsh retired from the Presidency in 1928 at age forty-six. He remained on campus as advisor, history teacher, a Father Chips who told droll tales, became more slender, more frail, with a softer voice and gentler smile, giving the impression of a man who had never asked for any of it, but had enjoyed every minute of it.

28. POETIC PRACTICALITY

IT is probable that almost every Catholic boy has at times in his grade-school youth thought of becoming a priest and decided against it because he did not think he would be man enough to pay the price. He thinks of the priest as a better-than-average man, worthy to stand somewhere above in his prayerful mediation with God. This explains "the glue," the respect Notre Dame men of all ages and eras have had for their priests. They know that in the years before his ordination the priest has been given every test and every chance to honorably withdraw. They know that no priestly life is harder than that of the teaching priest. The small-town pastor with the poorest congregation usually has his car, his television set, ordinary creature comforts, and reasonable freedom of action. The most brilliant teacher on the Notre Dame campus gets his keep and can reach into the faculty box for cigars; but he must ask for permission and money to travel, and cannot be sure of getting either.

(An old student favorite, living out his years, recalled plans he once had for spending a two-dollar offering for a Mass, and the disappointment when he was required to turn the money over to his superior, who needed it to satisfy a creditor; a poignant but not unusual incident in the early days or an institution whose working capital was once down to fifty cents; which, another time, had to sell two horses for food money.)

Why a boy, or a man, decides to devote his life to the service of God and his fellowman is a precious story each such individual might tell. This is *how* it was done by Charles O'Donnell, born at Greenfield, Indiana, November 15, 1884, the youngest of six, to Mary Gallagher and Neil O'Donnell.

Charles loved fun and roughhousing as well as the next, but it was obvious he was not an ordinary lad in the parish grade school at Kokomo. When he began to show an inclination toward the priesthood, his pastor suggested he write the head of the seminary at Notre Dame. He received a reply from Father John Cavanaugh:

> I am happy to tell you you may report to the seminary for study on September 5. From the cheerful tone of your letter and Father Lordeman's letter regarding you, I judge you will not only be happy yourself but will contribute materially to the happiness of others.

One of the satisfactions of a teacher is to spot the seed of talent, to nurture it and watch it grow. It is easy (for one who was later encouraged by both) to imagine Father Cavanaugh noting that Charles O'Donnell had the mark of a writer as well as a priest, perhaps of a future leader. Charles O'Donnell worked hard to find the exact word, which is the mark of a poet. He was an editor of *The Scholastic* and in his senior year (1906), editor of the first *Dome*, the University yearbook. (It made a profit of $1,500 which was turned over to President Cavanaugh for the building fund—and that was a significant arrow to the future, too.)

Graduation was a great triumph for his parents: their youngest wrote and read the class poem; he received the gold medal for the best English essay; but they could not take the medals home to show the neighbors because Charley had donated them to the Novitiate which was collecting gold for a new chalice. The young man went to Washington where he took his theology at Holy Cross, studied for his doctorate at Catholic U., and engaged in a research project. In Father Tom Crumley's poetry class he had been entranced by the work and personality of Francis Thompson. Now he wrote to people in England, especially the Meynells, for every scrap of detail about the tortured poet who had fled The Hound of Heaven down the corridors of time.

O'Donnell's doctoral thesis at Catholic U. was "A Study of the Prose Works of Francis Thompson." He took a "stiff course in Anglo-Saxon" at Harvard, and returned to Notre Dame and ordination in 1910 as the first of Zahm's new breed of educated priests come to full flower. For two years he taught English and lived among the hurly-burly as a hall prefect, before Father Cavanaugh switched his protégé to the quiet of the presbytery and the post he himself had occupied as assistant to Father Daniel Hudson on *The Ave Maria*. After seven years of this esthetic discipline, Father O'Donnell volunteered for chaplain duty, saw some action in France, was the first American Catholic chaplain to enter Italy. He was back teaching poetry at Notre Dame in the fall of 1919. The next year Morrissey became Coadjutor Superior-General, and O'Donnell was elevated to Provincial at the youthful age of thirty-six. He was involved in the academic and building programs of Father Burns and Father Walsh until 1926, when he was made First Assistant to the Superior-General. Two years later he succeeded Walsh as President. He had been around. He was ready. The poet became a builder; and most of the poet's building was done between 1929 and 1932, at the blue note of the Great Depression, when practical financiers were running for cover and guarding their hoards. Here is his score:

1929.... The Little Princes, favorites of Sorin and other Presidents, were dispossessed, amid much wailing of the traditionalists. The domicile of the Minims became the nucleus for the present St. Edward's Hall.

1929.... The golf course, a gift of William J. Burke, President of the Vulcan Golf Company of Portsmouth, Ohio, was built on land which had been farmed. No woman has ever played there. The ladies from the "matrimonial farm across the Dixie" made formal requests and Father O'Donnell, searching around for some justification other than tradition, remembered the toy "lake" on the St. Mary's campus. "Permission refused," he wrote, "because Notre Dame boys have never been allowed to swim in your lake." (The golf course may be moved to another location so that the valuable land can be used for college buildings.)

1930.... The stadium was informally opened by Southern Methodist October 4th. The next week, October 11th, Navy was the opponent for the formal dedication. G.K. Chesterton, on campus for a lecture course, listened as thousands cheered:

> He's a man
> Who's a man?
> He's a Notre Dame man.
> Chesterton! Chesterton! Chesterton!

"My, they're angry" Chesterton said to Johnny Mangan, the chauffeur who was steering him about.

"Hell, man, they're cheering you!" cried Johnny. Chesterton raised his bulk, bowed—and later wrote a poem about it.

1930.... The Law Building was dedicated October 7th. Cardinal Hayes came from New York to bless the $400,000 structure which replaced the cramped quarters in what had formerly been Chemistry Hall.

1931.... The church was renovated.

1931.... Alumni Hall and Dillon Hall, each housing 400 and costing $950,000, opened for the fall term. In these structures Father O'Donnell combined his artistic and practical talents. Worthy of inspection are the niches, inscriptions, statuettes, figurines, and plaques. The complex of Lyons, Howard, and Morrissey had been called by students The Gold Coast. Alumni and Dillon, much more pretentious, were tabbed The Platinum Coast. (These are the two halls just off the entrance circle which campus visitors pass en route to the dining-hall cafeteria.)

1931.... A new heating plant for the growing Notre Dame town was built near St. Joseph's Lake. It cost $250,000 and The Poet fired the first boiler.

1932.... The commerce Building. Edward Nash Hurley, Laetare Medalist of 1926 and Chairman of the U.S. Shipping Board during World War I, contributed $200,000 for the building "to be known as the College of Foreign and Domestic Commerce" because the University of Notre Dame is rendering valuable service to American industry by educating young men ... and features the great importance of foreign trade to the future industrial development of the country."

1932.... The John F. Cushing Hall of Engineering....

The erection of these buildings completed the outlines of the original quadrangle and added to the developing "new campus," facing the golf course. The total cost of $2,800,000 could hardly be duplicated for five times that amount today. Early expenses for the stadium were underwritten by the sale, for ten years ahead, of two hundred forty-four boxes, each seating six, at prices from $1,250 to $1,500. (The modest capacity of 59,000 has served well enough until recent years, when the increase in alumni, students, faculty, and student families, along with the inclusion of St. Mary's girls, has pretty well cut off public sales. There is talk of enlarging.)

Notre Dame has been built on the simple formula, faith *and* good works, by dreamers who could make the dream come true. Father O'Donnell obviously did not fear fear itself,

as President Roosevelt cautioned Americans not to do at that
time. The product was good, there was faith in the future,
especially in the good works of the football future. But, as
Bob Zuppke of Illinois is credited with first saying, "the football takes funny bounces."

29. "ONE FOR THE GIPPER"

TROUBLES come to the troubled. Injuries piled upon injuries. The 1928 Notre Dame squad limped into Yankee
Stadium with a 4–2 record and as 4–1 underdogs to undefeated Army, led by player-of-the-year Chris Cagle. The sports
pages of *The New York News* on the Monday following were
lyrical about the 12–6 Irish victory. Paul Gallico had a rave
column headed "Let Us Overemphasize!" The banner line
on the back page read: GIPP'S GHOST BEAT ARMY. The
exclusive story explained:

> Irish Hero's Deathbed
> Request Inspired
> Notre Dame
> by Frank Wallace

George Gipp beat the Army in 1920 and died that fall,
the football man of the year, mourned by his nation. Saturday, what was thought to be the weakest Notre Dame team
in fifteen years completely outplayed the Cadets, stopped the
outstanding player of the year and provided the biggest
upset of the campaign.

Football people knew that Rockne would fire up his boys in his speech before the game. This is what he told them: "On his deathbed George Gipp told me that someday, when the time came, he wanted me to ask a Notre Dame team to go out and beat the Army for him."

(The author intrudes), Rockne accused me of violating a confidence for the first time. I said Joe Byrne had given me the story, that it was not in confidence, that ordinarily I would have considered it so, "but I thought this one belonged to the tradition." Rock pondered a moment, nodded as if he hadn't thought of it that way. Later he used the incident in his own writing and speeches. And so "Win One for The Gipper" became a phrase in the language for the all-out emotional try; has endured in lore, been kept green in news stories and editorials, was inserted in the 1968 political primary because Ronald Reagan had played George Gipp in a movie.

Nineteen twenty-nine was expected to be difficult, because the stadium was being built, and all nine games were to be played on the road. The season had hardly begun when Rockne was put to bed with phlebitis. Tom Lieb was in charge, and Rockne coached by long-distance telephone before each game until Carnegie Tech, the self-proclaimed jinx. He ignored medical advice, made the trip to Pittsburgh. In the locker room Dr. Maurice Keady whispered to four others: "If he lets go emotionally and that clot breaks loose it could lodge in his heart or brain. There's an even chance he might not leave this room alive." Rockne let go, collapsed—but was on the sideline in a wheelchair, doing a psychological job on Joe Savoldi for a prized 7–0 victory. Later at Soldier Field before the Southern California game, the clot let go and lodged *in the other leg,* presumably having passed through the heart. In the finale, against Army, the Yankee Stadium temperature was twelve degrees above zero, but Rockne sweated it out at home until Jack Elder intercepted

156

a Cagle pass, ran it back over the frozen turf 96 yards for the national title.

In 1930 the stadium was ready, and Rockne was back on his feet, joking about the two "spare tires" (rubber bandages) around his legs. Again there was drama upon drama, before the finale against Southern Cal at Los Angeles, where, after winning 18 straight, Notre Dame was actually a 5–3 underdog. Rockne had jacked his tired squad up with psychological devices during the practice stop at Tucson. Bucky (now Dr. Paul) O'Connor scored two touchdowns before the Trojans even knew he was in the line-up; the supermen from Troy never got untracked. The 27–0 victory sealed back-to-back national championships.

That night at dinner with the squad Rockne was quiet, for only the second time in memory of those who knew him best. He was especially pleased because he had pulled a rabbit out of the hat in plain view of the Hollywood showmen. He permitted himself a rare moment of public self-appreciation. "They expect it of me."

In Rockne's "poor" year of 1928 the attendance mark had passed 400,000 for the first time. In 1929 it jumped to 551,112. In 1930 it "dropped" to 512,553, ironically because of the comparatively limited seating capacity of his own stadium. The saga of success had brought the customary *football factory* jibes. (After the 1928 Army game, W. O. McGheehan of *The Herald Tribune* had gone out to South Bend "to investigate the rumor a University was located there." He saw, was convinced and in New York became Attorney for the Defense.) Father Charles O'Donnell had a low boiling point about the *football factory* jibes. He wrote scathing letters to individual critics and in January, 1930, issued a statement which "opened the books" to the public. It revealed that total income represented only 70 percent of the instructional expense; that football profits helped to make up the deficit, made a direct contribution to the academic growth of the University, and even permitted little luxuries like the artistic furbelows in residence halls, the importing of prestige lecturers like Chesterton and Yeats, and a new seal for the University.

The old seal was hardly distinguishable from that of the Congregation of the Holy Cross. O'Donnell commissioned a new one from Pierre de Chaignon la Rose. It consists of a shield with a clear blue field and cross of gold—the colors of the patroness, the Blessed Virgin. At the base of the shield are two wavy lines of silver and above them, to the left, a silver star, another symbol of the Virgin, Star of the Sea. The waves indicate part of the University title *"a lacu"* (by the lake). The cross symbolizes the Community. In front of the cross is an open book representing the University as an institution of learning; and upon the book are written "Vita, Dulcedo, Spes," words taken from the Salve Regina, again symbolizing the dedication of all the University's activities to the Mother of God.

30. SORIN WITHOUT A BREVIARY

[by United Press]
BAZAAR, KANSAS, MARCH 31 (1931)—Knute Rockne, noted Notre Dame football coach and seven other men were killed in an airplane crash near here today.

Edward Baker, a farmer, was feeding stock on the Stewart

Baker farm and was watching the plane when it flew over.

Suddenly, he said, there was an explosion and the ship fell to earth.

The first flash to Emporia that Rockne was among the dead shocked the entire world, and business and industry halted while all the sources of communication were placed into service to determine the truth of the report.

THE family was at Coral Gables, Florida. The first wire to come was from Rockne himself, dated Kansas City, where he had been put on the plane by a close friend, Dr. D. M. Nigro.

LEAVING RIGHT NOW   STOP   WILL BE AT
BILTMORE   LOVE AND KISSES

The next was from Dorais, roommate, teammate, best man, best friend.

Little Jackie, playing around the house, asked: "Did my Daddy get killed in an airplane?" It was just another great thing his wonderful Daddy had done.

(We waited an hour for the kidding wire to come, explaining it was all a mistake. Finally the packing began. A football wouldn't fit in a trunk. I suggested we deflate it, but Bonnie cried: "Oh, no—Knute blew that up himself for Jackie." Somewhere Rockne's breath may be in an old football, as it is still in the game, and in Notre Dame.)

Father Cavanaugh wrote: "All day long it was all but impossible to reach Notre Dame by telephone, so clogged were the wires. Every student on the campus hurried to the church."

Messages were received from presidents and kings, from Douglas MacArthur and Babe Ruth, from Ring Lardner and presidents of unions; from a school for the deaf, from coaches and businessmen, actors and musicians. Editorials and poems

159

were written. His old players and opponents came for the funeral, which was broadcast over network radio.

As President of the University Father O'Donnell said in his sermon:

> I think, supremely, he loved his neighbor, his fellowman, with genuine, deep love. He made use of all the proper and legitimate methods of modern activity to be essentially not modern at all; to be quite elementarily human and Christian, giving himself, spending himself like water, not for himself but for others. And once again in his case most illustriously is verified the Christian paradox—he has cast away to keep, he has lost his life to find it. This is not death, but immortality.

He was buried in Highland Cemetery, near Council Oak. As his widow, his family, his "boys," his friends crowded round, an airplane roared above.

Rockne had been flying to Los Angeles on business. He could have taken his pick of offers which would have made him and his family rich in a very short while. But before he left South Bend he had left a pair of tan, hightop shoes with Augie Backus, a bellhop at the Oliver, to be half-soled. Nobody ever called for those shoes. Nobody has ever filled them.

W. Edmund Shea, Dayton lawyer, a Rockne halfback and man-about-Notre Dame through the years, relates: "Rock had a student secretary who was standing at a window looking out on a dreary day. Rock asked Andy what he was doing there. 'Just looking out the window and feeling how lucky I am just to be a part of Notre Dame,' Andy said. Rock went to the window and looked out and said: 'Yeah. Even on a cold rainy day.' "

There was a growing mystique. Joe McArdle, a Leahy assistant, was observing a game from the vantage point of a scoreboard when Joe Oracko kicked a crucial field goal. "God bless you, Oracko," shouted McArdle. And the word spread that the voice of Rockne had come from the sky. Another visitor asked, seriously, if that was Rockne up there on The Dome. Even the irreverent student editors of the sixties, who satirize Gipp and scorn "The Golden Dome image" have not demeaned his memory.

Who would succeed Rockne? Or *try?*

There were many capable men at his funeral, pupils who had absorbed his methods and proven themselves at other major schools, but who could hardly be asked to walk out on their jobs at the beginning of spring practice. It was decided to go with Rockne's two assistants for one season. Line Coach Heartley "Hunk" Anderson was to be Senior Coach; backfield coach Jack Chevigny was named Junior Coach; and Jesse Harper was brought back from his ranch as Athletic Director. A stopgap arrangement while the field was surveyed was sound enough, but the *troika* was unsound. In football there must be a head man, and the more autocratic, usually the more successful.

Notre Dame won the first seven games, to run the undefeated streak to 26. Southern California was coming; and as a gesture of confidence, Father O'Donnell announced that the stopgap arrangement had been made permanent. Notre Dame promptly lost the two final games, to Southern Cal and to Army. Football people were now dubious; they knew that the *troika* had been operating with *Rockne-trained* men; that the real test of a new coach came in his second and third year when he worked with men he had recruited and trained.

The 1932 record was also 7–2. In 1933 it was three won, five lost, one tied. This was not merely the first losing season in modern Notre Dame history; the squad had not scored in six of the games, had tallied only 32 points in the nine games.

There was that ultimate and deafening statistic, the verdict of the paying public. From the Rockne peak of more than half a million, the figures had dropped alarmingly: 1931—404,723; 1932—419,545; 1933—317,655.

This was what Father Walsh had feared: a big stadium, with a big debt, and no Rockne to fill it.

There is a fact that the purists concerned with simon-pure amateurism do not usually care to publicly admit: the football business is an amateur sport conducted for profit; the head coach is the general manager of the business; when he fails, he must be replaced. Every college which plays big-time football has at some time or other, and in some cases quite often, had to replace the general manager when profits, image, enrollment, alumni-giving, and other fringe benefits were threatened.

In the latter part of the 1933 season a few qualified people were confidentially informed that a change was to be made and asked to nominate five. The man chosen was Elmer Layden, one of the Four Horsemen who had made a very good coaching record at Duquesne in Pittsburgh. He had not been first on any ballot but had been named on every ballot. Here was the universally popular, middle-of-the-road coach to enforce the new pianissimo policy the University had in mind to erase the image of *football factory.*

The last years of Charles O'Donnell were also spent in Gethsemane. It had begun in 1931 with the same strep throat that caused Gipp's death and contributed to Rockne's phlebitis. The poison was arrested, but never quite defeated. "I am propped up in bed" he wrote to the widow of his good friend, Joyce Kilmer, "a hot water bottle at my back and at least seven devils of infection running riot through my ears and throat." From the Mayo Clinic he wrote: "The gentlemen have punctured my spine, taken out my tonsils, loaded me with serums, to say nothing of other indignities." At St. Francis Hospital on Miami Beach he seemed to be recovering, his letters were cheerful: but the seven devils brought seven more.

The Apostolic Delegate, Secretary of State Cordell Hull and Governor Paul McNutt of Indiana were on the stage at the 1934 Commencement, but Father O'Donnell couldn't make it. In the early morning of the following day, he died at age fifty.

31. JOHN FAITHFUL

JOHN FRANCIS O'HARA was born in (of all places for a Notre Dame man) Ann Arbor, Michigan, May 1, 1888. He attended the parochial grade school and public high school of Peru, Indiana, and in the ordinary schedule of future Presidents would then have departed for the Novitiate. Theodore Roosevelt had something to do with the detour, because he appointed John W. O'Hara to the post of United States Consul at Montevideo, Uruguay. His son John entered a Jesuit College there, but dropped out for the excitement of riding horseback and punching cattle on a ranch in the Argentine. At various times "El Restless" also served as secretary to his father and to Edward C. O'Brien, the United States Minister to Uruguay.

He finally arrived at Notre Dame in January, 1909, at age twenty-one, taught elementary Spanish while completing studies for a degree in philosophy, remained as an instructor in history and English, decided to become a priest, took the familiar trek to Washington for theology at Holy Cross, and Latin-American history at Catholic U., where he received his doctorate.

Ordained in 1916 at age twenty-eight, he was assigned to Wharton School of Finance, and to practical experience in New York commercial houses. In September, 1917, Notre Dame became the first American university to offer a four-year course in foreign trade, with Father O'Hara in charge of the seventy-five students. He became the first dean of the expanded College of Commerce in 1921; but he is most remembered at Notre Dame as "John Faithful," the Prefect of Religion, a post he inherited when Father Charles O'Donnell left to become a chaplain, and which he retained for sixteen years. This position required an understanding man whom a student in any sort of trouble would voluntarily approach. There was about his office all the secrecy and sanctity and humanity of the confessional.

Father O'Hara was Father Commonplace, tall, lean, with a very ordinary narrow face, a quick smile, a direct stare, a strong but neutral voice. He had neither the flourish of Cavanaugh, the wit of Walsh, the austerity of Burns, nor the intellectual remoteness of O'Donnell. His door in Sorin Hall was never locked; he was available at any hour to any troubled soul; he could be seen hurrying along the campus at midnight; and at six the next morning in the basement chapel of Sacred Heart Church (the crypt), distributing Communion. He would have been far, far down on the list of prospects who might one day become a university president, a bishop or Notre Dame's first cardinal. All these things came because he was content to be what a priest was ordained to be—a priest.

In the religious field he became nationally known for movements that spread to other colleges. It began when he

164

decided that a more personal spiritual program might help calm the animal spirits of the boisterous young colts in Carroll Hall. To the post of religious director for the preps he appointed Father Cornelius Hagerty, whom many old students remember as a husky walking-around saint who could also pitch a good baseball game for the athletes and near-athletes in his philosophy classes. (Father "Con" doesn't pitch anymore, but neither his faith nor his intellectual vigor has waned.) There were no cases of instant sainthood among the preps, but the general climate improved. At other halls the practice of Daily Communion increased, with the athletes leading the quiet move.

In 1921 the West Point publicist announced that Elsie Janis, a musical comedy star who had entertained troops in World War I, would ride the Army mule before the Notre Dame game. Father O'Hara told the football squad that Joan of Arc would kick off for Notre Dame, and he gave each a medal of the Saint. They would be traveling on First Friday, so they were whisked from the train at Albany and transported to Farrell Institute for Mass and Communion at the Grotto there. These things had always been done quietly, but a reporter, on hand to greet the team, sent the news and pictures across the land. On Saturday, Joan beat Elsie, 13–0.

Coaches of competing schools knew of the religious custom, and some even copied it for their Catholic players. Howard Jones of Southern California had an ambition "to beat the Irish with eleven Catholics"—and once he almost did. In the days when the Notre Dame party traveled to Los Angeles on a special train, there would be a halt momentary somewhere in the southwestern desert, during the Consecration of the Mass.

After the 1930 Penn game, President Charles O'Donnell received a letter from a Catholic attorney in Philadelphia, who told how his three teen-age sons on their own initiative, had "trudged and trolleyed the eight miles to see the arch-angel of the laity, Mr. Rockne and his squad," and how impressed they had been by the manly matter-of-fact devotion to the Blessed Sacrament. "Your men have done, unconsciously, more to back up parental example and suggestion than anybody else could possibly do. I now perceive the value and importance in this country, not necessarily of your remarkable football squad, but of their quiet influence. It is hard, indeed, under such circumstances, not to root for Notre Dame, even if one is a University of Pennsylvania man." (Heisman Trophy winner Leon Hart passed out religious medals along with autographs to grade-school youngsters. Before and after the 1967 Miami game, guests at the Key Biscayne Hotel might have followed a group of huskies into a private dining room off the lobby for the morning squad Mass.)

Daily Communion had become a fact of life on the Notre Dame campus. Periodic Missions was the next step; and after some misbehavior at one of these, Father O'Hara typed out admonishments in language the students understood, and posted them on the bulletin board in each residence hall. The approach hit the target, and thus began the daily *Religious Bulletin* which grew to a circulation double the enrollment, as six thousand mimeographed copies went to faculty members, alumni, and to other schools. The boys called it The Wit & Humor Dept., but they looked forward to it. O'Hara described it: "The Bulletin is an application of modern principles of advertising to the spiritual life. From day to day it hammers at student foibles, or suggests means of advancement in the spiritual life. It is a caricature rather than a portrait, for a portrait is too true to be comfortable, while the exaggerations of a caricature carry home a point without leaving too much sting. . . ." The language, neither pious nor polished, was more reminescent of a bull session than of a tract.

As usual with the new thing, there had been reservations among the traditionalists about promoting Daily Communion, and risking the laxity that might come with familiarity. O'Hara's next venture, *The Religious Survey,* calling for anonymous answers from students, supported his program. After alumni were included, the mailing list of *The Survey* went to fifteen thousand and was sought by alumni, educators, missionaries, psychologists, sociologists, and business corporations. In 1933 O'Hara regretfully resigned the in depth association with Notre Dame men to become Vice-President (and soon, President), and take over most of the executive duties during the long illness of Charles O'Donnell.

Notre Dame had long had a friendly interest in the Philippines, Catholic for centuries under Spanish rule. A celebration of Philippine independence was held December 9, 1935, the date selected by Franklin D. Roosevelt, who had consented to accept an honorary degree. (Encouraged by his friend, alumnus Frank Walker and by his Postmaster-General and National Chairman of the Democratic Party, James A. Farley, who had been a friend of Notre Dame since he had attended the first Army game on the Plains in 1913.) Sorin would have been delighted with the ceremonies attending the first visit by a President of his adopted and cherished country.

The Presidential Special arrived from Chicago at two in the afternoon. On it was George Cardinal Mundelein, an old friend of the President, who would preside at the exercises. Father O'Hara and other members of his administration waited at the New York Central station, scene of so much Notre Dame history. The procession proceeded through cheering South Bend to the old dirt-floor gymnasium, bedecked and festooned for this occasion like a dray horse impressed for a wedding party. Long accustomed to vocal explosions, the old place shuddered as the audience of five thousand students, faculty people, and dignitaries, really shook down the thunder when the band broke into "Hail to the Chief," and the President came on stage leaning on the arm of his aide. The speeches are remembered for two prophetic utterances:

The President said: "The United States, in restoring independence to the Philippines, is doing a thing human and just. So might the rest of the world, preparing so ominously for war, come to a like respect for the rights of man."

Carlos P. Romulo, representative of the Philippines, said: "If war comes or fresh conquest from whatever source, we shall oppose it to the death. . . . To the Philippines the United States has been a generous benefactor, a loyal and true friend; and if we can honor that debt in no other way, we can pay with our lives if need be." Notre Dame accounts rate Romulo's address "brilliant, heart-stirring, a song of hope and gratitude." Farley, more than thirty years later, remembered that "Romulo stole the show."

In 1936 Cardinal Pacelli, Secretary of State to the aging Pius XI, visited the United States and had scheduled Notre Dame for one of his flying stops. Sunday, October 25th, was a cold and rainy day and the students, already depressed by a 26–0 football defeat at Pittsburgh the previous day, waited glumly at the entrance. Somebody said, "Even when traveling on a plane, Rome moves slowly." Those who gave up lost the opportunity of boasting to their grandchildren how they had welcomed future Pius XII. The party, delayed by weather, proceeded to the church where the Cardinal fulfilled a prophecy of a sort by kneeling in prayer at almost the exact spot where, in 1875, Gregori, in a Main Building Mural, had imagined such a scene.

Father O'Hara presented the diploma, making the visitor an alumnus of Notre Dame *honoris causa*. Cardinal Pacelli read from a short, prepared statement, "in understandable English with a musical Italian accent" his words of appreciation. He blessed the kneeling throng and concluded: "And now, if there is no objection on the part of your superiors, I grant you a holiday. And to St. Mary's." The students nobly refrained from the mutual disparagement so noticeable in the adjoining cheering sections at football games, between the Notre Dame boys, and the girls from the matrimonial farm. (It is assumed that this is a lip service confined to daylight hours.)

32. FRESH RED ROSES

A GRADUATE SCHOOL is a luxury for a private university with minimal endowment. Costly facilities become obsolete, multiple experiments are outmoded, the whole package of equipment, library and highly trained faculty is so expensive that one graduate engaged in original work for one year might equal the cost of several undergraduates over the four-year period. Limited research help had been provided for the two Zahms, Jerry Green, and a few others. A graduate faculty, organized in the summer school of 1918, was abandoned in 1923 because of little demand during the regular terms. Thereafter research was confined for the most part to Nieuwland and Professor Henry Froning in chemistry, Father

Wenninger and Dr. Theodore Just in biology, and to J. Arthur Reyniers, whose work in the germ-free laboratory he originated would culminate in today's internationally significant *Lobund*.

Serious graduate work began in 1933 when Father Philip Moore returned to the University, after obtaining his doctorate at Catholic University and being engaged for three and a half years at the *Ecole des Chartes* in medieval studies. He and Father Leo R. Ward planned the program leading to a doctorate in philosophy. Critical studies began to be published at Notre Dame in the new *Publications in Medieval Studies.*

As other departments leading to doctorates were organized in physics, mathematics, and politics, Father O'Hara found himself in the unhappy position of trying to spread inadequate funds among such suppliants as Father Steiner, Dean of Engineering; Father Henry Bolger, a physicist who had studied four years at California Institute of Technology; Dr. Karl Menger, former professor of mathematics at the University of Vienna; and Dr. Waldermar Gurian of the Department of Politics, who in 1939, began the publication of *The Review of Politics,* the highly regarded quarterly.

Menger, Gurian, Arthur Haas, and Eugene Guth from Vienna; and Dr. F. Alois Hermens of Bonn and Paris, came to Notre Dame. Other distinguished scholars and visiting lecturers in various fields gave a shine to the graduate school, but had varying success with the American student body. Jacques Maritain had language difficulties, but his countryman, Etienne Gilson, was more successful. Arnold Lunn "provoked many a delightful controversy"; Christopher Hollis, a shy, eminent man of letters, and historian, got across very well. Shane Leslie of the *Dublin Review* made more of an impression with his eccentric straw hat and white cotton gloves than with his lectures. Best-liked "for solid thought and dexterity of speech" was Desmond Fitzgerald, who had been Minister of Foreign Affairs for Ireland, and whose "intimate knowledge of the struggle for Irish independence" gave his visit added popularity.

There had been a steady decline from the year 1931–1932 peak undergraduate enrollment of 3,227; but this was somewhat alleviated by a new University scholarship program totaling around a quarter of a million dollars each year, and by a government subsidy offered through the National Youth Administration. As enrollment began to move upward, the building program was resumed. In 1934 there was a new laundry and a new post office; in 1935, a new infirmary (with rooms for distinguished visitors); in 1936, a new biology building; in 1939, the Rockne Memorial (a physical education building); and an important addition to Chemistry Hall. Three new residence halls went up on the East campus: Cavanaugh Hall, 1936; Zahm Hall, 1937; and in 1939 Breen-Phillips Hall, in memory of two old students and benefactors, William P. Breen and Frank B. Phillips, both of Fort Wayne.

Father O'Hara was not a football buff, but like so many other people he managed to be in Columbus, Ohio, November 2, 1935 for a game which had captured the advance attention of the nation. Elmer Layden was doing the job for which he had been hired, conducting a low-keyed operation while fielding representative squads capable of drawing adequate crowds. Notre Dame had modestly won its first five games, but was underdog to Ohio State which had been spectacularly successful with a new "razzle-dazzle" offense brought up from the southwest by Coach Francis Schmidt. A record crowd of 81,018 came to the stadium, expecting to see the Buckeyes not merely beat Notre Dame, but smother it. In the first half it looked as if that might happen. Ohio led 13–0; Notre Dame had never been so thoughly stopped on offense.

In desperation, Layden started his second team in the second half. Senior Andy Pilney, who had never started a game, achieved gridiron immortality with a triple-threat performance. His final run of 32 yards was one of the jewels of football history. He was hurt and Ohio seemed saved; but as Pilney was being carried from the field William Shakespeare threw an artistic pass to Wayne Milner. It was Notre Dame's fourth touchdown in the final period (one had been lost by a fumble), for an 18–13 victory. Even the press box forgot its poised neutrality.

Early in December, 1939, Father O'Hara left on a trip to the West. He wanted to be away when announcement came that he had been appointed bishop and military delegate for the armed forces. In 1958, he became John Cardinal O'Hara, based in Philadelphia.

"Once he had any contact with you," Father Jerome Wilson, current Vice-President for Business Affairs, reminisced of O'Hara, "he had a great way of greeting you around the campus with, 'How about-cha Jerry, I haven't seen you around lately' which meant he hadn't seen me in the basement chapel for awhile. If you were to indicate that the spirit was willing but the flesh was weak, he would arrive in your room in the morning, flip you out on the floor, laugh and say, 'I'll see you in the basement chapel at 7:00.'. . . One student in the Corby basement locked his door, but Father O'Hara came in through the window. The next morning he blocked his door with his locker and desk but the Bishop kept after him. . . . Once O'Hara carried a boy, who had been sleeping through Sunday Mass, to the shower room and put him under the cold water. . . . He was simply great, a real hound for souls, and of course we called him the 'Pope.' The boys for whom he did these things have been eternally grateful."

Dan Young recalled his last meeting with Cardinal O'Hara. "It was on the walk in the rear of Sacred Heart Church as he left the Provincial's house. We talked of days of old, and turned and left each other. I took five steps away and turned at the same instant as he turned, as if a second had given a signal. He raised his hand and said 'Yea, I know. Quit smoking.' "

Bob Hamilton of Manhasset, New York, an Irish basketball man of the era, answered a query:

When O'Hara was Prefect of Religion I had a problem involving a matter of conscience and went to Sorin Hall to discuss the matter with him. He was reclining in his chair, chain-smoking and relaxed—and he invited me to sit in a big, overstuffed chair next to his desk. Both of us were dressed quite informally. As in any session with His Excellency an immediate air of freedom of thought and expression permeated the atmosphere. During the discussion I unwittingly put my feet on his desk, smoking a big cigar he had given me. When our discussion was over he asked me if I wanted to go to confession and obtain a clean slate to start over again. I started to kneel and go through the routine in preparation but His Excellency interrupted my preparation by requesting me to stay put where I was and keep the cigar going through confession. . . . He once offered five hundred dollars to a Walsh Hall group to anybody who could tell him something he hadn't already heard in a confessional. The sanctity and awareness of this man to everyone's problems related to confession is beyond belief. No wonder many of us think of him as a saint—yet his simplicity was extraordinary. As auxiliary bishop assigned to run the Military Ordinate during World War II, he chose to live in a Harlem ghetto parish, instead of Cardinal Spellman's residence on Madison Avenue. He was way ahead of his time in his concern for the poor and the problems relating thereto.

Fresh red roses, provided by a group of 1928 graduates, are kept in the niche at the left of the altar in Sacred Heart Church where John Faithful is buried.

173

33. "PEPPER"

J. HUGH O'DONNELL, son of Edward J. and Sarah O'Grady O'Donnell, was born June 2, 1895 at Grand Rapids, Michigan, and came to Notre Dame as an undergraduate in 1912. He was a sophomore member of the 1913 football squad which defeated Army. In 1915 he was the first-stringer. His football nickname "Pepper" clung througout his official career, because it described his personality. He was six feet, weighed only 175, but his speed, fire, and leadership compensated for the weight he usually had to give away.

Tradition casts the Prefect of Discipline as *the enemy* to all students, whether he is or not. So while he served in that office, it was not uncommon for Father O'Donnell to hear a siren-like voice blast from an open window: "Who lost the Yale Game?" And a chorus would answer: "J. HUGH O'DONNELL." It was not J. Hugh O'Donnell; but this was another case of the denial never catching up with the canard, especially when the target is juicy. Father O'Donnell would smile and bear it bravely. He would suffer worse.

Rockne called the annual Army game "the game where nobody quits and nobody cries." He cited an incident worthy of enshrinement among the annals of sportsmen. "In 1915 our center, "Pepper" O'Donnell, had a broken rib. Harry

Tuttle, the Army trainer, heard of the injury and came into our dressing room with a special pad. As play began, John McEwan, the great Army center, asked O'Donnell: 'Which side?' O'Donnell pointed to it—and played every minute of the game."

After receiving his bachelor's degree in 1916, the big football man entered the Novitiate, and the trail he followed indicated that the leadership and character he had shown on the football field had marked him for higher distinction in a higher field. His doctorate at Catholic U. was on American Church History. After ordination in his home parish of Grand Rapids he served one year as rector of Badin Hall, six as Prefect of Discipline, and three as President of St. Edward's University, a Holy Cross institution in Austin, Texas. After five years as Vice-President during the tenure of O'Hara, he became Acting President when the latter was made Bishop. In the chapter meeting in 1940 he was elevated to the Presidency.

There was surprise bordering on shock on February 4, 1940, when Elmer Layden resigned as head coach and athletic director to become Commissioner of the National Pro Football League. The stated reasons, family welfare and financial security, were credible enough; and health might have been added, because Layden had become known as The Thin Man under the pressures of the most demanding coaching job in football. Still, it was an unusual step for a Notre Dame immortal to take, unless gently urged; especially since he had done a very good job with what he had to work on under an austerity program that limited scholarships and hampered recruiting. As Athletic Director he had brought Ohio State to the schedule and resumed gridiron relationship with Michigan for the first time since 1909. Attendance had held around 440,000.

Critics said he could improve the schedule because he

averaged two or more defeats each season. He had won a national championship in 1938, but had contracted the bad habit of finishing poorly, of *losing games he was supposed to win,* a mortal sin at Notre Dame, and at most places. These things were happening, it was said, because he coached too conservatively, emphasized defense, was pale on offense. Meanwhile, waiting in the wings, was Frank Leahy, who was going great at Boston College . . . and Father O'Donnell was a football man.

Leahy was signed almost immediately. He had probably insisted that the school stop bending over backwards on recruiting; or perhaps that decision had already been made. Leahy, who seldom needed help of any sort from anybody, turned things around in a hurry. In three years, before going into the service, he won twenty-four, lost three and tied three, won a national championship and was voted Coach-of-the-Year by his colleagues.

All of the Administrative decisions made by President Hugh O'Donnell would be influenced by the cloud of war. There had been big plans for a celebration of the centenary in 1942; but as with every previous quarter-century anniversary, it arrived during a war; and as Notre Dame became an armed camp, the observance was subdued. The Civilian Pilot Training Program had begun in 1940. In September, 1941, a campus unit of the Naval Reserve Officers Training Corps (NROTC) was established, and those of the freshmen who passed the physical, mental, and aptitude tests (about one hundred fifty each year), were permitted to remain at the University for eight semesters to complete their college work. Early in 1942 the V-7 Naval Program was instituted, and Notre Dame was designated as a training center of four months duration for each group; after which the successful candidates received commissions which made them immediately available for sea duty.

Four residence halls—Lyons, Morrissey, Howard, and Badin —were placed at the disposition of the Navy, along with a classroom, cafeteria, and other facilities. The students displaced from these residences were doubled up in other halls, "cheerfully" it was recorded by a perhaps optimistic reporter. The vacation periods were shortened so that degrees could be granted in two and two-thirds years—to make the graduates available for military service that much sooner.

Father O'Donnell died young, after a long siege of cancer of the pancreas. He bore that as he had borne the broken rib in the Army game, with bandages, medication, and as much secrecy as he could arrange, while carrying on his official duties.

He is memorialized in football by The Reverend J. Hugh O'Donnell Trophy, emblematic of dominance in an era, retired by the University of Oklahoma, after having won national titles in 1950, 1955, and 1956. He and his fellow priests were also memorialized in a very positive sense, at his funeral in Sacred Heart Church. The sanctuary was crowded with men who would range from competence to intellectual brilliance. All could have done very well in the business or professional worlds, and some could have been national leaders. All could have enjoyed family life, Thursdays and Sundays at the Country Club, and other privileges of *oblige* and status. All had deliberately chosen to serve God and man—as Badin, Sorin, and all the missionaries before them.

34. THE HOUND OF HEAVEN

JOHN J. CAVANAUGH was another boy from Michigan, born at Owosso. After high school there he worked as a secretary for the Ford Motor Company, and left to go to Notre Dame on one of its "poor-boy" deals: He would work two years as a full-time secretary, after which he would receive a four-year scholarship. By accident or somebody's choice, he became secretary to the President of the University, John W. Cavanaugh, who was no relation.

His 1923 classmates knew him as quick to laugh, persuasive, and never known to display, publicly at least, any emotion beyond humor. He was of average height, with a good "black-Irish" face, a soothing voice, and a very practical, quick-thinking, tenacious mind. As a senior he was chairman of the Student Activity Committee, the first tentative move toward student government at Notre Dame, then in its second year of operation.

His brother Frank, also of the class of '23, was already in the Novitiate, but John seemed to elude both The Hound of Heaven and President Cavanaugh, who had had such influence in the early careers of Matt Walsh, Charles O'Donnell, and John O'Hara. He had spent a summer vacation in the engine room of a ship on a round trip to the Orient. He had occasionally written a column of campus gags and verse, substituting for a classmate. He was known to have broken some of the minor campus commandments of his own making. After graduation he went under the wing of Paul Hoffman at Studebaker and became engaged to a tall beauty from St. Mary's and Atlanta. Then he entered the Novitiate, and she the convent.

After ordination John Cavanaugh was awarded a Lector of Philosophy degree from Gregorian University in Rome, and went off on a holiday in Spain. There he was having dinner alone when he saw an elderly cleric, also alone. They ate together, and there was a mild discussion about who should pay for the check. "I thought from his appearance and speech he was a parish priest from Scranton or some such place, probably scratching out a vacation, so I insisted and he let me have my way." He was not a parish priest from Scranton, but a dignitary traveling incognito. When, as Cardinal Pacelli, he came to Notre Dame, the embarrassed young Prefect of Religion, Father John Cavanaugh, remained carefully incognito.

In 1940 John Cavanaugh became Vice-President and Assistant Provincial. He was elevated to the Presidency of Notre Dame in 1946, and faced the problem of reconverting the wartime training center into a civilian University. The students were flowing from the services into the school, and there was the customary influx of freshmen each year. During his six-year Presidency the enrollment advanced from the prewar 3,200 to more than 5,100. There were the same old problems of housing, feeding, teaching, and finding the wherewithal to do all this. There was an athletic problem created by the refusal of Frank Leahy to lose to anybody. There was the problem of spreading himself around as educator, fund-raiser, ambassador-at-large. These problems were solved; and during their solution Father Cavanaugh created more problems.

The Alumni Association, dormant during the war, began thrashing through the undergrowth as a new Board of Directors took over in 1947. A member close to athletics suggested that something be done to recognize the "synthetic" alumni and to convert their tremendous reservoir of good will. President Harry Hogan, a peppery, dapper bantam who had just retired from formal activity as a Fort Wayne lawyer and banker, thought the ideal way to do it would be to invite the "synthetics" to participate financially; and that was how the Notre Dame Foundation came into being. For two years Harry Hogan pursued the subject at Board meetings, aided by Secretary Jim Armstrong, and abetted by President John Cavanaugh. At the formal organization he became Director of the Foundation, and the Board was able to get on with setting up the procedures under which the Association still pretty much operates. Harry Hogan, one of Notre Dame's men-for-the-moment, died at the age of eighty-four while driving his own car.

A 1968 letter from Art Cronin of Detroit reveals things about the operation of the Alumni Board, about the recruitment of football players in the thirties, and the manner in which a mature Notre Dame man clings to his school:

"Some members of our high-school team were invited to spend a week at a fraternity house at Northwestern. I stopped off at Notre Dame to ask the coach, Hunk Anderson, if he was interested in me, and he told me to go see the Registrar. Years later I asked why he hadn't offered me a scholarship. He said he had heard my Dad wouldn't let me go anywhere else, so why should he waste a scholarship on me? So, with that attitude, you should have seen his face when Bill Steinkemper, to whom he did give a scholarship, showed up for practice in his father's Cadillac Sixteen—with a chauffeur! My first desire to attend Notre Dame had come when I was still in grade school and met The Four Horsemen at the cottage of Hank and Linc Wurzer in Canada.

"We used to settle our most knotty Alumni Board problems at the after-midnight sessions of The Bar Association. Father Vince Brennan, a Board member, had asked me to serve Mass for him. It so happened there had been a very late session of The Bar Association. When I brought him the cruets I had forgotten to take the tops off. His remark was: 'What do you think you're doing? Serving Manhattans and Martinis?'

"At one of these meetings we got into a discussion about secondary education. Joe Boland asked what I had studied in high school. I told him rather proudly that I had attended a Jesuit High School and had been required to take four years of Latin and Greek. Joe, who had been my line coach, answered: 'No wonder you could never remember the signals.' "

Cronin's latest credit came from delivering much sought-after Jim Seymour, All-American pass-catcher, to Notre Dame. A former Board member asked: "Does that Cronin still keep people up late?" Seymour chuckled: "Yes. My father." A member of that same Board was Jack Elder, hero of the 1929 Army game, a teetotaler who left the meetings early, but knocked on doors at seven every morning to make sure everybody got up for Mass.

35. BLUEPRINT FOR THE FUTURE

ON JUNE 5, 1948, at the annual Alumni Banquet, Father Cavanaugh reviewed the immediate physical needs; congratulated the Notre Dame Foundation for collecting a remarkable $551,803 in its first year; then he began dreaming a dream that accurately forecast a future which would be brighter than his brightest dream.

"In the young men who now storm our gates seeking Catholic higher education we have a priceless reservoir of youth trained in the rich traditions of American schools. If we are to exercise that moral leadership which the world sorely needs, we must look beyond the spiritual equipment of our graduates, beyond their power to reason well, to contemplate wisely. We can hope and work always for the day of more effective leadership, when Notre Dame men, imbued with sound principles of morality, will more largely influence the society of which they are a part. The graduates of Notre Dame must be equipped to compete for leadership with the same skill and coaching that produce the football teams that have brought first rank leadership to Notre Dame."

Some Notre Dame people criticized Father Cavanaugh for implying that Notre Dame was not already a great University and its graduates not men of great influence. Some alumni came to the Board to indignantly protest that their sons were being shut out of Notre Dame in favor of strangers with better academic averages. Some looked askance at The Great Books Movement which spawned The General Program, in which intelligent students became somewhat arbiters of their own pace and direction. Others questioned loosening of the tight discipline about which they had complained as students, but now thought was the very thing their sons needed in this changing world. They thought the school was moving too fast, going overboard on new ideas. Notre Dame had been built by people with vitality; so let the "double-domes" go to Harvard. Cavanaugh was getting entirely too chummy with Robert Maynard Hutchins, who had abolished football at Chicago. A gag was making the rounds: "Will Cavvy convert Hutchins before Hutchins ruins Notre Dame football—and Notre Dame along with it?"

Hutchins was not converted and Notre Dame football got bigger and better. Frank Leahy returned from the Navy in 1946 and greeted a squad swollen with veterans that included: Johnny Lujack, Emil Sitko, Jim Martin, Leon Hart, Terry Brennan, Ziggy Czarobski, George Sullivan, George Ratterman, Frank Tripucka, Jack Zilly, and George Connors, the lone transfer (from Holy Cross). The big objective was Army, which still had Doc Blanchard, Glenn Davis, and others who had beaten the impoverished wartime Notre Dame squads, 59–0 and 48–0. On the practice field they would stop and bellow:

> '59 and '48
> This is the year
> We RETALIATE.

The revenge motif developed into the first postwar Dream Game, but ended in a 0–0 nightmare of sorts. In four years— 1946–1949—Leahy won 36, lost none, and tied two games, was awarded national championships in '46, '47 and '49, and missed out in '48 when tied by Southern Cal in the final game. The attendance figures were: 1946: 548,401; 1947: 571,527; 1948: 580,268; 1949: 575,278.

All this at a price. The embarrassment of riches had returned. The cry of *football factory* was louder than ever. Frank Leahy became the center of attack; he was brought up on murder charges for such traffic violations as his players feigning injury to stop the clock. And so on. There began a flight of old and honored foes from the schedule: Army, Northwestern, Illinois. Again forced to roam (as Harper in 1913), Leahy came up with Oklahoma, Pitt, and Michigan State. (He professed not to worry, and saw no significance in grinding the cap off a tooth during the night.) Father Cavanaugh, who refused to throw him in as a sacrificial offering, said to alumni:

"Speaking softly among ourselves, much of the distress about Frank Leahy is due to the fact that he is admittedly the most able coach in America. For two of the finest years he has had as head coach, his first year at Boston College and his first year here, he had nothing whatever to do with selecting the material he coached. A few months ago most of these boys were scattered over the world, fighting for their country. Their devotion to Notre Dame brought them back.... This has always been the secret of success here at this University in all of its activities. When we in American sports hold the winner under suspicion merely because he is the winner, we come perilously close to the kind of dismal thinking that stigmatizes with suspicion the man who achieves outstanding success.... The condition of the loser is not improved in the estimation of the public by criticizing the winner."

Back in 1937 a Notre Dame student named Hal Williams worked in the athletic office. His family came on from Baltimore to see a game, and Hal introduced his eight-year-old brother to Elmer Layden: "Coach, this is Bobby. Someday he'll play quarterback for Notre Dame." Bobby did play quarterback superbly, filling the shoes of Lujack, then of Frank Tripucka. He was playing quarterback in the second game of the 1950 season when, after avoiding defeat for 39 games, Notre Dame lost to Purdue 28–14. A national holiday was all but declared; and as Leahy went on to a 4–4–1 season, followed by a 7–2–1 in 1951, Father Cavanaugh's prediction came true—most of the distress about Frank Leahy evaporated. Even a Frank Leahy (as Rockne in 1928) could not win without the "horses." Because there had been so many returned veterans, and Notre Dame was obligated to honor scholarships interrupted by the war, there had been fewer scholarships granted in 1948 and 1949. As a result, in 1950 the cupboard was bare.

In 1949 Father Cavanaugh had reorganized the administration, creating five Vice-Presidents. Father John H. Murphy was in charge of Public Relations and served as coordinator of the Alumni Clubs, The Notre Dame Foundation, The Department of Public Information, and the Department of Public Relations. Father James E. Norton was in charge of Academic Affairs; Father Joseph A. Kehoe of Student Affairs; and Father John J. Burke, Business Affairs. Father Theodore Hesburgh, age thirty-two, became Executive Vice-President, correlating the work of other administrative officers and serving as Chairman of the Athletic Board. At the same time Edward "Moose" Krause, head basketball coach and football line coach, was named Assistant Athletic Director. He was to take some of the load, and hopefully, the heat, off the beleaguered Leahy.

Television football had begun in a tentative way in 1949. All of the 1950 games were shown on the pioneer DuMont network. The 1951 Michigan State game, televised in Boston and as far west as Omaha, had drawn the biggest viewing audience to that time. Notre Dame, Michigan, Ohio State, Navy, Army, and Penn were leaders in the movement because they could televise and still draw capacity crowds. The Irish were the preferred people because of their demonstrated national appeal. But television was hurting the attendance at most colleges, and the Have-Nots were demanding controls. The annual meetings of the National Collegiate Athletic Association became debating soundboards as the question was argued. This was the first major job Father Hesburgh drew. "Red" Heard, athletic director of Louisiana State, said of him: "Notre Dame never sends a boy."

Released from administrative details, President Cavanaugh was free to exercise his considerable talents as Ambassador and Super-Salesman; to make high policy decisions and specific plans toward materializing the blueprint he had drawn in 1948. In all of this activity he drew on the advice and experience of the members of the newly created lay advisory councils of the various colleges; and primarily of the Board of Lay Trustees which included such men of national affairs as I. A. O'Shaughnessy, Joseph LaFortune, Charles Fisher, John P. Murphy, George Strake, Frank C. Walker, Ernest Morris, Bryon Kanaley, Joe Byrne, Terence Cosgrove, John Moody, Peter C. Reilly, John McCaffrey, Tom Beacom, Edward Doyle, Tim Galvin, Constantine McGuire, John Tully, Bernard Voll, Charles F. Williams, and Joseph P. Kennedy. Many of these would become material benefactors of the University.

Of all the buildings on campus today, none brings more student pleasure than the LaFortune Student Center; and to Notre Dame people of any vintage, there is no more heart-warming legend than that of how it came to be. Here is the story from Joe LaFortune himself:

"My family and I have been associated with the University in excess of one hundred years. My grandfather, Michael

186

Hastings, worked at the University for 37 years. My father, Louis R. LaFortune, was the tinsmith for 27 years and yours truly has been on the campus for 68 years.

"When I was about 9 or 10 my grandfather told my mother that one of the Brothers wanted a boy to come out and pick potato bugs and save the potato crop. I was elected to do the job. They paid me 75¢ a day which I turned over to my mother. Many years later Father Hugh O'Donnell, then President, asked me to visit his office after a football game. He introduced me to two Admirals from the Great Lakes Training Center as one of the new Trustees of the University. I told them it was one hell of a jump from picking potato bugs for the school.

"I went to work for the gas company in 1909 at the age of 14. Six years later it was suggested to me by a Mr. Winchell, head of the new business department, that I take up a short course at the University. My father advised me to see Father John Cavanaugh, the President of the University. That esteemed and brilliant man told me I could work at the University in my spare time to pay my tuition. The first year I was given the job of picking up papers on the campus and the second I looked after the art room for Professor John Worden.

"As I look back on those two years, I feel as though I kept plenty busy doing my studying at home with about eight other children in the living room at night; working for the Spiro Clothing Store Saturday afternoons and evenings; doing some work for the gas company on Thursday and serving drinks at the Elks Club Saturday night and Sunday. I think I lost five pounds during that period as I was on the go constantly.

"After moving to Tulsa in 1919 my connection with the University was not as close until I was asked to become a Trustee somewhere around 1944 or 1945. In 1946 I made a donation which later became the nucleus for what is now known as LaFortune Student Center. I have only missed one Trustee meeting in the succeeding years.

"One of the stories I recall was about my Mother and Dad. Mother was 100% Irish, and Dad, who spent most of his life at the University, was French-Canadian. He would often dwell on the fine work Sorin had done for the University. Mother would listen until he ran down and then she would say: 'Well, the French may have started the University but the Irish run it today.' "

At the expiration of his second term Father Cavanaugh, following Canon Law and the course of Father Burns thirty years previously, gave his entire time to directing the Notre Dame Foundation. He continued to serve as Ambassador-at-large, has been a close friend of Joseph Kennedy and the family, and said Mass at the White House on the day President Kennedy was buried. He is currently serving as chaplain at St. Mary's. Senator Ted Kennedy's wife, Joan, was there in 1968, speaking for the campaign of family friend Senator Birch Bayh of Indiana. After she had finished and began to walk away from the lectern, she turned and came running back: "Oh dear, I forget to mention Father Cavanaugh. And he was the first to know that Ted and I were going to be married."

PART IV

HESBURGH

36. DICK TRACY

THEODORE MARTIN HESBURGH, the sixteenth President, bowled over precedents from the beginning. He was not born in France, Canada, Ohio, Michigan, or Indiana. He did not have an Irish name and never knew poverty. He was an undergraduate at Notre Dame for only one year and did not receive his bachelor's degree from there.

Otherwise he conformed to the pattern. He was born May 25, 1917 in Syracuse, New York, where his father was an executive in a glass company. His mother was a Murphy. He decided to become a priest while in grade school, and favored an order like Holy Cross because, "I didn't want to be asking people for money as a secular parish priest has to do. Since I've been here at Notre Dame it seems I've done nothing but ask people for money." His parish priest advised him to take plenty of time to think things over. At Notre Dame the strong influence for him to become a priest was supplied by Father Tom Duffy of the Mission Band. He has "never given any thought" to the idea that he had early been marked for leadership. Father James Burns was the Provincial who made the unusual decision, after his first year in the Notre Dame seminary, to send young Hesburgh to Gregorian University in Rome.

Hesburgh was forced to leave Rome after three years, because of the advent of World War II. He wanted to become a chaplain, but was overruled and sent to Catholic U. where he received his doctorate in Sacred Theology; and during these years in Washington he served as chaplain at the Fort Meyer Army Camp and the Federal Reform School. He was ordained at Sacred Heart Church on the campus, taught "theology and marriage," was the chaplain of "Vetville," the barracks for married veterans which students christened Fertile Valley because its babies, diapers, and young mothers gave the masculine campus a supermarket aspect.

When President John Cavanaugh first asked if he would be interested in administration, Hesburgh said he would not. When the administrative setup was reorganized in 1949 Father Cavanaugh did not ask, but informed: "You are going to be my Vice-President in charge of Vice-Presidents." At age thirty-two Hesburgh thought that "idiotic." His intention then was to serve his time in administration, after which he would still be young enough to go on "with the things I wanted to do," in general, teaching and the problems of youth. He was characterized in the 1949 *Dome* as "the amiable young Vice-President who, through his many contacts with students, has won the love and admiration of everyone connected with the University." Young, handsome, with black hair, square jaw, intense eyes, and a darting mind, he looked and acted like a student, eager to challenge and be challenged. He was hep. He communicated, knew the score, made the scene, including the gridiron scene.

Football has been so intertwined with general administration that the Executive Vice-President of Notre Dame, as Chairman of the Athletic Board, functions in fact as Athletic Director on matters of major policy. When he moves up to the Presidency he is fairly well-insulated against mistakes common among those administrators who are inclined not to bother a successful athletic department until it begins to bother them. Hesburgh had been party to Cavanaugh's decision not to throw Frank Leahy to the coaching wolves, and to the other decision which temporarily limited new football scholarships until the flow of returning servicemen had ended.

In 1952, when Hesburgh became President, the gridiron situation was normal. Forecasters were again predicting great things for Leahy, who was gloomily seeing "one of Notre Dame's worst seasons because of the shortage of running backs." After six games he had won four, lost one and tied one; and coming up was Bud Wilkinson's finest Oklahoma squad with its famous backfield of Billy Vessels, Eddie Crowder, Buck McPhail, and Buddy Leake. A television audience of 15,000,000, saturation at that time, assembled to watch "gridiron worlds collide."

The worlds collided. From the moment Joe Heap gathered in the first kickoff until Paul Reynolds batted down the final Crowder pass, there was doubt. Vessels scored all three touchdowns for Oklahoma, two after long runs and the third with a pass, and clinched the Heisman Trophy that day. Notre Dame had a flock of hard-nosed sophomores directed by Ralph Guglielmi and led by junior Johnny Lattner, who gave a Gipp performance for the full sixty minutes. Wilkinson, in his letter to interested alumni, analyzed:

"The willingness to hit harder than the other fellow, to go all out for something you want and believe in, is one of the great lessons of the game. I thought Notre Dame exemplified it best on the seventh kickoff when Dan Shannon followed the ball down fast and struck Larry Grigg, our receiver, with such shattering impact that Larry turned a half-flip in the air and lost the ball."

Notre Dame held off a Sooner storm for the final thirteen minutes and defeated a superior squad 27–21.

In 1953 Purdue and Pitt had been defeated, and another

super-duper loomed with Georgia Tech, which had gone thirty-two games without defeat. The Irish led 7–0 at half-time, but Leahy walked toward the dressing room as if carrying a heavy load—which indeed he was, of chest pains. He blacked out, was given the last rites of the church by Father Edmund Joyce, the Executive Vice-President. The between-halves talk that day was a prayer that the coach might live. With the score Notre Dame 20 Georgia Tech 14 and minutes remaining, the Irish were on the opposing two-yard line, and the student body was calling the next signal: "Happy Birthday Dear Johnny." And Lattner celebrated his 21st birthday in the Tech end zone for the 27–14 victory.

Leahy's seizure was diagnosed as a severe intestinal spasm. He was back on the bench four weeks later, but it was no place for a sick man. With less than a minute to play in the first half, Iowa led 7–0, but Notre Dame was charging. Tackle Fred Varrichione was hurt. Time was taken out. Notre Dame scored. Exactly the same thing happened as time was running out in the second half. Iowa was tied at 14–14. And fit to be tied. After a 48–14 finale over Southern California, Leahy had his sixth undefeated season. At the annual football dinner Varrichione received an Academy Award from his team-mates as Best Actor of the Year. (Twenty years later, on Regis Philbin's network television show, he was still explaining: "If you were on the ground and looked at the scoreboard and saw your team trailing with time running out, wouldn't you feel sick?")

On January 31st, 1954, Leahy resigned. The medicos had given him an option: Give up coaching or give up living. There was a loud groan of relief from coaches on the Notre Dame schedule at the departure of The Dick Tracy of the Gridiron, who almost always got his man—and his boy, in recruiting competition. Rockne could beat them, and he would be invited back. Leahy would beat them and they hated his guts, professionally. Rockne was a genius at personal relations. Leahy, though nobody tried harder, was a dud. And therein was the coaching difference between The Master and his idolatrous Pupil.

Leahy football, with its drama ranging from comedy to tragedy, was box office. In the postwar years the annual attendance was always over 500,000, and peaked in the final season at 610,704.

Obviously Leahy had been doing the job he had been hired to do; but among the noises at his forced departure was a soft sigh of relief from segments of the official family, which could now look for the peace and tranquility which evidently couldn't be had with continual victory. The desideratum would be a new coach who would retain the winning tradition without tarnishing the shine of The Golden Dome. Any number of promising people were available, including Johnny Lujack, who had added a successful professional career to his college prestige. But the surprise choice was Terry Brennan, age twenty-five, who had done well in Chicago prep-school coaching, but whose college experience was one season as freshman coach under Leahy. Few were inclined to publicly disagree with Notre Dame administrators who had come up with Rockne and Leahy; especially after Brennan came up with 9–1 and 8–2 records in his first two years. Notre Dame was obviously launched on another victory parade under an ideal coaching type, a young, handsome, intelligent, impeccable Irish lad who could make friends rather than critics, while still drawing close to 600,000 each season. Hesburgh had gambled on youth and won—again—for Hesburgh was young, and behind the football curtain he had been burning up the academic league.

Buildings had gone up: a new Science Hall, and the reconversion of the old one into the LaFortune Center; a post office, bookstore, bus stop, and minor structures.

Hesburgh had taken an early aim on the development of the graduate school and the upgrading of the faculty. Beards and dialects mingled, as the faculty lounges and dining places began to take on the sounds of Oxford, Vienna, and Bonn. The many new people who were not Catholics were often astonished at the academic freedom permitted in this Catholic university, and delighted when all this was spelled out in 1954 in a Faculty Manual which brought the professors into the administration for advice, if not always consent. The first step toward effective student government had been taken in 1952 with the creation of the Student Senate, again for dialogue and recommendation, if not always consent.

"Following Father Cavanaugh's advances," Hesburgh recently said, "I saw the chance to make Notre Dame a really great Catholic university." He aimed at the top echelons, sought the m-o-n-e-y which would supply the housing, teaching, and researching for a future which would bring more students and require more buildings, bolder programs, more m-o-n-e-y. As he met and captivated influential people, they saw him as a coming man; and the school which could send him out as a coming school. In the manner in which such things are done, he used them and they used him for mutual advantage. The name of the President of Notre Dame began to appear in the places of prestige; the list would grow, and the growing man would absorb those opportunities, take them in stride.

"The time was ripe," he explained.

When Hesburgh's six years in the presidency terminated in 1958, the Chapter meeting of the Congregation bypassed Canon Law, in effect tore up the contract, and extended his term indefinitely. Hesburgh was also Dick Tracy.

There had been just one failure.

37. THE PRIDE AND THE PENANCE

THERE is no more peaceful place at Christmas than a college campus, made up with snow, after the students and faculty have vacated. This is especially true of Notre Dame with its bells, silences, chapels, and Grotto. But in 1958 a storm had blown in, with blasts of criticism from press, radio, and television. For the first time in memory the Notre Dame family was publicly somewhat divided. From the clamor it might have been concluded that the sheen had been stolen from The Golden Dome.

A football coach had been fired; a young Galahad who had represented the very image Notre Dame had sought for itself. The father of four young children had been sacked a few days before Christmas. Scrooge had come to the Main Building. The coach had won 32 and lost 18; wasn't that good enough? Couldn't Notre Dame stand an occasional defeat? Wasn't an annual attendance of 600,000 enough? Had Notre Dame surrendered to the alumni faction that had never been happy about losing Leahy?

President Hesburgh did not stand above the battle. He replied to *Sports Illustrated* which had climbed the highest Alp of criticism by charging that he could "no longer live with" convictions he had previously expressed in its columns.

His letter made these points: (a) He had approved the recommendation of the Athletic Board with "reluctance" because Terry Brennan, an old friend from student days, had been his personal choice for head coach. (b) He had made the decision on the same basis as any other change in University personnel—a commitment to excellence. (c) He and Terry had mutually decided to make the announcement before, rather than after Christmas, in the interest of assistant coaches who might be looking for jobs. (d) The new coach, alumnus Joe Kuharich, would be judged "not by any nostalgic calculus of wins, losses, and national championships," but only by the excellence of his teaching and the spirit of his teams. A team could perform miserably while winning or look magnificent in defeat. There was no *academic* virtue in playing mediocre football nor *academic* vice in winning a game that by all odds one should lose. "We make no apology for the will to win as long as it keeps faith with the honor and integrity that should characterize an educational institution."

Emotional sports columnists, radio and television commentators had heated up the athletic parody of the Christmas story, but the more realistic reporters had dwelt on certain gridiron facts. There were always firings between the end of the season and Christmas so that those let out, especially the groups of assistant coaches, would have more time to scurry about for other jobs, especially at the annual convention of the N.C.A.A. held early in January. . . . Notre Dame had probably made a mistake in picking so inexperienced a coach; and Terry had compounded that mistake by getting rid of Leahy's seasoned staff too soon. . . . He had won 17 and lost 3 in his first two seasons with *Leahy-trained* players and coaches; but in his last three seasons, he had won 15 and lost 15; and Notre Dame football success had not been built on winning one and losing one. Notre Dame might shrug off the $150,000 difference between the "gates" of the '56 and '57 games with

Southern Cal; but would Southern Cal? And other opponents on the gold-bond schedule Rockne had built?

Nobody but a Notre Dame man could know his frustration when the Notre Dame will-to-win was questioned, when it was implied or *privately felt,* that the Fighting Irish no longer fought. At stake had been not just a football game, nor a season, nor the career of a favorite son. At stake had been "The Image." They turned out hopefully for Joe Kuharich's first game. They were thrilled to see an imaginative, hard-hitting, old-fashioned *Notre Dame* squad win over North Carolina 28–8. Happy days were here again. The coaches would rank in history: Rockne. Leahy. Kuharich.

There was that pride again.

38. HESBURGH'S TEAM

FATHER HESBURGH was an "in" person: Civil Rights Commission, Ford Foundation, Rockefeller Foundation, International Atomic Energy Agency; President's General Advisory Committee, Freedom Award, and on and on. Calls from Nelson Rockefeller; from the Speaker of the House. Need help in a hurry? Call Hesburgh, out at Notre Dame.

The student *leaders,* feeling their new power, flexing the new muscles, were not overly impressed. *The Scholastic* printed a picture of The Empty Chair, thought it would be nice to have a President in residence more than half the year, suggested that if it were really that necessary to jet about the world in pursuit of the elusive buck and the erudite faculty beard, a Chancellor be appointed to mind the store. When work began for the Largest Library Building in the World, a student sign was planted at the summit of the first big pile of excavated soil: *Mt. Excellence.* It might well be said that the first stirrings of student protest at Notre Dame in the early sixties were directed at the Peripatetic Prexy; and the beginning of permissiveness was in his reaction: "Let them speak. Let them publish. This is a place devoted to the seeking out of the truth. Inquiry must be encouraged, dissent must be permitted." An ancient priest who remembered Sorin said of the new student freedom: "It might be modern but it is not Notre Dame."

The older alumni, products of the old Notre Dame, were confused and disturbed; but they marched loyally along, establishing a fine record of financial contributions, hoping Hesburgh knew what he was doing, knowing that, regardless of the wise-cracking students, he did have a very good team minding the store.

Father Edmund P. Joyce, Executive Vice-President and Treasurer, was a solid product of old Notre Dame. A native of South Carolina, he had majored in accounting while earning a bachelor of science degree in 1937. He became a certified public accountant, but after six years in the business world had entered Holy Cross in Washington, and later studied at Oxford University in England. He was ordained at Notre Dame in 1949, immediately named Assistant Vice-President for Business Affairs, became acting Vice-President in 1950 and Executive Vice-President when Hesburgh was elected President in 1952. Obviously he had also been spotted and brought along. Notre Dame might sometimes make a mistake in picking a football coach, but Father Joyce was another proof that it never missed in selecting an administrator.

Joyce was as big as Sorin, impressive as the elder Cavanaugh, pleasant and self-effacing as Matt Walsh, efficient as John O'Hara. He inhaled work. In addition to coordinating the work of the six functional Vice-Presidents, serving as Chairman of the Athletic Board, and pinch-hitting on ceremonial occasions, he was Chairman of the Building Committee, followed through on all major construction, took part in planning for the future. He made the football trips and could often be found watching football practice. He was approachable, unflappable, and could be depended upon to see that the campus trains ran on time, while the President was out selling the product that took on a new dimension in 1960 with the return of a man who was about as much *Notre Dame* as could be packed into one person.

George Nauman Shuster was born in Lancaster, Wisconsin, graduated from Notre Dame in 1915, served as a sergeant in the AEF, returned to the campus to receive a master's degree in French literature in 1920. During the next four years he was head of the English department, associate editor of *The Ave Maria* and faculty supervisor of *The Scholastic*. He was an amiable, incisive teacher who could inspire: he caused one student to abandon the security of the law for the perils of the slot-machine business of writing. He married Doris Parks Cunningham of the matrimonial farm, and when they moved to New York their flat in Flatbush became a haven for youngsters from both their schools who came adventuring to The Big Town.

Shuster served as managing editor of *The Commonweal* from 1929 to 1937; was awarded a two-year fellowship to study the Weimar Republic, returned to earn his doctorate at Columbia. He was President of Hunter College for twenty years, was detached to serve as State Commissioner of Bavaria in the U.S. Zone of Germany during 1950–51, has been American delegate to UNESCO, and other international cultural conferences, holds many impressive degrees and decorations.

In 1959 twenty-nine college Presidents attended a special convocation when Shuster was awarded the third honorary degree in the ninety-year history of Hunter College, from which he was retiring. He intended to do some writing. Father Hesburgh, who searched the world for talent, was not likely to overlook this bonanza. So Dr. George Shuster became Professor of English at Notre Dame, Assistant to the President, was given a chunk from a Ford Foundation grant, and an open-end assignment to pursue his own curiosity about The Study of Man in Contemporary Society. He has become the driving force behind the University's surge in social science and humanities research. He also jets about the globe on business of the State Department and Notre Dame. He still communicates with students, talks in simple language, and he anguishes like other Notre Dame men over gridiron defeats. When he meets an old friend after a quarter-century they take up from where they left off, as if it were yesterday. One described him: "A Christian gentleman who has retained humility, simplicity, good humor, and invincible youth."

For business decisions on Hesburgh's team there were the Trustees; for technical advice the members of the six Advisory Councils. Together these groups, chiefly, but not entirely Notre Dame men, composed a formidable phalanx of hard-headed business and professional achievement. In the background, shepherding the VIP's, planning the campaigns, serving as dynamos and shock absorbers, were home-growns, some from as far back as the twenties: Art Haley, Director of Public Relations; Jim Armstrong, Alumni Secretary and Director of Publications; Herb Jones, Business Manager of Athletics; Ed "Moose" Krause, Director of Athletics; Father Jerome Wilson, long-time Vice-President in charge of business, Father Philip Moore, and others of the changing group of back-up Vice-Presidents; and Jim Murphy, Department of Public Information. Jim Frick would become the first lay Vice-President with prime responsibility for the financial drives. Dr. Frederck Rossini, a "rather rare compound of top-rated scientist and able administrator," would occupy the new post of Vice-President for research and sponsored programs. There would be Special Assistants to the President like Dr. Tom Stewart for planning; and lawyer Phil Faccenda for general administrative duties. There were the deans and heads of departments to meet expanding programs and new developments. The office of Vice-President in charge of Student Affairs would so grow in importance that the students would somewhat resentfully call Father McCarragher "the second most powerful official on campus."

So Father Hesburgh sailed into the sixties not always certain about the hazards ahead, ad-libbing brilliantly toward the future he knew was there—damn the torpedoes, full speed ahead.

39. REGILDING THE DOME

THE Golden Dome, symbol of hopes and accomplished dreams, was regilded for the eighth time in eighty years in 1961. The previous renovation in 1948 had cost $20,000. This one totaled $50,000. It began with the removal and salvaging of the tarnished gold leaf. The entire sheet-metal base over the wooden frame was replaced by monel metal, a nickel-copper alloy that was heavier, stronger, and more corrosion resistant. The supporting structure, extending down into the fourth story of the Main Building, was repainted. The monel metal was prepared with several compounds, the last a sizing to which the leaf adhered. The 23-karat gold leaf cost $10,000, was one ten-thousandth of an inch thick, came in tissue-paper back rolls three-quarters of an inch wide and 67 inches long. Each roll covered about 16 square feet of The Dome's 3,500 square feet of surface. A workmen could sit in the outstretched hand of the 19-foot cast-iron statue while regilding. Weather was an unpredictable problem. Rains and high winds delayed the project, causing the fragile gold leaf to blow about. Unexpected frost prevented the leaf from adhering properly.

The Golden Dome became famous as a landmark.

Early planes used The Golden Dome for directional bearings. Millions of travelers have glimpsed it from the Indiana Toll Road. (Exit 8 is nearby.) Tourists use it to find the campus. Returning sons look first to The Lady, and the motto on the base of The Statue: *vita, dulcedo, spes;* "Our life, our sweetness, our hope." None of the new buildings rise (as yet) nearer the sky.

The University image was also regilded June 5, 1960, with ceremonies that would have delighted Sorin. It was the Feast of Pentecost, and the Solemn High Pontifical Mass was celebrated by His Eminence Giodanni Battista Cardinal Montini. He donned the mitre, took up the staff, and during his sermon spoke of Truth. He attended the luncheon also honored by the presence of Dwight D. Eisenhower, President of the United States. Before delivering the Commencement Address the President, in an unusual gesture, left his seat to congratulate the youngest man among the distinguished gathering of international figures to be honored. He said: "Few if any men that I know have equaled his example of complete self-sacrifice, faith in his God, and readiness to serve his fellow men."

The young man had received his bachelor's degree at Notre Dame just fourteen years before. He had already become world famous for his humanitarian work as a jungle physician in Laos and Viet Nam, and as cofounder of Medico. He wore his mortar at a rakish angle, as a young man would. He bowed his head and smiled when he shook hands with the President. He bowed and his eyes were closed as he received his degree from Father Hesburgh. He already had terminal cancer, contracted during his work. He knew that barring a miracle, he would be dead in six months. Who knows what Tom Dooley might have hoped from The Queen of Heaven, along with his degree?

Vistors to The Grotto, replica of the scene of miracles, can read the glass-framed letter to Father Hesburgh, written from a Hong Kong hospital by Doctor Tom Dooley during his last illness:

> The Grotto is the rock to which my life is anchored. Do the students ever appreciate what they have while they have it? I know I never did. Spent most of my time being angry at the clergy at the school ... bed check absurd for a nineteen-year-old veteran, etc. etc. Did just want to communicate for a moment and again offer my thanks to my beloved Notre Dame. I must return to the States very soon, and I hope to sneak into the Grotto before the snow has melted.

Cardinal Montini's gift to Father Hesburgh was a huge limited edition quarto volume containing 248 drawings and sketches by Renaissance masters, from the collection of Milan's Ambrosian Library. It has an inscription in which he describes himself as "bound forever with chains of esteem, friendship and devotion to a glorious American Catholic University in gratitude and benediction."

If public pride is a sin, Father Hesburgh was obviously guilty, as he stood in the photograph between the President and the Cardinal Archbishop of Ambrosia. Dr. Shuster became the only man to receive the Laetare Medal from a future Pope. (Eugene Cardinal Pacelli had also become an honorary Notre Dame man three years before he became Pope Pius XII. Eisenhower's degree came twenty-five years after that conferred on Franklin D. Roosevelt.)

Notre Dame has conferred its greatest number of honorary degrees on American prelates who have preached the baccalaureate sermons; on educators, statesmen, and other public men who delivered the commencement addresses; on lay trustees, advisors, and other benefactors who had also given long and faithful service. In recent years those from the public sector have included Earl Warren, Supreme Court Justice William J. Brennan, Jr., Robert S. McNamara, Henry Cabot Lodge, Admiral Arleigh Burke, Herbert Brownell, and Sargent Shriver; and men whose names are linked with major buildings on campus: I. A. O'Shaughnessy, Ernest Morris, Frank J. Lewis, James F. Keenan, Joe LaFortune, J. Peter Grace, and Thomas Pangborn. Pride is taken on early recognition of future stature, as Cardinal Spellman, who expressed special affection for the University which "honored me when I didn't amount to much."

In 1915 the University bestowed an honorary Doctorate of Laws on Hon. John F. Fitzgerald of Boston.

In 1941 it awarded the same degree to Joseph P. Kennedy, son-in-law of "Honey Fitz," and brother-in-law of Joe Gargan.

In January, 1950 the same doctorate was conferred upon Joe's son, John Fitzgerald Kennedy, then a member of Congress, who gave the address at the midwinter graduation.

In 1957 Senator John F. Kennedy received the Patriot of

the Year Award, conferred annually by the senior class on Washington's Birthday. He urged the seniors "to act with the same steadfastness and courage that characterized an unhappy politician named George Washington just 161 years ago tonight, who was willing to oppose the people in order to save the people." He called uon them to remember the words of Daniel Webster inscribed upon the wall behind the Speaker's desk in the House of Representatives: "Let us develop the resources of our land, call forth its powers, build up its institutions, promote all its great interests and see whether we also, in our day and generation, may not perform something worthy to be remembered."

In 1958 the Patriotism Award went to Robert F. Kennedy.

In 1961 the Laetare Medal was awarded to President John F. Kennedy.

The Last Hurrah, a novel thought to be based upon the twilight of "Honey Fitz," was written by Edwin O'Connor of the class of 1939. Each year he would visit the English classes of Professor Frank O'Malley, to whom later he dedicated his Pulitzer prize novel *The Edge of Sadness.* O'Connor was a shy writer whose visits were without fanfare but the word always got around and his readings of his current work always drew capacity. In the '39 class notes in *The Alumnus* he was just another guy. ("Ed O'Connor has written another book. Hope you make a million with it, Ed.") He died suddenly and much too young, as did another writing alumnus, James Metcalfe; and James A. Reyniers, whose memory the University honored in 1968 by officially giving the name Reyniers Germ Free Life Building to the facility in which he carried on the research that has already been helpful in the fight against cancer.

40. TED'S MAHAL

IN 1960 the Ford Foundation selected Notre Dame as one of five rapidly improving Universities which would receive a $6-million grant if $12 million could be raised from alumni and friends. The University called it Challenge I, and teams from the Notre Dame Foundation spread out to raise the matching amount in three years. Previously Notre Dame alumni had been responding about fifty percent to the alumni drives; but eighty percent contributed to Challenge I and raised one-third of the money. The rest came from friends, corporations, and other interested agencies. Eight million dollars was earmarked for the 14-story Memorial Library, four million for two graduate residence halls, three and a half million for the faculty, two million for student aid, and half a million for the Administrative Fund.

The Memorial Library has been called The Silo, a not altogether derisive description, because it is a bank of knowledge where 2,000,000 volumes will eventually be stored. Its tower looks like a big, oblong box, secured on top of a much bigger, square flat box. The first floor is devoted to the humanities, with a goal of 60,000 volumes in the stacks, and seating capacity for about 800. The second floor, devoted to the social sciences, has 140,000 volumes and seats 1,300. Ten floors of the tower are used as a research library, primarily by faculty and graduate students, though open to undergraduates. The book collection is augmented by 120 small, closed study rooms called carrels, and 250 open carrels. Director Victor Schaefer spent more than a year preparing to move the half-million volumes from the old library by the lake. The selection and arrangement of furniture was facilitated by the use of toys in working models.

The staff includes professional librarians, full-time clerical personnel and part-time student workers

Derisive students call the Library Mt. Excellence and Ted's (Hesburgh's) Mahal. Students of architecture have other descriptions, and old Notre Damers have considered it a maverick, because it is such a world apart from the prevailing Gothic. But it also looks out upon a different world, the world of the future, exemplified by its neighbors, the Computing Center and the $2,200,000 Radiation Building, recently erected by the U.S. Atomic Energy Commission. These grim invaders of rustic charm use great quantities of water for air conditioning from nearby St. Joseph's Lake, and have already rendered it deadly for fish and warm for humans who swam off the dock near the old boathouse in the good old days of the "tight little boarding school."

There is nothing sinister about the architecture of this new East campus. Even in this period of affluence, Notre Dame still has to consider the cost sheets. It would take entirely too much money to try to match up the new buildings with all the intricate curlicues, gables, and turrets of the Main Building and, in less degree, of other campus buildings. A student of architecture could read economic history in the structures of Notre Dame.

The ground beneath the Library was once trod in athletic practice by folk heroes with the quaint names of Rockne, Gipp, Steers, Anson, Reulbach, and others. Now their deeds, and those of athletes from all the innings of time and all parts of the world, will be preserved at Notre Dame in the International Sports & Games Collection—a Notre Dame first.

Challenge I also provided funds for a number of significant academic changes: 1.) A new Freshman Year program expected to keep ninety percent of the incoming class in college through graduation. 2.) An Area Studies Program, which permitted an undergraduate to concentrate on subject matter concerned with a particular area of the world. 3.) A Collegiate Scholar program which would allow superior seniors to engage in a special subject instead of the regular curriculum. 4.) An Inter-Institutional program which would permit a Notre Dame student to study special subjects at other universities. (This is already in effect with St. Mary's and Notre Dame may eventually go co-ed.)

Joseph Lawrence Kuharich was a local boy who hung around the practice field as a grade schooler and idolized the great Rockne. He was personally recruited by Elmer Layden, as a light-weight lineman who made up in spirit, brains, and leadership what he lacked in size. After graduation he helped coach the freshmen, while working on his master's degree. He won all-pro honors as a guard for the Chicago Cardinals, spent four years in the Navy, shuttled successfully back and forth between college and pro ball, had an undefeated season at San Francisco University (where Pete Rozelle, now czar of pro football, was his public relations man). He was Coach of the Year with the Washington Redskins. In 1959 when he came back home at age forty-one, he seemed the very man to put Notre Dame back where it belonged in football.

After six games the count was three won, three lost; but the games had been exciting, and Notre Dame had become the scene of another interesting experiment—the introduction of pro techniques into the college game. Between halves of the Georgia Tech contest, with the score 7–7, attention went to the band, which was putting on a show celebrating the Golden Anniversary of *The Victory March*. The two brothers who had written it, Father Mike Shea and John Shea, were being honored; and some history of one of the great college songs came to light.

The Victory March had its first "tryout" on the organ of a Congregationalist Church. It was a marching song for Notre Dame men in World War II. At a German prison camp where national songs were not permitted, programs were opened and closed by a gramophone rendition of *The Victory March*. An infantry captain wrote President Hugh O'Donnell: "The big offensive toward Rome begins soon. Tonight the band is playing *The Victory March*." It was defiantly played in a Japanese prison camp as a substitute for the forbidden National Anthem. It has been selected as "neutral" music at joint Army-Navy affairs. It has been adopted by countless Catholic high schools which sometimes also use The Fighting Irish nickname. Its familiar strains have been heard by most Americans on television, radio, and motion pictures.

> Cheer, cheer for old Notre Dame
> Wake up the echoes cheering her name
> Send a volleyed cheer on high
> Shake down the thunder from the sky
> What though the odds are great or small
> Old Notre Dame will win over all
> While her loyal sons are marching
> Onward to victory.

(Notre Dame has four other songs, all familiar to its people: The alma mater *Notre Dame Our Mother; Hike, Hike, Hike; Down the Line;* and *When Irish Backs Go Marching By*. The music for all was written by Joseph Casasanta '23, who received the first bachelor's degree in music, and remained as Director of the Glee Club and of the Band. The alma mater was composed especially for a memorial program following the death of Rockne. The lyrics were by Father Charles O'Donnell. Vince Fagan, Casasanta's brother-in-law, did the lyrics for the *Hike Song,* and *Down the Line.* Lyrics for *The Irish Backs* were by Father Eugene Burke. The Glee Club sang and the band played at the 1968 funeral of Joe the Music Maker.)

Georgia Tech seemed more inspired in 1959 by *The Victory March* than Notre Dame, which lost 14–10. It looked more than miserable against Pitt the following week, but recovered for two spanking victories over Iowa and Southern California. Football fans of today, especially the pro addicts, will find it hard to believe that the 1960 squad which lost eight straight games included Darryle Lamonica, Myron Pottios, Red Mack, Nick Buoniconti, Mike Lind, and George Sefcik. The unhappy fact is that Joe the Pro had installed "the shuttle system" of win-one-lose-one.

After the second year (2–8), Notre Dame extended Kuharich's contract. All it got for that generous gesture was another avalanche of criticism. Notre Dame seemed intent on proving that it was *not a football factory.* After '62, the four-year record was 17 won and 23 lost. Winter dragged toward spring. The recruiting cop was in the barn and spring practice was about to begin when the ice jam broke. Kuharich announced that he was returning to pro ball as supervisor of officials. His 1963 farewell speech: "This insatiable appetite to win has become ridiculous."

Again, as in 1931, it was too late to hire a new coach away from another school. Hugh Devore was temporarily elevated from freshman coach to head coach, and for a brief while it seemed as if he might make it permanent; but it was another 2–7 season, shortened by the death of President Kennedy. An odd and surprising situation arose: "The best coaching job in football" was going begging. Word passed through the fraternity that Notre Dame either had had it, or no longer wanted it. Then Ara Parseghian, of whom nobody but himself had thought, made a phone call to Father Joyce, and began immediately to prove to all those coaches how wrong they had been.

41. "KIRUNGI"

PRESIDENT HESBURGH was writing for *The Notre Dame Alumnus* in the summer of '62:

"I'm writing this in August, during what is supposed to be the dog days. Actually they are very busy days here. No sooner had the 1961 Summer School nuns left (about 1,500) when another 1,600 Sister Superiors came in for a week's course. This week-end we've had five retreats going—women and teen-agers, as well as laymen this year. It was also the reunion week-end for the Vetville couples and children. As their former Chaplain, I guess I enjoyed this week-end as much, if not more, than they did, although I'm slightly bruised from the football game we had. Next week there will be thousands of high school students here—boys and girls of the Catholic Students Mission Crusade.

"And so it goes. Earlier this summer I made a quick trip to Africa to review the work of six universities—at Dakar, in Senegal, Accra in Ghana, Ibadan and Nsukka in East and

West Nigeria, Lovanium in the Congo and Makerere in Uganda. These are most interesting universities that contain much of the hope of these new countries, all of which were born in the past ten years. We also saw all of the ambassadors and cultural affairs officers in connection with my latest government assignment: The United States Commission on International Educational and Cultural Affairs. Notre Dame men, Holy Cross priests and brothers, are doing great work there, *kirungi* as they say in the Rutoro language."

Back home in Indiana it was *kirungi* too in the early sixties as traffic flowed outward and inward, as Notre Dame scholars and scientists visited all parts of the globe, as others came to Notre Dame for professional meetings, seminars, and symposia. Vetville folded its barracks, other old landmarks were obliterated to make way for the buildings beginning to take form on drawing boards. When the Ford Foundation repeated its offer of $6 million, the University called it Challenge II and went after $18 million, the big chunk of which would be earmarked for the long-awaited new field house which would be twice as long as the football stadium with an even longer name, Athletic & Convocation Center.

The pages of *The Alumnus* carried the customary news about the Spotlight Alumni who were being promoted to prestige positions. More and more space in the magazine was being given to the doings and opinions and demands of students.

On the football practice field Ara Parseghian was reading a letter to his squad as the 1964 spring training began in preparation for his first season as Notre Dame's head coach. The letter was from Don Hogan who would have been the backfield star of this squad had he not been badly injured in a car accident while returning from a Christmas Midnight Mass two years previously.

"One last thing. I'll be out there this spring and fall watching. When things get rough remember that a guy named Hogan would give anything to trade places with you—and if he could, he would never quit—then after you think it over, give it that second and third effort. Bring Notre Dame football back where it belongs. Someone in the stands will get the message of that extra effort and that someone will be mighty pleased and proud. Best of luck. Don Hogan, Class of 1965."

Straight out of Rockne; out of Sorin and his wheelbarrow after the fire, and his crowbars on Holy Thusday; out of Gipp, the sophisticate; Chevigny, the expendable Marine; Johnny "One-Play" O'Brien; Johnny "Tape and Guts" Niemiec; to a squad who had messages of their own, received and filed during the years of gridiron penance: John Huarte, Jack Snow, Jim Lynch, Jim Carroll, Bill Wolski and sophomores Nick Eddy, Alan Page, Kevin Hardy, Tom Regner....

The 1964 season:

```
Notre Dame 31 Wisconsin 7
Notre Dame 34 Purdue 15
Notre Dame 34 Air Force 7
Notre Dame 24 UCLA 0
Notre Dame 28 Stanford 6
Notre Dame 40 Navy 0
Notre Dame 17 Pittsburgh 15
Notre Dame 34 Michigan State 7
Notre Dame 28 Iowa 0
```

In the Los Angeles Coliseum, at half-time, it was Notre Dame 17 Southern Cal 0. The Irish were sitting on perhaps the greatest comeback story in football history. With five minutes gone in the third period, it was Notre Dame 17 Southern Cal 7. But the Irish had come storming back toward the clinching touchdown. With first down on the Trojan eight, Huarte called the play that had worked so well all through the season. . . .

Fumble. Trojan's ball.

But the Trojan fire seemed to be out. Again Huarte drove. Joe Kantor, subbing for the injured Captain Jim Carroll, got to the one-foot line. Notre Dame thought he had actually scored, but with second down on the one-foot line, who worried? *Holding! 15 yards.*

With 9:30 remaining in the game the Trojans took over on their 12-yard line. Four plays later they had scored on four successive passes.

With only 5:09 left, now leading by only 17–14, and against a red-hot foe, it was crucial that Notre Dame control the ball. They hadn't really been stopped on offense all afternoon. But now they couldn't even make that one first down. Snow punted to Garrett, who was snared on his own 23. With three minutes left, all Notre Dame had to do was give them the short game and protect against the long passes.

Wait! The red kerchief again. Holding!

Garrett brought back the next punt to the Notre Dame 40! The underdogs were now Supermen. They played that way.

Notre Dame gave up 25 yards in bitter fighting. It was fourth and eight on their 15. All they had to do to preserve the miracle, the perfect season, the No. 1, was to stop the next play.

Touchdown! The Notre Dame defender had slipped, had got *almost* close enough to bat the ball down. 21–17. Nothing so final as a final score. For the Cinderella team the clock had struck. Football is that way, a game of inches.

Back at Notre Dame Hesburgh was writing:

"It's dark and cold outside. I'm too old to cry and not old enough not to feel hurt. . . . We can never be sure of total victory, not even of eternal salvation until we've won it. Life goes on, the challenge remains and it will really be a dark day and a cold place here if we ever lose the desire to be No. 1 in everything we do, or lack grace and style and humanity in doing it."

The players went to Disneyland as planned. Seven thousand students welcomed them home. They dropped to No. 3 in the final ratings, but the annual football dinner was celebrated with grace, style, humanity, and wit. Then, after the season had been put to bed (call it Lazarus), it rose again most joyously. The Football Hall of Fame at its annual dinner in New York awarded the MacArthur Bowl:

"For consistency in championship performance, winning its first nine games against major colleges from East and West by an average of 21 points and leading in its 10th game for 58 minutes and 25 seconds, when Southern California rose to insuperable heights to win the game 21–17, Notre Dame has been adjudged the outstanding team of the year."

A veteran observer had this theory: "It might have been a big break when Notre Dame went outside its family to hire a coach. A Notre Dame man, after inoculation through eight years of defeat, might have found himself unconsciously contaminated by that gas that came down from the top, that it was no longer necessary to have championship teams; that 7–3 seasons were permissible. Parseghian and his staff hadn't been exposed to that. They came in believing in that Notre Dame spirit they had heard so much about and had seen in operation as opponents. They counted on it, built upon its presence, and they were right."

42. A VERY GOOD YEAR

"ONE always begins a new year with a surge of hope" the President reported, "and we have far-ranging hopes for 1966. The University is at a new threshold, thanks to Challenges I and II. One could outline a long list of developments that resulted from the infusion of some $36 million during the last six years. In a sense our appetites have been whetted for what can yet be at Notre Dame.

"A great new School of Theology, with special studies in ecumenical, liturgical, and pastoral theology for both priests and laymen, Catholics and non-Catholics, is in the offing. A new Center for Higher Religious Studies will operate ecumenically on an intercultural as well as interreligious basis. At least God is not dead at Notre Dame.

"Planning is under way in all our colleges. Science has now planned an interdisciplinary, graduate approach for the years ahead. We are installing a new and more powerful atom smasher. A Life Science Building and a new chemistry addition to Nieuwland Science Hall are on the drawing boards. Engineering has its new master plan too, involving another building for expanding graduate research and teaching. Both of these plans run over $10 million apiece, which is a new challenge in itself.

"Business Administration is also looking to a new graduate program in business and public administration. There is no outstanding Catholic graduate school in this field. Not yet. We are hoping. Another challenge.

"The Humanities and social sciences have recently been neglected in American higher education, with most of the outside support going to science and technology. We tried to correct this at Notre Dame by allocating one-third of the last Ford grant, $2 million, to these fields. We are inauguating this year a new social science laboratory and have allocated a whole floor in the new Memorial Library to our on-going projects (another $2 million worth) in humanistic research.

"The new Psychology Department is growing, as are our overseas programs in population studies, university development, Peace Corps, and exchange of students.

"On the material side, thanks to very generous alumni support, we are getting into the ground in the spring on three new projects, The Athletic and Convocation Center, The Faculty Club, and a new post office. High on our list of priorities are new graduate and under-graduate residential halls to make this university completely residential; a new liturgical chapel on the East Campus, a Half-Way House between here and St. Mary's for both classes and social activities.

"So run some of our hopes for 1966. I have only touched the surface, but enough to indicate that, as Tom Dooley loved to quote from Robert Frost:

"We have miles to go
And promises to keep
And miles to go
Before we sleep."

There were implementations from the backup men: James W. Frick, Vice-President for Public Relations and

Development: "It has always been said that you can't run two capital drives back to back. 1966 will prove that wrong. There is little doubt that we will complete the Challenge II $20 million program well in advance of the Ford Foundation deadline."

Rev. Joseph Simons, Dean of Students: "The role I have in mind is that suggested by the title *Student Personnel Services*. Although "in trouble" has always meant one thing at Notre Dame, a young man may be "in trouble" a number of ways: disciplinary, financial, emotionally, medically, and so forth. The long-range hope is to provide "a place to turn" when other avenues are closed."

Rev. Joseph W. Hoffman, University Chaplain: "We shall identify our religious program with the attitude of search, so apparent in students, because Christianity is not a status but a process. More and more students are looking for ways to give witness to this faith."

Edward W. "Moose" Krause, Director of Athletics: "In addition to the varsity sports there is amazing interest in club sports: hockey, lacrosse, rugby, soccer, sailing, skiing, rowing. The new Athletic and Convocation Center will enable us to expand the whole program tremendously. Every boy will be encouraged to take part in some form of athletics."

The plush Center for Continuing Education was opened in late March, 1966, with a historic first as Catholic *periti* and hierarchy from Vatican II came from all parts of the world to have frank theological discourse with leaders of the Jewish, Protestant, and Orthodox faiths. The agenda included discussions on a wide variety of Vatican II-related topics, including the liturgy, revelation, ecumenism, relations with non-Christian religions, the role of the layman and the church in the contemporary world, marriage and family life, culture and politics, religious freedom, economics, international affairs, and the impact of Vatican II on theology in America.

In his dedicatory remarks Father Hesburgh noted that through the beneficence of the W. K. Kellogg Foundation "Notre Dame now adds a very special dimension to the total substance of learning: becoming a crossroads that welcomes traffic from every intellectual direction. Of course, one could say that of every great university. But Notre Dame is a crossroads in a very special way. We are clearly, openly and unashamedly interested in the spiritual and moral dimensions of man's main problems in our times."

Mr. and Mrs. Patrick F. Crowley, organizers of the worldwide Christian Family Movement, became the first couple to share the Laetare Medal. Both were from families having long-standing ties with the University.

Rev. Joseph Schneiders, a former Catholic who turned Unitarian, defended atheism before an overflow crowd on campus. When Father Gomar DePauw, founder of the Catholic Traditionalist Movement, was denied permission to speak or celebrate Mass at Notre Dame, a student organization, Young Americans for Freedom, sponsored his appearance at a downtown hotel, after being turned away by two other establishments. He called for returning Latin to the Catholic liturgy and denounced the "Protestanized hootenanny Mass" which had found a welcome on the campus. Rev. Schneiders said the Church should teach more St. Francis and less St. Thomas, thus substituting charity for an emphasis on faith and justice. . . . Dr. Charles Appel, President of the American Medical Association, discussed "four contemporary medical problems: mental health, alcoholism, drug addiction, and venereal disease." He drew a similarity, showed a deep relation to rising mental health problems among college-aged people. . . . The University's Academic Council cleared the way for more than one hundred former three-year pre-med students to receive bachelor of science degrees from Notre Dame. One of these, Dr. Charles Moran, of Louisville, Kentucky, joining the class of 1923 at its 45th reunion, said: "I must be the dumbest student in the history of Notre Dame, because it took me thirty-seven years to get my degree."

The Class of '66 had a 7–2–1 season in football; the "worst season in Notre Dame basketball history"; and "in a quite unprecedented move," started a class bar in the basement of a downtown restaurant. At the Student-Faculty Cocktail Hour, politics, class matters, and other subjects were discussed in "a natural, enjoyable atmosphere." The Class of '66 had the "distinct pleasure" of being the first to enjoy co-exchange classes with St. Mary's classes, "causing many a senior to wonder what he's been missing for three years."

The Voice, a bi-weekly newspaper of Student Government, editorialized against "the special academic treatment offered athletes at Notre Dame, in the areas of course scheduling, honor code violations, and grade preferences." Some metropolitan papers picked up the editorial. *The Voice* then denounced their "exaggerations and misquotes." The more venerable *Scholastic* chided *The Voice.* A University official recalls: "It was a spectacular untruth by a student publication which soon went out of business because of its lack of fairness and objectivity. It is very unusual for student editors to criticize each other."

The 1966 Sorin Award, for service to Notre Dame, went to Bernard J. Voll whose qualifications were: Advisor to Presidents from Cavanaugh to Hesburgh; Lay Trustee; Past President Alumni Association; South Bend civic leader available to the campus in myriad situations. (The Sorin award was inaugurated by the Alumni Association in 1965 with Father Hesburgh as the first recipient.)

Sixty-one percent of the 1,274 members of the class of '66 planned to continue in graduate or professional school. The Peace Corps outranked the business world 16 to 15 in future plans. The armed services claimed 189. Nineteen opted the priesthood. Two headed for nuclear power school. One hundred five planned to go to work on jobs. The Committee on Negro Enrollment contacted over 1,500 students. Of the 300 who replied, 65 applied for admission and 12 enrolled. ... Rev. James Blantz, '55, a missionary to Uganda, revealed that "a touch of homespun sorcery (magic tricks) helped attract crowds."

Alumni Notes: "Jap" Lawton, '11, sat on Sorin's knee and pulled his whiskers at age five; studied under Nieuwland; organized the Century Club of 56 members, each of whom gave $100 to the University in its 100th year. At the funeral of Joe Bach, one of the Seven Mules and later, Pittsburgh Steeler coach, his parish priest revealed that Joe had not only gone to Mass and Communion each morning, but remained to say the Stations. John Fox, '38, was made captain of the aircraft carrier, USS Independence. Tom O'Brien, '53, wrote: "Joan just delivered a new baby boy and the count is now ten —five boys and five girls—how is that for Planned Parenthood?"

Dr. Thomas Carney, Alumni President, wrote after the sudden death of Mort Goodman, member of the Alumni Board: "The first time Ara Parseghian met with us he told of a football prospect whose mother feared Notre Dame might make a Catholic out of him. The French-Armenian Presbyterian couldn't remove her fears. Mort Goodman volunteered to give testimony that it was possible to avoid conversion. He wrote a letter and the boy arrived. One day before a Board luncheon Mort offered a prayer in Hebrew. Thereafter the prayer was part of our meals. He was a living example of ecumenism before the practice became popular. *Tanuah nishmato besh shalom.* May his soul rest in peace."

43. #1 ... AND #125

ARA PARSEGHIAN is a candid fellow who consistently violates the first canon of The Perilous Profession: "Never tell 'em how many you've got coming back. Tell 'em how many you lost." He told 'em like it was at the beginning of 1966: "Our passing game in '65 was our weakest suit and it has been encouraging to view the performance of several freshmen. A rebuilding job must take place, but with the Notre Dame spirit prevailing, I have every confidence Notre Dame will be a representative team in '66."

No ambitious season ever got off to a more ghastly start, as a Purdue sophomore named Leroy Keyes plucked an Irish fumble from the air and fled 94 yards for the opening touchdown. Seconds later senior Nick Eddy returned the kickoff 94 yards and it was a tie ball game. Minutes later sophomore Terry Hanratty passed to sophomore Jim Seymour, who took the ball over his head in full stride and finished an 84-yard picture touchdown on national television that introduced the Dynamic Duo who would rewrite the Irish record books. From that moment on the forecasting scopes were turned toward East Lansing where Michigan State, the defending national champions, with Bubba Smith, George Webster, and a passel of other Jolly Green Giants, would be awaiting the Fighting Irish. It was the most ballyhooed contest of modern times. The national television audience was estimated at 33,000,000.

Before the first period ended, Parseghian was without Eddy, his game-breaker, Hanratty, his quarterback-and-passer and George Goeddeke, his center and principal blocker for the passer. The stout Irish line broke down for the first time during the season. The Spartans scored 10 quick points and humiliation loomed. (Actually, though none could even suspect it at the time, Michigan State was through offensively for the day.)

Coley O'Brien, a diabetic quarterback who had to take compensating food during the game, replaced Hanratty and led a steady march climaxed by a 34-yard perfection touchdown pass to Bob Gladieux just before the half ended. Early in the second half safety man Tom Schoen intercepted a Spartan pass and O'Brien led a 69-yard march into the barbed-wire defensive territory from where Joe Azzaro kicked a 28-yard field goal to tie the score. Michigan State never got beyond the Irish 45-yard line thereafter, but was ever dangerous because its kicker, Kenney, had already booted a field goal from the 47. Kevin Hardy, punting for the first time, was doing a magnificent job of keeping the Spartans in poor field position.

The carnage had taken a heavy physical toll. In the final minutes fullback Larry Conjar was the only regular left in the Irish offensive backfield. Any sort of a miscue could lead to the disastrous field goal which would ruin one of the great spiritual comebacks of Notre Dame's proud history. Parseghian played it safe, ran out the clock, accepted the 10–10 tie and brought forth a storm of scorn which has not completely abated through the succeeding years. The next week his quilted squad, bruised and abused and with strange faces in the line-up, beat a strong Southern California squad 51–0, and won the national championship. The performance in the final two games would have delighted Rockne himself. Gallant Coley O'Brien had cut himself a slice of that instant immortality Andy Pilney had won at Ohio State (1935), Nick Lukats at Army (1933), Norman Barry at Indiana (1920), George Gipp at Army (1920), and Dan Shannon against Oklahoma (1952).

Students laid aside concerns and causes to welcome the ninth National Champion, but the first since 1949. Townfolk came to the old gym to help shake down the thunder. Faculty people came, including some of the bearded imports, whose understanding may have been limited to the knowledge that young men they knew to be scholars demonstrated that academic and athletic excellence could coexist. And for everybody, the pure if fleeting joy of being some part of perfection.

> Breathes there a man with soul so dead
> Who never to himself has said
> We're *Number One?*

Nineteen sixty-seven was birthday one hundred twenty-five. Sorin would surely have celebrated with a most elaborate gala; but a mature alumnus who claimed, during the Reunion weekend, to have interviewed the statue of The Founder, reported that the patriarch was thinking of taking off on another of his famous world tours in search of the real Notre Dame. The Beautiful Lady was still up there on The Golden Dome, but she now wore a cloak of many colors that was changing every day.

Lay Governance. . . . Four days of closed-door debate by 44 Holy Cross priests in January ended with the announcement that Notre Dame would henceforth be governed by a Board of Trustees, in which laymen would outnumber the clerics. The President would continue to be a Holy Cross priest nominated by the Provincial. Six of the twelve Fellows who made final decisions for the full Board would be clerics; and since a two-thirds vote would be necessary for any substantial change, and the lay trustees would be mostly alumni, it was thought that the essential character of the University as a Catholic institution would be guaranteed. Only 84 of the faculty of 598 were priests. Fifteen priests were in the administration. They would "hereafter exercise an even more effective role as administrators, as teachers of theology and philosophy and in the pastoral role most remembered and treasured by alumni."

Edmund A. Stephan, '33, Chicago attorney, was Chairman of the new governing Board, with Paul F. Hellmuth, '40, Boston attorney as Secretary. The ten other Fellows were Father Howard McKenna, the Provincial; Father Hesburgh; Father John Cavanaugh, past President; Father Joyce, Executive Vice-President; Father Charles McCarragher, Vice-President for Student Affairs; Father John Walsh, Vice-President for Academic Affairs; Robert W. Galvin, Chairman of the Board of Motorola, Inc.; J. Peter Grace, President of W.R. Grace and Company; I.A. O'Shaughnessy, President of Globe Oil and Refining; and Bernard J. Voll, '17, Chairman of the Board of Sibley Machine and Foundry.

Summa. The new Board recommended another five-year drive for $52 million which would be called *Summa*. These funds would be allocated for five high-rise residence halls; 40 endowed professorships; graduate education; and special research projects including the Institute for Advanced Religious Studies. Under the guidance of James Frick, lay Vice-President for Public Relations and Development, two top-level teams, led by Father Hesburgh and Father Joyce, and supported by a nationwide advertising program, went out to get the money. (By March, 1968, 81 percent of the total had been subscribed.)

Faculty Manual. Faculty-administration relationships at

Catholic colleges had been under close scrutiny from the American Association of University Professors since the strike against tight administrative controls at St. John's University in New York City. Surveys had given Notre Dame a top rating. The faculty included non-Catholics and non-Christians. The only line drawn against an atheist was that he should not "openly display a skeptical disbelief in the ultimate truth of God's existence on which Notre Dame education is based." There had been no such problems. "It is hardly likely" Father Hesburgh said, "that a teacher who disagreed with our basic beliefs would want to work here." "The thorny 'publish or perish' controversy had been 'conspicuously inconspicuous,'" said Professor James Robinson, "because the incoming classes at Notre Dame have never gotten so big that we had to take on inadequately equipped teachers and then lower the research-requirement boom to get rid of them."

A faculty relationship had been part of the over-all plan, conceived in 1960, for the internal development of the University. The first meeting of the new Board approved a Faculty Manual which had been two years in preparation. Typically, the introduction by President Hesburgh had been written from Southern Chile, where he was in attendance at the annual meeting of the Council on Higher Education in the American Republics. "Faculty involvement in academic administration is here to stay," he wrote. "It is high time that past academic paternalism gives way to present academic participation. The Manual reveals little that would not be equally true of academic procedures in any university." (The "little" did not include his own turnback of an early draft of the faculty manual: "I see nothing here that says Notre Dame is a *Catholic* University," he said.)

Student Life Council. The student leaders of the sixties had been following the national trend toward assertive self-government. The early force had depended very much on the

SBP (Student Body President), and one leader likened the annual student protest to a balloon that rose swiftly at the beginning of each first semester and then slowly deflated. The 1967 balloon had not deflated. The first student General Assembly brought out 1,500 people to Stepan Center. As a result of this meeting, Notre Dame became the last Midwestern University to demonstrate against Dow Chemical Company; about two hundred, including priests, nuns, St. Mary's girls, and volunteers from South Bend, ignored an order from the Dean of Students to stop the demonstration.

SBP Chris Murphy dispatched a letter to Father Hesburgh, peremptory in tone, demanding an immediate meeting to "negotiate issues voted by the Student Assembly." In a published reply, the President deplored "the ultimatum tone," and said such policy matters were now decided by the Board of Trustees. A statement from the Board to the SBP is here paraphrased:

The Board did not believe that the student desire for informal meetings with young women on the campus required visitation in men's dormitory rooms. On student life and disciplinary procedures, the Board approved equal representation of faculty, administration, and students on a legislative University Student Life Council, with a comparable structure for adjudication and review in serious disciplinary matters. ... The Dean of Students would continue to have authority to act promptly in emergent situations, subject to review procedures. The Board did not accept the student requirement that the legal doctrine of "double jeopardy" had valid application to student disciplinary proceedings that followed violation of criminal laws.

The Board looked to the President as its day-to-day representative. Actions taken by tripartite bodies should stand unless the President in good conscience could not approve them, in which event the right to appeal to the Board might

229

be granted. While the Board recognized the need of the University to adapt itself to a changing world, it firmly resolved to hold fast to those values that had made Notre Dame an enriching experience, intellectual and spiritual, for so many thousands of her sons. Finally, the Board recognized that every human institution must have its creative minority and welcomed Notre Dame's "despite its occasional incivility in the published word."

Four students ran on as many tickets for SBP for the '67–'68 term. The one who said he would abolish most student government as a pompous nuisance finished third. The others were student-power advocates. The winner was Richard Rossie, a history major from Clarksdale, Mississippi. Here are various quotes from Richard Rossie:

> Student power means ability to make decisions as well as influence them. It is committed to help make decisions pertaining to the curriculum and quality of teaching.... Legislation passed by the Student General Assembly shall be kept before the Administration with diligence. And we shall expect them to act both positively and responsibly upon it. We insist on being treated as adults.... Notre Dame students are asking the Alumni for help which they know will be hard to give ... and for faith in us and this new Notre Dame we are creating.

In September, 1968, at a meeting of the Tripartite Committee with members of the Science and Engineering Advisory Councils, Richard Rossie might well have considered himself an alien among The Establishment, but he was magnificently unperturbed. In a soft voice he put the Administration on notice that it had better give serious heed to student "apprehension," because the movement was not isolated but part of a nation-wide protest. At later meetings with freshmen and other groups he spoke with similar frankness about the need to "restructure" the University. Fifteen hundred students, about one-fifth of the undergraduate body, signed a petition of impeachment. At a consequent election Richard Rossie was returned by 75 percent of the students who voted. His speeches thereafter were muted, and it was accepted by most that the students had intended only to slow him down. At least one University official thought "Richard engineered the impeachment in order to get a mandate."

Richard Rossie resembled the late Heywood Broun, in attitudes and physical displacement. He was definitely no deflating balloon. In the eyes of some students, most older alumni, probably a majority of the faculty, and very probably almost all of the administration, he was a sterling justification for the compulsory disarmament of campus rebels known as graduation. If political parties drafted recruits in the manner pro clubs draft football players, Richard Rossie might very well, in the Notre Dame tradition, have wound up No. 1.

44. THE LODGE

MILT BEAUDINE, Secretary of the over-thirty-but-hardly-ancient class of 1954, appealing to his classmates to attend their 15th reunion, warned: "It might be your last chance. Mr. Rossie may decide to abolish the custom." (If, in their "restructuring," some group of students should decide to picket the Reunions, they might be advised about the Monogram Men. These come back one day ahead, have their own golf tournament, cocktail party, dinner, and business meeting. It is not likely that tactics which succeeded with students would work with the men of Rockne or Leahy. If pickets should lie down before the door of the bar and invite the Monogram Men to "make a moral judgment" about walking over their bodies, it is possible that the huskies might pick up the bodies and not stop walking until they reached the lake.)

On Friday the complete Reunions begin with golf, bus trips, class dinners, followed by beer busts, and lantern-lit talk that goes on well into the night. Saturday has the memorial Mass for deceased members, class luncheons, more golf, seminars, and the main event, the Alumni Banquet, where the state of the University is discussed, and later dissected. Sundays it's Mass again and the noises of goodbyes, with the older ones wondering, but never out loud, which ones will never make the next one. And in among all of this are the tales of the old days, for that's what it's all about, Youth Revisited, with no titles, no failures—as when the fellow in the wheel chair was being pushed by his old buddy who happened to be Jack Scallon, President of the Pullman Company.

A very famous football star told of the time he was so busy picking up awards and making banquet speeches that he didn't get around to doing the thesis needed for his degree. He paid a shark student $50 to write one. It was a beautiful job which the Dean immediately spotted as a phony and told the star to write one himself if he wanted to graduate. The footballer went to a priest who was a philosopher and confidante of athletes. "You could stand by your guns and they couldn't prove a thing," the padre said; "or you could have your friend write another thesis, and you could rewrite it

in your own style, and that would make it reasonably legit."
And so it happened.

Bill Schmitt came to Notre Dame to take civil engineering, because it stirred images of pioneers building railroads and fighting off Indians. He played in that 1909 game with Michigan, was track captain, later did enough of those romantic things well enough to make a few million. He comes back from Portland, Oregon every football season, makes the trips with the team; and the fact that he has to use two canes never slows him up. The extra bed in his room at The Morris Inn was always reserved for drop-ins by old teammate, Red Miller.

Red Miller told of the time they couldn't sleep, and Schmitt said: "I think I'll give the University a quarter million." So Bill lit the lights and wrote out the check. And another night they couldn't sleep, and Bill decided to write out another check for a quarter million. And that's how part of the $8 million Athletic and Convocation Center got built. It took a week of celebration to get it opened in late '68, featured basketball, ice hockey, shows by Andy Williams and Bill Cosby. Because it's also a South Bend showcase its roof has twin domes; and the students call it The Golden Bra.

During the 1968 season a friend asked Bill Schmitt, "How's Red?"

"Well," Bill said, "he hasn't been well lately but I talked to him last week. Suppose I call him and you can talk with him?"

The call took a little while to get through. Red's son answered the phone. "I'd like to talk to your father," Bill said.

"I'm sorry," the son said. "My father just died."

The Millers are the most famous Notre Dame clan. Five brothers played football. Red was a DuPont lawyer. Ray was Rockne's substitute, Mayor of Cleveland, an Ohio political power, and one of the early sponsors of John F. Kennedy. He died mowing the lawn of his 50-room house. Walter played fullback alongside George Gipp. He became famous for his white borsalino hats. The Millers traveled from Cleveland for big games in caravans. Once Ray came upon a car on fire. It was Walter's car, and Walter seemed to be trapped; but it turned out he had just gone back into the burning car for his spare hats.

Don Miller was one of The Four Horsemen. He coached at Ohio State and Georgia Tech, practiced law, was mentioned as a possibility for a judge in the Nuremberg Trials. One of his daughters said, "Daddy, you know you shouldn't. After a little while you would wind up saying Goering was the best man who ever walked in two shoes." Don thinks well of everybody, except sometimes, his pal Jim Crowley, who persists in referring to Don as his blocker. Somebody sent Don a clipping, in which Rockne was quoted as saying that Don Miller had been his best running back. Don sent the clipping to Crowley, who replied: "I had heard that in his later years, Rock had a slipped disc in his head." After five girls, Don sired a son. And began bragging. He was telling how his son, only four months old, had thrown a block through a window. "I'm glad to finally hear of a Miller who could throw a block," Crowley said.

The Four Horsemen became the most famous unit in gridiron history, because they "rode together" for almost forty years after graduation, until Harry Stuhldreher's death. The fun seemed to go out of it after that. Don now comes to Notre Dame games surrounded by grandchildren and fellow judges he brings from Cleveland, where he is a referee in bankruptcy. One night two carloads of Millers and friends were riding into South Bend. Gerry, the fifth brother halfback, said: "If anybody had ever told me that on the Friday

234

night of my 25th Reunion I'd be riding into town looking for the best dish of ice cream ... "

Roger Kiley, Judge of the 7th District Appellate Court in Chicago, leading figure in The Great Books Movement, and a member of the Law Advisory Council said: "When I went out for the squad nobody seemed to know me. One day George Gipp said, 'Hello, Rodge!' I hurried to my room and wrote to my mother, telling her 'George Gipp called me by name today.' "

Rodge spoke of Joe Brandy, the gamecock quarterback of 1920. "He only weighed one hundred thirty-seven pounds but he could lick anybody on the squad. If you missed a block you had to answer to him before Rockne ever got a shot at you." Brandy publishes a newspaper in Ogdensburg, New York, still gets back to reunions, plays golf, still looks— and acts—like he could lick anybody in any club. Privately, the old quarterback probably thought Notre Dame should not have settled for the 10–10 tie against Michigan State. Publicly he roared: "And if they don't stop changing the liturgy I'm going to join the Holy Rollers."

Hunk Anderson, one of the very toughest of Our Lady's tough guys, and none more loyal, never became a Catholic. Gently twitted by teammates, he said: "You guys never taught me my beads."

Larry "Moon" Mullins was of that rare breed, a man who spoke his mind and whom everybody loved; not merely at Notre Dame, but in all of football. A member of the Library Sports & Games Committee, he was unable to attend a meeting of the Chicago group in the steak house of Johnny Lattner, in the Marina. Moon lived in the Marina complex, and ten of the old Notre Dame blues, including Kiley, Harvey Foster, Dave Condon, Joe Petritz, and Bud Dudley, walked in when he was sick. He died ten days later.

Chet Wynne came for the 45th Reunion of his 1922 class.

For one hour. Kiley and Ojay Larson looked after him. Chet died the next week. Unlike Hunk, somebody had taught him his beads.

Doctor Dom Nigro looks as sturdy as the morning he put Rockne on that plane in Kansas City, March 31, 1931. At the '68 Reunion he had Rockne's son and grandchildren in tow, taking pictures, as always. He has done more than any one person to keep Rockne's name alive. The old athletes always look up Father "Bernie" Lange, once pictured in *Strength Magazine* as having the biggest chest in the world. He doesn't cut holes in the ice to swim anymore, but still teaches weight lifting.

The Clan gathered in the new Convocation Center in January, 1969, to honor ailing Frank Leahy with a belated testimonial dinner. It packed them in, and the one thousand old players, friends and coaching rivals hoped that it might inspire college football to honor one of its great figures by electing him to its Hall of Fame. Jake Klein and Alex Wilson, the veteran baseball and track coaches, were already honored in '69 by election to the Halls of Fame of their sports.

Football holds the spotlight at Notre Dame but the other sports have maintained consistently high ratings. The Irish chose Madison Square Garden and N.Y.U., in February, 1969, to secure their 900th basketball victory. Coach Johnny Dee pointed to other all-time distinctions: "Tenth in the number of wins; played before more people than any other college basketball team; traveled more miles; two national champions and 17 All-Americans."

There is pride in any member of the Notre Dame "Lodge" who makes his letter anywhere: Carl Yastrzemski in baseball; Daryle Lamonica in football; Jack Schneider, President of Columbia Broadcasting; John Cunningham, Executive Vice-

President of the New York Stock Exchange; Harvey Foster, Vice-President of American Airlines; Nordy Hoffman, a Labor intimate of LBJ; Walter Kennedy, Commissioner of the National Basketball League; John McHale and Jimmy Gallagher of the highest councils of baseball; show-biz personalities like Charlie Butterworth, Walter O'Keefe, Tex Rickard, Regis Philbin, and Tony Bill; writers like Harry Flannery, Red Smith, Dave Condon, Bill Fox, and John Patrick; editors like Charles Hecklemann and Hal Williams.

Class rivalry and pride is expressed by boisterous applause at the Alumni Banquet; and none more sincere through the years than that of the class of '42 in '67, when two of its members were introduced: Archbishop Paul Hallinan of Atlanta (who would die shortly after), and Rabbi Albert A. Plotkin of Temple Beth-Israel, Phoenix, Arizona. The Rabbi and three Jewish classmates have long had their own motto: "Hold Aloft The Star of David Even While You Bear The Cross."

Julius Tucker never went to any college but has had a unique association representing Notre Dame athletes, from Leon Hart and Paul Hornung through to Hanratty and Seymour, in their negotiations with pro football, and without commission. (Several of the big bonus gridders have donated $5,000 each to the recent Challenge drives.) Julius, a South Bend businessman who has been advisor to every coach since Leahy, seldom misses a football practice. He is a long-time President of Sinai Synagogue where, in a 1964 testimonial, Ara Parseghian, John Dee, Paul Hornung, Father Tom Brennan, and others sat, wearing golden-domed jarlmulkes. The athletic relationship has blossomed into spiritual levels, with classes in Hebrew at Notre Dame; and annual observation of the Jewish Passover by 120 seminarians, priests and nuns at Holy Cross Seminary. The influence has spread to St. Mary's College and St. Mary's Academy.

Every so often, in the social center of the Morris Inn, the story is told of how "old" Father John Cavanaugh made it possible for young Ernie Morris to get an education; of how Ernie later handed to "young" Father John Cavanaugh a check for $1 million to build the long-needed Morris Inn. Ernie's widow was Chairman of the Women's Advisory Committee until her recent death. She was succeeded by her daughter, also an Ernie, known formally as Mrs. O.C. Carmichael, whose husband "Mike" is national chairman of the *Summa* drive.

The Notre Dame Lodge has millions of members who have never seen the place, but also exult when "we" win and suffer during Periods of Penance. Writers, broadcasters, and coaches who have come to Notre Dame for professional reasons, have found things about it to like. A national columnist recently wrote about the time "those dirty Trojans who'd snatched victory from defeat with a last-minute field goal 16–14; and suddenly there was this little Irish kid sniffling his way along the picket fence on the way to the store in the gathering gloom of a chill autumn evening, with clenched fists, occupying himself with visions of himself, resplendent in Notre Dame Green and Gold, making those incredibly long gains through stacks of bewildered Trojans." Jim Murray, syndicated columnist of the *Los Angeles Times* is not always now so reverent about the Irish, but there was his true heart in 1931. Westbrook Pegler was another whose true heart belonged to the Irish when he wasn't feuding with Rockne or being indignant about such things as the Laetare Medal going to Labor's George Meany.

And from Lindsey Nelson:

"When we chose up sides and played football on vacant lots I wanted to be Notre Dame or maybe Carideo because I thought they were the best. . . . I was a Southern Protestant (wasn't everyone?) and if I knew that Notre Dame was a

Catholic School it was of no consequence one way or another to me. . . . Working sports and radio through the years I have been impressed by the fact that many of my partners—Jim Crowley, Terry Brennan, George Conner—were Notre Dame men. As a reporter I've learned to be objective about the outcome of all football games.

"In September of 1967 I flew in to do the opener between Notre Dame and California. I got to the campus about 9 a.m., parked my car near the exit of the lot so that I could make my accustomed dash to the airport, then walked to the sports information office. There was just a touch of the Midwestern fall in the air. Students (younger each year to me) were scurrying from classroom to classroom, The Golden Dome was glittering in the sunlight, the program and banner hawkers were already about that business, and I was about to telecast another football game from the campus of Notre Dame! I never felt better in my life."

Grand Master of The Lodge for 41 years was Jim Armstrong, renaissance man, Alumni Secretary, editor of *The Alumnus,* writer, speaker, spark plug, shock absorber. When he was retired in 1967 they discarded the usual program for the annual Alumni Banquet, made Armstrong listen for hours to the good things ordinarily said about an Irishman only at his wake. They gave him the Sorin Award, made him a Doctor, named a scholarship after him, gave him a car, and a trip around the world for him and his wife, Marian. They recited the Alumni Association growth under Armstrong: From 39 local clubs and 4,000 members to 183 international clubs and 43,000 members, Universal Notre Dame Night, Notre Dame Communion Sunday, Placement Bureau, Notre Dame Foundation, Class Reunions, Alumni Senate, President of the American Alumni Council, Distinguished Service to Education Award by Columbia University. . . .

The next issue of *The Alumnus* fulminated with all these and additional personal tributes to Notre Dame's Mr. Chips. The cover had his picture; a caption *Passing of an Era;* and a top banner advertising the lead article: *Has Change Run Away with The Church?*

The conjunction was coincidental, but historically true.

45. THAT OLD-TIME RELIGION

A RECENT *Scholastic* cover depicting various student leaders and St. Mary's girls in an irreverent parody of The Last Supper brought a storm of protest from outside the University. The student editor could not understand "such a lack of a sense of humor on the part of old-line Catholics." He said he would do it again. The policy toward student publications is one of "no prior censorship," but Father Hesburgh has been pushing for a more responsible editorial board which would review written articles and statements. This student attitude in an assumedly old-line Catholic University can be better understood after a feature in *Insight,* an *Alumnus* spin-off quarterly which gives in depth treatment to specific subjects. The spring issue of 1968 carried an article: *4 Years 4 Lives in a Changing Notre Dame.* Reporters were assigned to follow four students, not typical, but representing significant types in the changing Notre Dame:

A. After one year in a seminary he had opted for the lay apostolate. A pre-med major, headed for the Harvard Medical

School, he also took humanities subjects which would help him prepare for a career as a ghetto doctor.

B. Another seminary dropout. A Danforth Fellow aiming for graduate theology study in Princeton. He wore sandals and long hair. Summered as civil rights worker in Chicago.

C. A Negro who never knew poverty. Cited by his Woodrow Wilson Fellowship for outstanding potential as a college teacher. Spent sophomore year studying in Austria. Intended to teach year in slum before entering graduate school.

D. Three-year linebacker headed for "graduate work" in pro football. Majored in economics. Interested in Russian language and would like to spend a year with Russian people. Had little time to become involved in campus politics or causes.

Some basic attitudes:

B. He had several complaints with structured Christianity, "particularly the trend to stress divinity of this one-god man." He had decided to replace membership in an institutional Christianity with "my own search for meaning and truth." He enjoyed going to Mass "to celebrate with my friends— a man needs to celebrate his God and his religiosity with his friends." He was no hippie: "I no longer feel the need to look weird. That's one reason I shaved my beard—I feel sufficiently removed from this whole bag (society) that I no longer must show it externally." He was Chairman of the Campus Coalition for Peace and had applied for draft status as conscientious objector.

C. "If Notre Dame is going to do anything for the Negro problem, she's going to have to get a whole lot more Negroes. You don't talk to people about giving Negroes justice if they've never known any Negroes." In his four years at Notre Dame he had not felt any extreme racial prejudice but had cringed at overhearing "nigger."

D. "One thing about a Notre Dame education—it isn't

handed to you. I'd liked to have spent less time on football; but there's a sense of satisfaction in doing a good job on the field. . . . And at all times you must set an example if you're a Notre Dame football player. The coach insists on a certain standard of conduct off the field and if you don't live up to it, you're in as much trouble as if you'd missed a tackle. . . . Ball players realize that if you want to attain success in athletics you've got to discipline yourself and follow a routine. If you're hungry enough, willing to sacrifice enough, you'll succeed. . . . Students should be aware of such things and discuss them, but I don't think the world's problems should pervade the student's every action and thought."

Quotes from a "bull session" following the question: Would they return to Notre Dame if they had it to do over?

A. "Yes. I think there is something happening here that just isn't happening in other places. . . . I'm talking about the interaction between the students and the clergy, men like Fathers Dunne, Burtchaell, Bartell, and Pomerlau—and the ideas that are being thrown back and forth."

C. "Yes. The only reason is because of the people, certainly not the buildings. There's a certain mystique. From a purely academic point of view I could have got an equal, in some places, much better education elsewhere."

D. "I'm very satisfied and feel exuberant about what has happened to me. I've really formed a base in this, my fourth year. In the next fifty years or so I'll find out just how good a base it is."

B. "Yes. A year ago I would have been surprised at saying that. . . . Because of the people. Not just students. I just couldn't be sure I'd run into a Burrell, Burtchaell, and Dunne somewhere else. My old man always told me, 'There's something unique about the place that is really great.' I really like what's happened to me—whatever it is and however it came about."

C. "When I was a freshman I was interested only in status. I'm not impressed by that sort of thing anymore. I'd limit myself to one or two extra-curricular activities and give my all." [Author: This is the attitude the Notre Dame Admissions Office currently emphasizes in sorting out applications.]

B. "Newman was not such a dumb cat even if he was such a legalist. You put a bunch of guys together with all the best books in the world . . . and you put them in with a couple of smart men for four years."

C. "Notre Dame is not enough of a university. Its too provincial . . . a monolithic structure: middle class, white Catholics. . . . I would recommend the increase of minority enrollment. I'd make it coed . . . varied religions, varied races. . . . That would destroy the University as it is now, but I'm not afraid of that. . . . I sort of live on two levels: the one is the here-and-now existence within my Christian community of friends. The other is that nostalgic level—Notre Dame, all men, rah, rah. I would go through it again because of the people. I wouldn't want my son to do the same."

A. "There are times when I feel we're just trying to compete with the Ivy League schools. You just don't say you're great. You work at it and let others decide."

B. "I don't think Notre Dame has the corresponding vision to its ideal of greatness."

C. "It's the Administration. Perhaps it was great fifteen years ago. But those progressive ideas are conservative today. . . . I don't think a great university puts ads in *The New York Times* apologizing for what the students have done. You never hear of Harvard apologizing." [Author: The *Times* ad rebuked James Kavanaugh for using a student invitation to speak as a springboard for announcing his defection from the priesthood, and as a plug for his book.] "To become a great university you might have to be willing to give up a couple of the prejudiced million dollars."

A. "From a purely pragmatic view ND needs all the financial support it can get. The operating budget every year is more than half the total endowment. Harvard can run for the next twenty years without having another donation. ND would have to go out of business."

C. "I don't believe that. If the alumni really loved the place . . ."

A. "That's it. They don't love the *real* place. They love 'The Golden Dome image.' "

C. "Then maybe it should go out of business."

A. "I think it should go on. It's in a period of transition."

C. "If it has to perpetuate some sort of a 'Golden Dome image' I don't think it should go on."

A. "When you come here you should stop learning and start to think. . . . I don't think it matters if you're shocked when you come out into the real world. You should confront yourself and be shocked within yourself, and things should make you get shook up a little."

B. "The mass of students around here don't think past their noses. I'm not saying they should have to run the place. I wouldn't want to figure out who was going to get what money. Students should have complete control over their own lives."

A. "That sounds like Boys' State or something. Do you think that sort of opportunity will 'make' the kid who doesn't give a damn about anything anyway?"

C. "I thought Jacqueline Grennan had a good idea. She has students on every board."

A. "I don't know whether students are mature enough."

C. "I compare the University to the Legion of Decency. If we can't make decisions it's because we have decisions made."

B. "Breen-Phillips is the standard old freshman hall with rah-rahs. There are a few upperclassmen, and the rest of them

244

are sophs who are as bad as the freshmen. The whole attitude is to get around the rules as much as they can."

A. "So you take away the rules? They must make decisions about whether to drink, whether to study. Those are decisions."

B. "I'm not talking about small things—like drinking and women. A freshman should have as much voice as a senior."

D. "Put yourself in the position of the Administration. Do you open the floodgates hoping the freshmen will come in, accept the spirit of the law, forget the letter of the law? Can we afford to take this chance?"

B. "If you want legalism . . . go ahead. You hope for the kind of students who are going to accept a challenge."

A. "There are people whose lives are just parties, and the movies, and dates, whose lives are pretty screwed up. I'm in pre-med and there are guys who are way ahead of me in lab, but they couldn't care less about all kinds of relevant issues. It's just 'gotta get to med school, gotta get to med school.' "

B. "The professors should live on campus . . . so they wouldn't have to throw a party to give the students a chance to talk to them outside of class. They should not have a guy come out of the laboratory and slap down his notes and sneer at everybody for forty-five minutes. I've got a course like that right now."

[And about religion:]

B. "Notre Dame should be directed away from a primarily Catholic orientation. . . . I'm more concerned about religiosity than Catholicity."

A. "The thing that held people to Catholicism through the centuries was that it was so legal, so solemn. You always knew where you stood. Today Catholicism is just one base of a pyramid. The University must first be Christian and then catholic, with a small 'c'."

46. CATHOLIC OR CHRISTIAN?

Religion on Campus: To Be Catholic or Christian?

THE lead article, unsigned, in the March-April 1968 *Alumnus,* which carried the above title, began by having "Alumni" ask, "in a resentful sort of way" what had happened to religion on campus; and students replying: "It's dead. It's not so much the Catholic religion anymore as it is Christianity." The article went on from there:

> The answer stuns Notre Dame parents and grads. And the gulf widens because the point in question is that aspect of a Notre Dame education which has meant most to alumni from the days when Notre Dame was a model Catholic university, where glowing reports told of the thousands of students attending daily Mass. Religiosity was then measured by the endless lines before the confessional. Visitors were always impressed by the host (Communion) charts that were faithfully tallied each day in each hall chapel. May devotions to the Grotto were something to behold. The entire student body poured into the shrine every evening to say the rosary. Underlying this spiritual fervor was a unique brand of discipline which, in the eyes of Notre Dame followers, produced a unique kind of man. People had admiration for an educational system that demanded morning Mass checks, bed checks, no girls on campus after dark, no cars, no lights after midnight. . . .

In those terms Notre Dame has indeed changed. Religion's sacrosanct ritual has been dispelled and will not likely return. Students now search for a more qualitative life. The new sense of religion is reflected . . . by the student's disdain for the institutionalized Catholic Church and its purely legalistic outlook and for the double standard observed by most Catholics today. Instead, students are looking for a personal Christ-centered way of life, an existence that attempts to live the story of the gospels.

The *Alumnus* article continued to spell it out for the alumni:

A freshman usually comes to Notre Dame steeped in the traditional Catholic background fostered by his family and his earlier formal education. But after a year or two in the academic community he comes across new ideas about religion. There is quite likely no average Notre Dame student; instead there are categories in which most students find themselves. These include:

1. The intensely religious who look upon their mission as being simply Christian. Their number is growing through their more progressive liturgical services and by enlisting other students.

2. The traditional Catholics who merely fulfill Sunday obligations. Their religious faith has been formed more out of ritualistic habit than by personal ascertainment.

3. The indifferent for whom personal convenience guides religious activities. They don't try to think out their lives as Christians. They just exist.

4. The rebels who detest the hypocrisy and ambivalence they feel is widespread in Catholic society. They react negatively to the institutional church.

5. Those who find no personal meaning whatever in the life of the church.

The article concluded: "God is very much alive at Notre Dame but no longer in the May processionals nor at the late

Sunday morning Masses. Rather he (small h) is found in the emerging Christian community of the halls; the ghetto schools of South Bend; the slum-ridden neighborhoods of Chicago. Old-time religion is gone. But Christ is not."

Father John S. Dunne graduated from Notre Dame in 1951, studied at Gregorian University in Rome, now teaches theology at Notre Dame, where he has become influential and popular among students by "dismissing the old traditional dogmatic teaching that the existence of God and the immortality of man's soul can be proven by logical reasoning." (Columnist Jimmy Breslin wrote: "Father John Dunne instructs his theology classes not to believe everything in the catechism books on which nearly all Roman Catholics were raised. His views, and the views of his students, would cause old Diocese of Brooklyn worshippers to light banks of candles for his soul.")

"The old system of teaching theology here was to start by taking all the important things for granted," Father Dunne stated. "They were presented as established truths by ingeniously reconciled arguments which nobody really questioned. Now we start by questioning everything. Thus faith is no longer blindly accepted. It's reached for in a spirit of inquiry. . . . The young man who comes here goes through a transition, a developmental process. He is passing from the faith of childhood, which is really not his own faith, but that of his parents and teachers, to a faith that is his own. There is a kind of apparent agnosticism which you find in colleges which is not real agnosticism at all. I think our students, especially the bright ones, are not agnostic; they are highly concerned religiously. What they are going through is a discovery process."

A former Dean of Students, then working with the Counseling Center: "Today's student is a troubled one. He's in conflict with his parents. His inherited religion turns him off. He's confronted with the draft. He asks: 'Now that I need help, what does Catholicism do for me?' The University can help most by encouraging him to continue his search for himself." In this context Father Joseph Fey, University Chaplain, sees the need for hall chaplains trained in psychological counseling. "The campus has grown by leaps and bounds, except, unfortunately, for the number of priests."

Father James Burtchaell, Chairman of the Theology Department, was quoted: "The real hangup in teaching theology is that we have to undo all the religious education the students have received in high school. They aren't ready to explore theology. As far as they are concerned, theology is a hard and fast set of teachings from which there is no recourse. Actually, theology courses should not be preachings but subjects in which students learn what yesterday's and today's Christians have thought." What Student *A* called "Burtchaell's Mass" was described in *Insight:*

Father Sorin would be somewhat perplexed by the dialogue homily Mass with guitar music which was held Saturday at 11:30 p.m. this year in the Dillon Hall Chapel. Celebrated by Father Burtchaell it was usually attended by 50 students from all over the campus and a sprinkling of St. Mary's girls and women graduate students. One night, after hearing confessions, the Mass began, a girl strummed her guitar, and the group sang:

> "Here we are—all together
> As we sing our song, joyfully
> Here we are, joined together
> As we pray we'll always be...."

The gospel of the day was on loving neighbors. Father Burtchaell opened the dialogue homily with a question of whether it is more difficult to love a stranger than to love members of one's own family. A boy in the fifth row raised his hand and other students discussed the problem.... At the consecration of the Mass everybody left his seat and gathered together closely around the altar table, singing, "Eat His Body, Drink His Blood, and We'll Sing a Song of Love." Before distributing Communion Father Burtchaell shook hands with a student near him who in turn passed the handclasp—a contemporary gesture akin to the "Kiss of Peace"—around to the rest of the group. When Mass ended Father Burtchaell joined everybody for coffee and doughnuts in a room down the corridor before hurrying off to spend the night with a dozen students from Dillon Hall who were on a weekend retreat at the Old College Building.

Father Burtchaell graduated from Notre Dame, received a degree of sacred theology at Gregorian in Rome, a licentiate in sacred theology from Catholic University, a bachelor's degree in sacred scripture from the Pontifical Bible Commission in Rome and his Ph.D. from Cambridge in England. He aligned squarely against the Pope in the controversy over "The Bitter Pill," called the encyclical "grossly inadequate and largely fallacious," stressed that it did not "allege infallibility" and was open to debate. He called the pressure being exerted by bishops and cardinals to force priests to conform "plainly blackmail."

At thirty-five, Father Burtchaell is obviously a man of the future at Notre Dame unless (as did Father John Zahm) he should project too far entirely too fast. He has darting bird-like eyes, rubber-band responses, and the sometimes terrifying certitude of invincible youth. There is nothing of the dreamer, the actor or the egotist about him. He has the gift of tongue which has served both Father Hesburgh and Father John Cavanaugh so well, the ability to translate lofty concepts, difficult for any but the scholar, into easy workingman's language. He obviously likes and is interested in people; when informed of the intention to do this book, he replied: "Don't forget the little people." Specifically, he meant people like Johnny Mangin, the chauffeur-character favorite of Notre Dame Presidents and Provincials.

Father Burtchaell said he was confessor of "three of the four" students profiled in *Insight.* He definitely does not encourage or condone violent dissent. He did not approve of the priests picketing bishops who were in conference in Washington about the encyclical. He is a personable, enormously talented young man who has been brought to the intellectual summit, who is doing what he was trained to do on that level, and would like to keep it there. He said he would feel very badly indeed if any waves he made should spill down into the parishes and dampen the faith of parishioners.

Father Dunne, thirty-eight, one of the recipients of the Harbison Awards for distinguished teaching in 1968, was to use the $10,000 grant to take time off and write his third book. In an interview at the time he said he had never been criticized by higher authority at Notre Dame for any of his teaching views; but he knew they were criticized by some.

The questioning of everything, and the encouraging of immature minds to question everything, is itself questioned by older priests. One was quoted in *Insight:* "I wonder if Hesburgh's plan to turn the University over to laymen was not really a cautious move to protect Notre Dame against the increasingly liberal views of some of the younger Holy Cross Fathers."

The Alumni Association conducted a campus seminar on the subject: *Is Change Running Away with the Church?* It later "took to the road" in a few major cities. Much of the content was philosophical and theological. Here are conclusions of the finalists on subjects most disturbing to what might be called "the troops" of the Catholic Church, including most older Notre Dame alumni:

Father Charles Sheedy, Dean of Theological Studies and

Institutes, finished his discourse on *The New Morality:* "Think of being a Catholic in all the old ways. Don't think of the Church as going soft or Protestant. The new morality will actually be harder, not easier, because it will be less covered by detailed rules, less open to minimalism, more requiring of generosity and extra action. Love the Blessed Mother, say the Rosary, go to confession and Holy Communion frequently, be a Catholic and be known as a Catholic, in the parish, the neighborhood, and the office. And do all of these things with the large, forgiving and humble heart that is the gift of the Holy Spirit."

Father Albert Schlitzer, discussing *Wanted, Dead or Alive: GOD:* "Men are frightened at the absence of God from the world. They are terrified at God's silence, at His withdrawal into His own inaccessibility. . . . This experience which men think they must interpret as atheism is a genuine experience of the most profound existence. . . . In this age of the 'Death of God,' God has become more truly Godlike."

Father James Burtchaell on *Authority vs. Conscience:* "No authority exists which can force a man to disregard his own conscience. The Second Vatican Council did flinch a bit in hesitating to apply this even to the society which we call the Church. I don't think this was good. No man, not even the Pope, can ask or should want to ask any of us to act contrary to our best conscience. . . . Authority in the Church does not reside in a few, but in all of us. . . . There is a problem in the Church today, as people break away from the officers of the Church who dislike the loosening hold they have on people's consciences. . . . I compare this to the situation of a family whose children are beginning to emerge from adolescence. . . . Conscience craves the thought that everyone of us . . . would feel quite lost if we did not have the Church to rely upon. Not that our instructions are all sealed in an envelope for us, but that we depend very much on that corporate and common explanation, that wisdom which is to be found here, there and everywhere in the church."

J. Philip Gleason, Assistant Professor of History, on *Why Bother Being a Catholic?* ". . . The question constitutes a direct challenge to faith itself. . . . A period of upheaval such as the present one tends to muddle things previously thought settled . . . might cause a person to wake up some morning and find that he didn't care any more. . . . The way to arrive at firmness of faith is not to be always cross-examining ourselves. . . . Deliberate self-analysis of a mental state is the surest way to destroy the mental state that is the object of analysis. How many happy marriages would we have if husbands and wives constantly interrogated themselves and each other about . . . whether they had a happy marriage? . . . One must confront the present situation in the light of his own experiences. . . . Can he find something better? Better than what he has had? Where can he go?"

The full texts of the seminar were published in *The Alumnus*. All of Father Burtchaell's opinions quoted in this book were issued previous to the Vatican strictures in December 1969 against such dissent.

47. THE LOST IMAGE

AMBROSE "BUD" DUDLEY came to Notre Dame from Philadelphia. He played baseball and football, was President of the class of 1942. In World War II he flew 54 missions in an Air Force B-24 Bomber and was awarded the Distinguished Flying Cross. He was Athletic Director of Villanova for four years, and emerged as an imaginative promoter. He created the Liberty Bowl in football, nursed it through sickly infancy in the Philadelphia climate, brought it through to stability in Memphis, Tennessee. In 1964 he was in charge of the United States ice hockey team that played a series of games in Russia and Czechoslovakia. He is the father of six, has spent a lifetime dealing with youth, has been in demand as a speaker for high-school, college, and other young audiences.

Through the years he evolved a speech which deplored the corruption of American youth by "intellectual malcontents and beatniks," especially on the college campus. He called upon athletes to "assume their normal roles as leaders and men of responsibility," to take a leading part in every student activity, to react politically on campus against the small group of students, "basically jealous of athletic ability," who had been creating "a distorted image of all men of brawn and brains." It was a very popular speech in the early sixties, frequently reprinted. When Dudley became President of the Notre Dame Alumni Association in 1967 it was reprinted in the *Alumnus*.

It brought down the thunder from the student sky at Notre Dame. One of the younger alumni letter-writers wanted to "impeach" the President. For months *The Alumnus* was kept busy reiterating that the article represented the private views of Ambrose Dudley. Louis Buckley, former member of the Alumni Board, outstanding secretary of the Class of '35, as beloved to Notre Dame people as Bud Dudley, but of opposite viewpoint, registered his dissent while mildly deploring that few letters of protest had come from the over-forty group of alumni. The inference was that these probably agreed with Bud since they were also products of the times and teachings of John (Faithful) Cardinal O'Hara in the era of

"The Golden Dome image." Mature *status quo* people ordinarily do not write as many letters as young Image Breakers; but some were printed in *The Alumnus.*

An unidentified San Franciscan replied to an Alumni Survey:

"There is another trend in progress I wish had appeared on your questionnaire. It is the growing official sanction of secularism and spiritual decline among students and faculty. Or perhaps it should be expressed as a more or less conscious departure from Catholic orthodoxy and worship. This, I think, is almost satanic, and if it is allowed to continue at a recent pace, I fear it will wreck all the good things in the intellectual order. . . . I hope it will not be necessary to decide whether to be good at being Catholic or good at being a university. If this is necessary, I would opt for the first because it is more transcendentally important to individuals and to society at large."

From Leo C. Heringer, '24: "Today some lay people, including wearers of Papal Decorations; straggly-haired, miniskirted nuns; and Catholic clergy, including wearers of the black, the purple and the red, are reaching for the "bottle" of public dissent. . . . The catch-all term 'conscience' is but the weakest possible alibi for REBELLION AGAINST DISCIPLINE at every level of society, including Catholic schools and the Catholic religion. . . . Without obedience to Pope Paul VI and his successors there cannot be a Catholic Church. If Notre Dame denies this truth then Notre Dame is a fountain of heresy and *The Alumnus* is an accomplice."

William Mitsch, '35, long-time Secretary of the Notre Dame Club of the Ohio Valley, quoted an editorial from the Wheeling, West Virginia *News-Register,* which deplored the Last Supper cover of *The Scholastic,* and wondered about "continued financial and vocal support." Mitsch said Harry Hamm, the writer of the editorial, was a friend of Notre

Dame who frequently attended club affairs. He added: "We have had no club meetings since last fall because the local alumni have been succesively shocked by such *Alumnus* articles as *Religion on Campus,* which was evidently not written by someone who lived there during the time described."

Mitsch, father of two student sons and a frequent campus visitor, concluded:

"The students of yesterday were confused as those of today. They looked to their instructors and to the administration for guidance. Today's students are guided by other students who have to be controversial to maintain their positions. Because the present-day students do not have faculty leaders to turn to, radical student groups seize the opportunity to expound their ideas. The public is led to believe that all of the ideas and activities which get into print are approved by the Administration. We still have a hard time proving around here that Kavanaugh was not a former President of Notre Dame."

A veteran campus observer arrived at much the same conclusion separately:

"Father Hesburgh followed the move begun by President John Cavanaugh to get the University into the mainstream. He did that just about the time all hell broke loose in the mainstream. And by this time Hesburgh himself was so caught up in the mainstream in most laudable activities for the University that he was away half of his time. Students have been testing authority around here for 125 years. This crop moved into a partial vacuum, found the customary administration defenses just not there; and they've been having a ball. Hesburgh is trapped in the backwater of the very freedom of thought he encouraged. . . . Something of the same testing has been happening with some of the younger priests. In this field it would seem to be up to the Provincial rather than the President to draw the lines."

The Advisory Councils meet in the spring; and in the fall, on a football weekend. In addition to their specific interests, there are group sessions attended by top-level administrative people; and talks by either Father Hesburgh or Father Joyce about the state-of-the-University. Here are the author's general observations gathered from such sources:

On campus there were roughly five groups of students:

1. *The Students for a Democratic Society* (SDS), militants, assumedly with outside guidance and financing. There were about thirty actual members. They could attract from two hundred to three hundred people, some from downtown. Their probable purpose was to repeat at Notre Dame, a most excellent background for television news programs, what they accomplished at Columbia.

2. *The Activists....* Those who took campus politics seriously, joined campus parties, campaigned and elected the SBP and other student-body officers. At Notre Dame they are not formally allied to the NSA (National Student Association), but seem to follow its general policies. Their power comes from control of a budget of over $90,000 student fees collected by the University. This budget permits them to invite sometimes controversial "name" speakers. In the 1968–1969 election, Richard Rossie received 2,485 votes of the 4,197 (of about 6,000 eligible) who voted for SBP.

3. *The Passively Involved....* Assumedly most of the 2,485 who voted for Rossie; the "troops" who do not turn out for all meetings but rally to the support of the student officers and generally follow the NSA (non-violent) line.

4. *The Non-Involved....* The 1,800 or so who did not bother to vote; assumedly included most of the "gotta get into med school" people who left the political field to the "serious guys." (These will probably become the non-voting

257

citizens who will permit political minorities to control elective offices.)

5. *The Athletes.* . . . Much too busy to bother with campus "causes." They are subject to the athletic discipline (previously mentioned by Student D). They want to "make the team" for a) personal pride; and b) collect the future financial rewards in professional sport for college graduates with athletic fame and superior talent.

Coaches from visiting schools have always been envious of the enthusiasm shown by Notre Dame students and consider it an asset. But there are indications that the traditional fervor is cooling. An editorial in the *South Bend Tribune* during the 1968 season was headed "An Old Friend Is Sick." The old friend was identified as the famous Notre Dame Spirit. Notre Dame students still go to games and make loud noises at pep meetings, but they no longer make those long marches in the snow to meet a losing team; or a winning team. Sports writers made quite a point in 1968 that Notre Dame, which made its reputation winning the ones it was supposed to lose, was now blowing big football games it was supposed to win. They laid it to some deficiency in Coach Parseghian. Some alumni see a possibly deeper, more disturbing cause. They point out that spirit thrives on faith; that the squads began to fold spiritually at about the time in the last few years that Catholic began to be spelled with a small *c* and God with a small *g;* when "philosophers" like Kavanaugh and Hefner began to become more chic on campus than Aquinas; when a Playmate-of-the-month in 1968 was awarded as a prize in a class raffle; when The Last Supper became a gimmick for a gag; when the class of '68 discarded the traditional Patriot-of-the-year for a Senior Fellow because "it was the feeling of many seniors that love of mankind is a prerequisite to love of country" and anyhow "patriotism was so hard to define."

Student activists have given widest latitude to the Open Speaker ruling admitting anybody "whose message might have some value to the academic process." Some of these, at fees up to $2,500, seem surprised to find themselves (as Norman Mailer was) at Notre Dame. Many would seem to add no shine to the Golden Dome. Official policy rests on the premise that since students read about controversial people they should be permitted to put them under the personal microscope, and that such close study might produce something like the results achieved by isolating a virus in the Lobund Laboratory. In some cases this seems to have worked out. In recent appearances standing ovations have been common; but Kavanaugh's emphasis on sex seemed unseemly from one who, at the time of his speech, was still technically a priest; Dr. O'Leary gave evidence of being high on his own drug petard; Tom Hayden threw mud on the image of Dr. Tom Dooley who had (he said), "created a popular feeling about intervention in Viet Nam by using the philosophy of charity." Jacqueline Grennan, admired by student C, carved out a new character of campus mother-in-law by carping about the residential aspect of Notre Dame which has been singled out by many newcomers to the faculty as one of its most impressive strengths. A 1968 *Scholastic* editorial implied that all this importation of page-one names was sophomoric showing off; that the money and time might better be spent on promoting campus art and student artists.

Notre Dame was comparatively free of student demonstrations until November, 1968, when, before the Georgia Tech football game, a mournful group marched solemnly in the rain as the crowd gathered, displaying bedsheets that informed "Ara" that "the day of the all-white backfield" was past, as O.J. (Simpson) and Leroy (Keyes) had proven. Ara replied that there were eight blacks on the combined varsity and freshmen squads, and he would be very happy if another

O.J. or Leroy turned up among them. (Notre Dame had been actively recruiting blacks with or without athletic ability for several years and had provided an office from which the group could organize for self-expression.)

Two weeks later a threatened disruption of the UCLA-Notre Dame basketball game, which officially opened the new Convocation Center, was averted by campus diplomacy. There was an orderly demonstration against recruiters for the Dow Chemical Company; but on the same day, access to the room where the CIA was interviewing was blocked by a layer of demonstrators. Father James Riehle, Dean of Students, warned the offenders that they could be suspended from school and subject to arrest by civil authorities. His order to move was ignored but the CIA averted further disturbance by closing up shop. Father Hesburgh was not on campus. When he returned he characterized the action as "tyranny" and called upon all formal organizations of Students, Faculty, and Alumni to express themselves, with the hope that a united community front would serve as a warning to the demonstrators and avert the necessity for severe unilateral action by the Administration.

During Thanksgiving vacation a national conference on Institutional Racism, sponsored by the NSA, was held at the Center for Continuing Education. Father Hesburgh as host and a charter member of the Civil Rights Commission, was a speaker. For the first time in its one hundred twenty-five-year history, Notre Dame heard one of its Presidents heckled. After the disturbers had left there was a long question-answer period. *The New York Times* reported that Father Hesburgh said he could see no connection between Reserve Officer Training Corps classes and racism. The basic question was a tough, grinding job not to be solved by emotion. "If you really want to help, for the love of Mike, get competent about the problem."

The situation finally erupted in early February, 1969, during a sanctioned week-long student seminar on Pornography. On the second day a motion picture was shown. The public had been invited. In its coverage of the event *The Alumnus* said: "The film had been judged by the Supreme Courts of New York and Michigan as 'hard-core pornography.' The U. S. Supreme Court had refused to review the New York decision. As a result University officials felt the film would probably be in violation of the applicable laws of the state of Indiana. Student leaders then banned the film."

A group of dissident students showed the film. James L. Clancey, legal council for the Citizens for Decent Literature, swore out a warrant to seize the film. They were physically attacked and defended themselves with chemical mace. No arrests were made, although a few minor injuries were treated after the scuffling for the film. The hard-core activists had turned out their usual complement of two hundred to three hundred, including some St. Mary's girls and "townies."

Father Hesburgh released a letter to students and *their parents* proclaiming what the headlines and television programs called "Notre Dame's Tough Policy." It spelled out several points: a) Dissent would be permitted, even encouraged. b) Interference with the rights of others would not be permitted. c) If it happened again, the identity cards of the students would be lifted, meaning they would no longer be classed as students and would be subject to civil arrest as intruders. It would be assumed that those who did not surrender student cards were not students. The letter denied the "myth" that a college student, or member of the faculty, could not be arrested for civil crime while on college property. Father Hesburgh made it plain he would stand by it: "I have no intention of presiding over a spectacle. Too many people have given too much of themselves and their lives to this University to let this happen here. Without being melodramatic, if this conviction makes this my last will and testament to Notre Dame, so be it."

His eight-page letter was accompanied by endorsements from the Student Life Council, Faculty Senate, Academic Council, and alumni. The glue had held.

The ultimatum was widely publicized and acclaimed. President Nixon endorsed it in a "Dear Ted" letter and asked that the Notre Dame head direct his comments on campus unrest in general to Vice-President Agnew who was convening a meeting of the fifty state governors in Washington. In doing this Father Hesburgh urged that universities be allowed to settle their own problems whenever possible. He said that a disrupted school should not hesitate to summon any outside assistance "necessary to preserve the university and its values," but that only the university should make a decision.

College officials interviewed by the *Wall Street Journal* were inclined to doubt that Father Hesburgh's "fifteen minutes to meditate or else" policy would work anywhere but Notre Dame. As the Irish campus remained peaceful during disruptions at Harvard, Cornell, California, and elsewhere, Hesburgh became a household name and a hero in many quarters, some of which embarrassed him as a practicing liberal. In March, when he moved up to the chairmanship of the Civil Rights Commission, he said "Too much emphasis has been placed on the fifteen-minute business. Whether it is fifteen minutes or fifteen hours, a student must make the decision to respect the values of a community. If not, he forfeits his right to be a member of that community."

Hesburgh did have certain things going for him—the traditional "glue" of the student body; a reasonably contented faculty; a sophisticated group of trustees. But in typical fashion he had seen what was coming, united his community beforehand, and made his pronouncement in an atmosphere of reasonable calm. The militants, caught with their emotions down, made no further moves during the remainder of the term. Student editors continued target practice, charging that their Prexy had been pressured by the fund-raisers. Visiting speakers paid their disrespects. Dick Gregory advised Hesburgh to "look to his recruiting practices"; Adam Clayton Powell, as one clergyman to another, observed that Hesburgh should "go to the mourners' bench until he sees the light." Eugene McCarthy, a member of the Notre Dame Library Council, on campus to become the first Senior Class Fellow, wondered whether such a pronouncement had been necessary, said it reminded him of a band leader who had threatened dismissal to any member of his all-girl orchestra caught chewing tobacco.

Richard Rossie told a Rotarian audience he opposed violence but went along with the Yippies because "it's better to take the wrong path than not to become involved at all." His successor as Student Body President, Philip McKenna, went into action in May with a twin broadside: 1) Withdraw all academic recognition of the campus R.O.T.C. programs, and 2) Open up meetings of the Board of Trustees to "any member of the community" and publish the minutes of such meetings. The student R.O.T.C. groups responded with a campus poll in which 61 percent of 2800 students who took part had favored "retention of academic credit for voluntary R.O.T.C. at Notre Dame." Father Hesburgh announced that the trustees would hold "open forums" four times each year at which representatives of students, faculty, and administrators would be welcome. Following a request by the Student Life Council, the trustees relaxed a previous decision by agreeing to allow women visitors in dormitories on weekends for a one-semester trial period.

48. THE LANDSCAPE OF GOD

FATHER HESBURGH has magnificent health, which with-
stands the vagaries of climate and food as he logs about
130,000 miles a year. In one week in 1967 he attended Atomic
Energy sessions in Vienna, visited Pope Paul in Rome, met
in Jerusalem with Jewish, Orthodox, and Protestant scholars
to discuss the operations of a new interfaith center there;
and kicked off the *Summa* financial drive in New York. It is
not unusual for him to spend the business day in New York,
Washington, or the West Coast, fly home and put in six hours
in his office on routine affairs, including an average of two
hundred letters a day which he answers in any of several
languages. He has a sparsely furnished cubicle in Corby Hall
where he may get six hours sleep between three and nine
a.m., but he lives in his office in the Main Building. If the
light is on at night, a student knows the President's door will
be open.

Father Hesburgh is a foremost exemplar of his own policy
of Continuing Education for adults. He is aware of the latest
moves in science, philosophy, civil rights, the revolution
within the Church, the student ferment. It is doubtful if any
one individual has had more opportunity to personally observe recent important events throughout the world. He gets

his exercise from moving around; his only sport is fishing, which he seldom gets to enjoy. He thrives on coffee, smokes cigarettes through a holder, gives interviews in odd moments and places, talks freely, answers quickly and in man-on-the-street language.

A supporter of celibacy, he points to the demands on his own time as a major reason why priests should not marry. He favors the new freedom for nuns; has nothing against student beards; thinks the ferment in the Church will settle down in about ten years with all the fundamentals strengthened. The only subject in which he has withheld a public personal opinion was the controversy about The Pill. In a press conference shortly after Father Burtchaell's lecture on that subject but before the Vatican statement of January, 1969, he said: "All the various sciences will be examining the encyclical at all the universities in the world. The best comments have not yet been made."

He said he had "personally and privately" conveyed his reactions to the encyclical to "the highest authorities" in the Catholic Church. Some deduced that he had withheld comment because of his close association with Pope Paul. (*The Alumnus* printed an article by Dr. George Shuster in which the latter, as a loyal Catholic, pleaded with His Holiness to grant "an indult that would permit the use of The Pill until the rhythm method was scientifically perfected." Dr. Shuster said there was ample precedent for such an action which would "not alter the Pope's moral position nor question the privilege of the magisterium.") There have been no further statements from high level Notre Dame people following the Pope's warning against public dissent.

"I'm against half the stuff around here," Hesburgh said in a 1968 interview, "but we're in the world of ideas. Ideas are going to be discussed and none are out of bounds. But we're not going to turn the University over to the students to run." In all this the President obviously has the firm backing of the Lay Trustees whose chairman, Edmund Stephan, told the Advisory Councils: "Academic freedom obviously includes the right of anybody to say the latest thing that pops into his head. . . . Students are difficult, lazy, occasionally lovable. . . . After two world wars there have been some breakdowns in family life and within the Church. . . . The Order has sweated out this place for one hundred twenty-seven years. . . . Change when necessary but hold fast to proven values."

Father Hesburgh is firm in the belief that Notre Dame has always found its man to fit the times. "Can you imagine" he asked [the author], "Father O'Hara going over to the library and cleaning out books with four-letter words in these days?" He thought the current student body was the best ever at Notre Dame; more knowledgeable, but not necessarily more mature. In a *South Bend Tribune* interview he said that less than five percent could be described as dedicated activists, but by capturing political offices and editorial control, these gave a false impression of student thought.

He was not worried about any lasting effect on the religious faith students brought with them. "Students start to change a half-hour after they graduate." He named a recent campus leader who had been anathema to traditionalists. "Where do you think he chose to become engaged? In the Grotto at midnight." (And he was joining a distinguished segment of the Notre Dame family.) The more recent graduates, Hesburgh added, had a better proportionate record than the older groups in supporting the financial drives.

At the Convocation celebrating the 125th Anniversary of the University President Hesburgh delivered what he called "in many ways the most important talk I have ever given." It was printed in a booklet of other addresses and titled "The Vision of a Great Catholic University in the World

Today." He has included its main points in shorter speeches on other occasions, significantly during the *Summa* campaign. It has been called "Hesburgh's Idea of a University," especially since it incorporated the thought that Cardinal Newman's classic of that name would not be viable in the climate of today. In it he touches upon most of the subjects which have made Notre Dame controversial among some of its own people and conservative Catholics. What follows is a repertorial digest (by the author), of his policies, thoughts, and hopes regarding the University which, forsaking all others, has become his life:

The great universities of the Middle Ages, Paris, Oxford, Cambridge, Bologna, and others had been Catholic and often Papal foundations. They turned to the Church for the charters that would guarantee a freedom they could not then have from the State.

In all of them there had been a faculty of theology and around "this mistress science" their intellectual life had turned. The conjunction of the Church and the University was ruptured in the years following the Reformation and especially the French Revolution. When restored as State universities they became academies for the exploration and exposition of natural truths alone.

Today we are trying to re-create great Catholic universities; but in a different world and climate of opinion. Newman's *Idea of a University* can no longer be a complete model. To his exclusively *teaching* British institution we have added the German concept of *graduate* and *research* functions; and since the end of World War II, the new function of *service* on local, state, national, international levels.

The internal structure of the American university has undergone further change. Freedom and autonomy are still central but are buttressed by a system of governance that involves diverse layers of power and decision: Board of trustees, faculty, administration, alumni, and students. All are not equal, but each group has its say. This is the world into which the Catholic university is being reborn.

The Church did not create this modern university. If the Church is to enter, it must observe the reality and terms of the modern world.

George Bernard Shaw called a Catholic university a contradiction of terms. Dr. Harvey Cox says the institutional church should stay out. This negative attitude is also found within the Catholic Church. Miss Jacqueline Grennan, in secularizing her former Catholic Webster College, said: "the academic freedom which must characterize a university would provide continuing embarrassment for the Church if the hierarchy were forced into negating the action of a university."

One now sees the clear value of the initiative Notre Dame took in placing the University under lay governance. Under the new form, fully approved by the Holy See, Notre Dame is totally governed by a largely lay Board of Trustees, comparable to any other university board.

A quotation from Vatican II's *Church in the World Today:* "In order that they may fulfill their function, let it be recognized that all the faithful, whether clerical or lay, possess a lawful freedom of inquiry, freedom of thought, and freedom of expressing their minds with humility and fortitude in those matters in which they enjoy competence."

The university is not the Church. It might be said to be *of* the Church as it serves both the Church and the people of God, but it certainly is not the magisterium. It is not the Church teaching but a place—the only place—in which Catholics and others meet on the highest level of intellectual inquiry, seek out the relevance of the Christian message to all of the problems and opportunities that face modern man and his complex world.

A great Catholic university must be a great university that is also Catholic . . . and something more.

All human intellectual questions, if pursued far enough,

reveal their philosophical and theological dimension. The university, as Catholic, must deepen this dimension of discourse so badly interrupted, to our loss, several centuries ago. Without a deep concern for philosophy and theology there is always the danger that the intellectual and moral aspects of human knowledge become detached and separated; that *technique* can become central, rather than the human person for whom technique is presumably a service. Social scientists can close their eyes to human values; physical scientists can be unconcerned with the use of the power they create. The presence of philosophy and theology moves every scholar to look beyond his immediate field of vision to the total landscape of God; and man; and the universe.

Some scholars are committed to agnosticism and a host of other positions. Is the commitment to a university as Catholic less sacred or permissible in a university world, if made freely and intelligently? Should a commitment to universality of knowledge by whatever means . . . be looked upon as retrogressive?

Notre Dame can perform a vital function in the wide spectrum of American higher learning by doing what many other universities cannot or will not do—give living, vital witness to the wholeness of truth from all sources, both human and divine, while recognizing the sacredness of all truth, from whatever source; and the validity and autonomy of all paths to truth.

What kind of a place will Notre Dame be in the years ahead if we accomplish all we have in mind?

1. It will bring to light, in modern focus, the wonderfully traditional and ancient adage: *intellectus quaerens fidem*— the mind of man reaching out for a faith—and *fides quaerens intellectum*—faith seeking in the university community an expression of belief that will be relevant to the uneasy mind of modern man, cowering behind a mushroom cloud of his own creation. . . . We cannot be satisfied with medieval answers to modern questions. . . . Faith is unchangeable in what

it believes, but there are many ways of expressing what we believe; and today the words must be directed toward the utter confusion in the heart of man. . . . If the Catholic university can fulfill this function—of the human mind seeking faith, and faith reaching out for an expression adequate to our times—it will indeed be a great light, faithful to the wisdom of the past, relevant to the present and open to the future.

2. The Catholic university must be a bridge across all the chasms that separate modern man from each other; the young and old; rich and poor; black and white; believer and unbeliever; potent and weak; material and spiritual, scientist and humanist, all the rest. . . . To be such a mediator it must build a bridge of understanding and love. So that the name of the game will be peace, not conflict.

3. The Catholic university must be a place where all the intellectual and moral currents of our times meet. Here should be the home of the inquiring mind, and whatever the differences of religion, culture, race, or nationality, here should be the place where love and civility govern the conversation and the outcome.

Let us now return to where we began, the possibility of a great Catholic university in our times. . . . All universities are totally committed to *human* progress in the natural order of events. This endeavor, left to itself, is fraught with frustration and despair. The Catholic university has that *something more* to offer: Call it faith, call it belief, a simple belief in an ultimate goal surpassing all natural endeavor, the recapitulation of all things in Christ.

We commit ourselves to something more. We must be ourselves at Notre Dame, in keeping with our tradition. Hopefully, being ourselves will mean that we may add something to the total strength of what we most cherish: the great endeavor of the higher learning in our beloved America and in our total world.

49. QUO VADIS?

IT was the morning after the Friday night dinners and reminiscences at the 1968 June Reunions. The old boys and young boys were coming from the morning memorial Masses when word was passed of an unscheduled luncheon in the East dining hall. Father Hesburgh had received an unexpected summons from the Vatican. He must be in Rome tomorrow and could not give his usual state-of-the-University address at the Saturday night dinner. But this was the 25th anniversary of his ordination, a major day in the life of a priest. It should be observed. Hence the luncheon. And the old boys and the young boys streamed from the various halls, in their class hats and sport shirts. They had been told to come as they were.

Father Hesburgh talked, not as a President nor as a world citizen jetting out to see the Pope, but as a Notre Dame priest talking to the Notre Dame family.

He spoke of the blessings of the place; of the sense of peace on the campus; of the grown men who, in times of personal crisis, had come back to find peace where they had known peace, at a place where the spirit had rooted; and uplifted everything it touched.

The place had values and standards. It would keep them.

271

"Let your lives show the touch of God from The Dome."

The greatest temptation of a priest, he said, was to become selfish and professional in the sense of trying to find and take the easy way.

The ordained place of an ordained priest was to stand somewhere between man and God.

"I've had a fairly mobile life. In twenty-five years as a priest I missed saying Mass only once. I was in a hospital."

The alumni, the old boys and young alike, but especially the old, left feeling good about Hesburgh and Notre Dame. This was exactly what they had been waiting to hear. As long as a *priest* was in charge, Notre Dame would continue to be Notre Dame.

But . . .

The physical plant would soon be built. The endowed faculty would be complete. Notre Dame would be ready to become that great Catholic University Hesburgh had hoped for, perhaps the future No. 1 University of the world. It would need careful tending. Father Joyce, another *priest*, had recently given a sober warning in a *Summa* campaign speech: "As we grow in the days immediately ahead of us, we must do so in a very careful and selective way. These things have a tendency to explode. I think you will find that in the future major moves will be in those areas in which we want to move the most and in that which we can do the best."

All right. Hesburgh and Joyce had built it, the new Notre Dame; they would continue to tend it and nurse it and keep it moving.

Hesburgh was at the top of his power and influence.

Suppose the Congregation of the Holy Cross said: "All right, you have done your job at Notre Dame. We now call upon you to follow the path of Sorin. You can still live at Notre Dame and keep an eye on its growth, but your major responsibility will be much wider. You will be Superior-General and manage our affairs throughout the world."

Or...

Father O'Hara was made a bishop, then a Cardinal, after one visit of a previous Pope to Notre Dame. Father Hesburgh had been closer to the present Pope than any American priest had ever been to any Pope. Would it be too surprising, after a future sacred consistory, to read that henceforth it would be Theodore *Cardinal* Hesburgh? With specific responsibility to take full advantage of talents of which His Holiness knew full well?

For that matter (alumni pride now speaking) if, in the way the world was turning, they ever got around to electing an *American* Pope, who would be better qualified by intellect, experience, contacts, and performance?

If any of these things happened, who would succeed Hesburgh?

Father Edmund Joyce, Hesburgh's executive Vice-President and deputy on every step of every operation?

Father John Walsh, Vice-President for Academic Affairs, who had made most of the customary stops on the way to the top?

Father Charles Sheedy, the seasoned academician and administrator, almost the image of the composite Notre Dame President from Sorin to Hesburgh?

Father Burtchaell?

Which way, Notre Dame?

In Rome the smoke from a chimney indicated the election of a new Pope and the path of the future.

At Notre Dame, it might also be well to keep an eye aloft; to see if, as up to now, and for symbolic realism, that Beautiful Lady, high on The Golden Dome, was still highest of all "for all men to know why we have succeeded here."

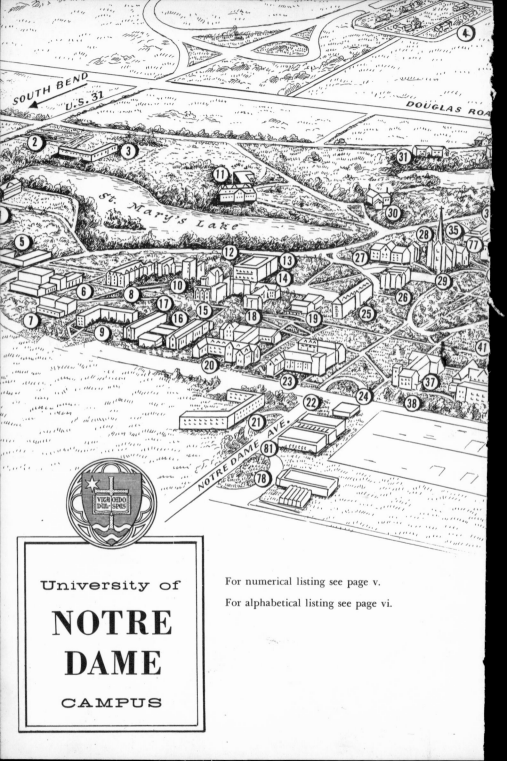

University of

NOTRE DAME

CAMPUS

For numerical listing see page v.

For alphabetical listing see page vi.